American Film Melodrama

GRIFFITH, VIDOR, MINNELLI

By Robert Lang

PRINCETON UNIVERSITY PRESS, PRINCETON, N.J.

Copyright © 1989 by Princeton University Press
Published by Princeton University Press, 41 William Street, Princeton, New Jersey 08540
In the United Kingdom: Princeton University Press, Guildford, Surrey

LIBRARY OF CONGRESS CATALOGING-IN-PUBLICATION DATA

Lang, Robert, 1957–
American film melodrama : Griffin, Vidor, Minnelli / Robert Lang.
p.   cm.
Filmography: p.
Bibliography: p.
Includes index.
ISBN 0-691-04759-6 (alk. paper). ISBN 0-691-00606-7 (pbk. : alk. paper)
1. Motion pictures—United States—History. 2. Melodrama in
motion pictures. 3. Patriarchy in motion pictures. 4. Griffith,
D. W. (David Wark), 1875–1948—Criticism and interpretation.
5. Vidor, King, 1895–1982—Criticism and interpretation.
6. Minnelli, Vincente—Criticism and interpretation. I. Title.
PN1995.9.M45L36 1989
791.43'09'09355—dc19   88-17936

Publication of this book has been aided by the
Whitney Darrow Publication Reserve Fund of
Princeton University Press

This book has been composed in Linotron Palatino

Clothbound editions of Princeton University Press books are printed on
acid-free paper, and binding materials are chosen for strength and
durability. Paperbacks, although satisfactory for personal collections,
are not usually suitable for library rebinding

Printed in the United States of America by Princeton University Press,
Princeton, New Jersey

For Paul

Contents

Preface

AT ONE time I thought a good title for this book would be *Hollywood's Family Romance*. That title would not only evoke the notion that Hollywood has (or has had) a romance with the family, but it would refer to a way of making movies, an ideology, which could be called "romantic." Also, it would refer to a genre I could loosely call the family romance. The title would have been misleading, though, especially for those who associate the term "family romance" with Freud, who uses it to describe the experience of the child who "imagines that he was not born of his real parents, but rather of noble ones; or that his father was noble and—to explain this—that his mother has had secret love affairs. Or again, that while he is legitimate his brothers and sisters are bastards."[1]

A more accurate title from Freud's repertoire might have been *Hollywood's Family Neurosis*, but that loses some useful connotations and supplies a few negative ones, such as maladjustment and illness. With this term, however, one comes closer to some of the distinguishing features of the family melodrama—the American cinema's dominant genre—for I assert that the family is Hollywood's one true subject. By *Familienneurose* Freud referred to a number of fundamental psychoanalytic conclusions: "the central role of identification with the parents in the constitution of the subject, the Oedipus Complex as the nuclear complex of neurosis, the important part played by the

---

[1] J. Laplanche and J.-B. Pontalis, *The Language of Psycho-Analysis*, trans. Donald Nicholson-Smith (New York: Norton, 1973), 160. The films discussed in this study are not of the type Freud had in mind when he coined the term *Familienroman*, although several of them do in some ways resemble this notion of the family romance. For example, Ruby Gentry, in Vidor's film of that name, is "born on the wrong side of the tracks," but lives to become the richest woman in town; and the poor, bastard son Rafe in Minnelli's *Home from the Hill*, is really the rich Wade Hunnicutt's son. For a detailed interpretation of the way fantasies grouped under Freud's term "are taken up—and transformed" by *Home from the Hill*, *Splendor in the Grass* (Kazan, 1961), and *Written on the Wind* (Sirk, 1956), see Richard de Cordova's recently published "A Case of Mistaken Legitimacy: Class and Generational Difference in Three Family Melodramas," in Christine Gledhill, ed., *Home Is Where the Heart Is: Studies in Melodrama and the Woman's Film* (London: British Film Institute, 1987), 255–67.

relationship between the parents in the genesis of the Oedipus Complex,"[2] and so on.

Nonetheless, Hollywood has had a veritable *romance* with the notion of the family, bordering sometimes on obsession. The Oedipal drama has been its chief represented object for more than eighty years; the familial is its favored mode, although not always even consciously. Whether it has been a neurosis or a romance (a *roman* it has certainly been—always a story)[3] probably depends more on how we watch the films than on which films we are watching.

In this book I try to come to some conclusions about what the film melodrama is, and what constitutes the melodramatic in film—to investigate a hunch I developed within a short time of coming to America ten years ago. What I sensed, but could not for a long time put into words, was that the most remarkably distinctive, and valuable, thing about American culture is the pervasive presence of the melodramatic in its representations. And the American cinema, I felt, could explain it all. The Hollywood movie, as one of America's greatest achievements in the arts—certainly a richly and vividly melodramatic one—could tell me what it means to live in America or to be an American.

I shall not try in a sentence to sum up here what I have found, but I should say that, like Peter Brooks, whose superb book on the "melodramatic imagination" I wish I had found much sooner, I see in the melodrama "a central poetry" of our time. Some understanding of the nature of this poetry has given me a "radical freedom" which should not have been mine if I had never come to America— to which country this study was written as a kind of thanks, in the mode of an investigation, a tribute, a dialogue, perhaps even a romance.

And there are those American friends who offered me various kinds of support during this project; I offer my grateful thanks to them all. They are: Cora Harris, Karen Kelly, Victoria Knopf, Barbara Leaming, Greg Martino, Maitland McDonagh, Roz and Stan Morrow, Marty Rubin, Martin Schwarzschild, Mark and Lore Singerman, Thom Taylor, Kate Waugh, and Vivian Wick. I should also like to thank E. Ann Kaplan for her enthusiastic support of my endeavor,

[2] Laplanche and Pontalis, *The Language of Psycho-Analysis*, 159.
[3] Cf. Sandy Flitterman, "That 'Once-Upon-a-Time . . .' of Childish Dreams," *Ciné-Tracts* 13 (Spring 1981): 14–25.

and for her valuable suggestions for rewriting. I am grateful to Foster Hirsch for suggesting ways to shorten an overlong manuscript, and to Sandy Flitterman-Lewis—not only for the many hours we spent talking about melodrama and the "ways of the world," but for giving my manuscript a thorough going-over. My greatest debt of gratitude is to John Belton, who suggested the topic and who, with exceptional generosity and a scholar's passion, lent me films, read several drafts of my manuscript, and was tireless in his efforts to steer me from illogical arguments and infelicities of organization and style.

My thanks also go to Noël Carroll, Ann Douglas, Carolyn Heilbrun, Sylvère Lotringer, Phil Rosen, Andrew Sarris, Stefan Sharff, and Robin Wood, to Anita Lowry and Eileen McIlvaine of the Columbia University Libraries, to Charles Silver of the Museum of Modern Art, to Howard and Ron Mandelbaum of Phototeque for film stills, to the Library of Congress, and to the New York Public Library Performing Arts Research Center. I thank Alexandra Penney, who has launched me on so many adventures, and my dear friend Marge Sullivan, for keeping the faith. I am indebted to Elisabeth Weis, who was always a source of cheerful encouragement, and who recognized enough virtues in what I had written to recommend my manuscript to Princeton University Press, where I have been expertly and graciously assisted by Joanna Hitchcock, her staff, and my copyeditor extraordinaire, Jane Lincoln Taylor, in preparing this book for publication.

Across the ocean, I send my thanks to Tim and Elizabeth Birley, and to Pam Burl, who many years ago in Central Africa was, and is still, an inspiration to me.

Finally, with love, I offer my profound thanks to June, Vic, Lesli-Sharon, and Gordon Lang, who provide that indispensable familial perspective.

PART ONE

1. Melodrama and the "Ways of the World"

MELODRAMA understands the "ways of the world" in a highly codified way of its own. This way, paradoxically, resonates with urgency and self-doubt, in the pressured attempts of the form to make sense of the world, to make experience conform to a melodramatic structure, to give textual, aesthetic existence to a moral articulation of difficulty and difference.

In this study I examine the construction of human subjectivity as it is defined by the melodramatic discourse in three of its major phases of development in the American cinema: the religious, the social, and the psychoanalytic. I have found that, in selected films of three major American filmmakers, D. W. Griffith, King Vidor, and Vincente Minnelli, the melodramatic imagination that structures the films understands experience in Manichaean terms of familial struggle and conflict. The struggle in the Griffith melodramas tends to be against "fate" (the Christian moral universe) and against social injustice. In later melodramas, those of the 1930s, 1940s and 1950s (the films of Vidor and Minnelli), the moral universe loses its overtly Christian inflection and the struggles tend to focus on the extent to which social conditions determine characters' destinies, before it becomes understood that the essential struggle is one for individual identity within a familial context.

It becomes apparent in the course of the American film melodrama's development through these phases that the conflict, finally, is with our patriarchy. The term "patriarchy" only becomes truly apt for the later films, since it contains in its etymology the recognition that ours is a "man's world," and only after Griffith does the cinema begin consciously to reflect the gathering conviction that a great deal of what is wrong with the world is owed directly or indirectly to the fact that we live in a patriarchy. Patriarchal ideology represents and constructs relations of domination of women by men, and awareness in America of this fact was given new impetus by the widespread influence, at the time Griffith was making films, of the discoveries of Freud. What psychoanalysis eventually discovered was a truth about female sexuality—that, as Luce Irigaray has put it,

the feminine occurs only within models and laws devised by male subjects. Which implies that there are not really two sexes, but only one. A single practice and representation of the sexual. With its history, its requirements, reversals, lacks, negative(s) . . . of which the female sex is the mainstay. This model, a *phallic* one, shares the values inscribed in the philosophical corpus: property, production, order, form, unity, visibility . . . and erection.[1]

To settle on the contemporary term, then, the melodrama represents a struggle against, or within, the patriarchy, and what seeks release and definition is a repressed identity. I investigate the universe of the family melodrama and some of the assumptions on which it is founded (the philosophical corpus to which Irigaray refers) in an attempt to discover how film spectators are both liberated and oppressed by melodramatic texts.

Most critical work on melodrama as a genre is relatively recent and concentrates on the form as it flourished in the British, French and American theater in the nineteenth century. In the most important recent work on melodrama, *The Melodramatic Imagination: Balzac, Henry James, Melodrama, and the Mode of Excess*, Peter Brooks maintains that his concern is, "not melodrama as a theme or a set of themes, nor the life of the drama per se, but rather melodrama as a mode of conception and expression, as a certain fictional system for making sense of experience, as a semantic field of force."[2] The exemplary melodrama, for Brooks, is the French "boulevard" melodrama of Pixérécourt, Caigniez and Ducange, and the great upheaval that provided the origins of and model for the melodrama is the French Revolution of 1789:

This is the epistemological moment which it illustrates and to which it contributes: the moment that symbolically, and really, marks the final liquidation of the traditional Sacred and its representative institutions (Church and Monarch), the shattering of the myth of Christendom, the dissolution of an organic and hierarchically cohesive society, and the invalidation of the literary forms—tragedy, comedy of manners—that depended on such a society.

[1] Luce Irigaray, *This Sex Which Is Not One*, trans. Catherine Porter (Ithaca: Cornell University Press, 1985), 86.

[2] Peter Brooks, *The Melodramatic Imagination: Balzac, Henry James, Melodrama, and the Mode of Excess* (New Haven: Yale University Press, 1976), xiii.

Melodrama does not simply represent a "fall" from tragedy, but a response to the loss of the tragic vision. It comes into being in a world where the traditional imperatives of truth and ethics have been violently thrown into question. . . . [It] becomes the principal mode for uncovering, demonstrating, and making operative the essential moral universe in a post-sacred era.[3]

This notion of melodrama as a "semantic field of force" in which the melodramatic mode exists largely "to locate and to articulate the moral occult"[4] informs my project in its attempt to bring to light the ideological underpinnings of the melodrama as a social form.[5]

Specifically, this study is concerned with the family melodrama. The family melodrama articulates a moral universe from within the familial sphere, or turns on the logic of the familial, of "personal life," of Oedipal structures, even when the locus of the action is not always literally or exclusively in a family. This domestic sphere, generally dominated by women, is distinct from the world of production, generally dominated by men.

The bourgeois domestic (i.e., family) melodrama is a historically specific form that emerged with the rise of capitalism. The bourgeois era, as Chuck Kleinhans has observed in a summary article on melodrama and the family under capitalism,[6] contrasts with all earlier historical epochs in that it designates the family as "the central area of personal life, a place of respite from productive life, from the alienated labor that workers must face." There, in the family, apart from the world of action, production and rational order, the melodrama of passion explores a familial world of subjectivity, of emotion and feeling, of problems of identity and desire.

Unlike the melodramatic forms that are constructed essentially for the traditionally heterosexual male viewer (the gangster film, the western), the family melodrama is constructed ostensibly for the traditionally heterosexual female viewer. In the "male" genres that are melodramatic, the sphere of conflict is public (the small town, the

---

[3] Ibid., 14–15.

[4] Ibid., 5.

[5] These ideological concerns are those of Griselda Pollock, Geoffrey Nowell-Smith, and Stephen Heath in "Dossier on Melodrama," *Screen* 18, no. 2 (Summer 1977): 105–19. The article summarizes a set of social and psychic determinations of the domestic film melodrama of the 1950s and indicates how they conjoin with a formal history of the genre.

[6] Chuck Kleinhans, "Notes on Melodrama and the Family under Capitalism," *Film Reader* 3 (February 1978): 40–47.

mob, the business), the focus of interest is on an external dynamic of action, and the familial is often repressed. It is a sphere that largely avoids the troubling, contradictory nature of sexual desire, and it represses the truth about repression. Above all, it conceals the fact that the patriarchy is founded on the repression of women.[7]

The evolution of the western is instructive in this regard. Always a "male" genre, the western after World War II began to deal with conflicts in terms of desire, but significantly, the films (such as *Red River* [1948] and *The Searchers* [1956]) transpose the issues outward, into the landscape, and the conflicts are resolved by action. The family melodrama, on the other hand, turns conflicts inward. Characters tend not to *act* in order to resolve conflicts; they are, rather, *acted upon*. Although the melodramatic postwar western does (like the family melodrama) grapple with questions of desire and identity, it is not defeated by those issues. The family melodrama, by contrast, as Thomas Elsaesser observes,

more often records the failure of the protagonist to act in a way that could shape the events and influence the emotional environment, let alone change the stifling social milieu. The world is closed, and the characters are acted upon. Melodrama confers on them a negative identity through suffering, and the progressive self-immolation and disillusionment generally ends in resignation: they emerge as lesser human beings for having become wise and acquiescent to the ways of the world.[8]

The family melodrama, as I use the term, is meant to comprehend four generally distinguished types of melodrama of passion: the "woman's film," the romantic melodrama, the family and/or small-town melodrama, and the Gothic melodrama. The Hollywood family melodrama from the teens to the 1960s has articulated its concerns, primarily the question of female subjectivity, in three major discourses: the "ways of the world" have been understood by the form successively—i.e., simultaneously, but at different times domi-

---

[7] See E. Ann Kaplan, "Theories of Melodrama: A Feminist Perspective," *Women and Performance* 1, no. 1 (1983): 40–48. Kaplan's article is brief, but in 1983 it was a timely call for "a theory that first, distinguishes between the different types of melodrama according to the gender of the spectator each constructs; second, that analyzes the conservative functions of the genre for both the male and female spectator; and finally, that exposes the particularly damaging aspects of melodrama for women, while acknowledging the powerful subversive moments that it contains."

[8] Thomas Elsaesser, "Tales of Sound and Fury: Observations on the Family Melodrama," *Monogram* 4 (1972): 9.

nantly—in religious, social, and psychoanalytic terms. In the three Griffith films I have chosen for this study (*Way Down East, The Mother and the Law*, and *Broken Blossoms*) the dominant melodramatic discourses are religious and social; in the three Vidor films (*The Crowd, Stella Dallas*, and *Ruby Gentry*) they are social and psychoanalytic; and in Minnelli's films (*Madame Bovary, Some Came Running*, and *Home from the Hill*) the discourse is psychoanalytic, with a degree of irony that is generally absent in Vidor.

My attempt to theorize about the film melodrama, and my decision to concentrate on selected works of three major American filmmakers, has been guided by the contention that the Hollywood cinema is informed by a melodramatic aesthetic whose formal basis is "over and above everything intensely *theatrical*."[9] Not only is the American cinema attracted ideologically to the melodramatic (and was so attracted from the start, for economic and social reasons), it is *formally* melodramatic also. It is so, as Michael Walker has pointed out, because the aesthetic which evolved in Hollywood is "dominated by action, spectacle, dynamic narrative, theatrical heightening and the externalizing of emotions"—an inheritance from the traditional melodrama (of the stage, primarily) which was "designed to arouse the same kind of intense emotional involvement."[10] I attempt in this book to investigate the way in which the ideology of emotionalism and the aesthetics of spectacle interact in the evolution of the melodramatic form as it flourished in Hollywood, from the time of Griffith to the collapse of the studio system.

In observing the constitution of some fictional subjects (and their discursive realities) in the melodramatic "field of force," one finds that the evolution of the form corresponds to shifts in the dominant ideology, since the melodrama is an aesthetic that makes ideological contradiction its subject matter. The struggles and contradictions of bourgeois capitalist ideology within which the Hollywood film is located take place in highest relief, it is immediately apparent, on the field represented by women, although not all the main characters of the films chosen for this study are women.

[9] Mark Le Fanu, "Pageants of Violence," *Monogram* 4, quoted by Michael Walker in "Melodrama and the American Cinema," *Movie* 29/30 (Summer 1982): 38.

[10] Michael Walker, "Melodrama and the American Cinema," *Movie* 29/30 (Summer 1982): 28.

The melodrama, I contend, is first a drama of identity. A woman (or a woman's point of view) often dominates the narrative of the family melodrama because individual identity within the patriarchal context—always defined by a masculine standard—is problematic for women. The dominant ideology asserts that, whether or not a woman is at the center of the narrative, what is at stake in the melodrama will be a question of identity—of a failure to be masculine, or a failure to accept the repressive, subjectivity-denying terms of patriarchal femininity. Patriarchy, it should be reiterated, understands femininity as a failure to be masculine. Feminine subjectivity is an impossibility according to the logic of the patriarchy, which defines it, with an inevitably negative connotation, as "not-male." We might think of "true" feminine subjectivity—feminine subjectivity on its own terms, not defined negatively—as being a possibility that is still evolving. But since any notion of the feminine really cannot be separated from a notion of the masculine, what constitutes the feminine, if it is emergent, will have the effect of modifying our concept of the masculine, and thus of the patriarchy. However, our whole system, our society, requires us to understand the concept of the patriarchy as absolutely fixed, incapable of modification. The bind, as Laura Mulvey has put it, is "how to fight the unconscious structured like a language . . . while still caught within the language of the patriarchy."[11] The family melodrama is a genre that addresses this problem. In the family melodrama the villain changes over time, but in one way or another the villain is some aspect of the patriarchy. By showing how the melodramatic form modifies its understanding of villainy, this study seeks a better understanding of how our moral universe is constructed along patriarchal lines.

The nine films discussed in the following chapters all show the workings of bourgeois patriarchal culture, and they reveal the melodramatic vision of this culture to be in some sense neurotic and paranoid. The struggles and contradictions of bourgeois capitalist ideology are usually most vividly represented in the melodrama, as has been noted, by the life or point of view of a woman who endures as a maladjusted subject. The melodrama, however, does not propose a comprehensively better substitute for the patriarchy; the most that a subject (female *or* male) can hope to achieve is some sort of adjust-

[11] Laura Mulvey, "Visual Pleasure and Narrative Cinema," *Screen* 16, no. 3 (1975): 7.

ment to the dominant culture. While there is always hope for change, even the most violent protestations of the melodrama are not a call for radical change.[12]

The melodrama recognizes that we are all—men and women—subject to the Law. What the analyses of these films should establish is the nature of this Law—"the legally established social order"—as founded on and based in the difference between the sexes. Sexual difference was used by monotheism, which laid the foundations for capitalism; this, in turn, has magnified the significance of sexual difference for the question of personal and moral identity.

Under capitalism, as Kleinhans notes, the individual's sense of worth cannot be achieved in productive labor.[13] This has the effect of dividing social from economic life and putting "a huge burden" on "the family and the area of interpersonal relations." It is this area of interpersonal relations on which the melodrama traditionally focuses. That this province should be dominated by women is to be expected, since the patriarchy has relegated women to the "negative term of the social entente,"[14] the sphere of human activity that is considered by the capitalist patriarchy to be less important, since it is not engaged in the symbolic operations of exchange and material production. Women traditionally have taken care of children and home life while men have worked to bring home the bacon. The consequences are thus: Women have been expected to make the home a haven from the workplace, to safeguard the emotional well-being of the family, in short, generally to absorb the contradictions of this separation of production and consumption, work and play, public and private spheres.

In this division of labor required by capitalism, the "work" of women is hidden and their desire subordinated to masculine imper-

---

[12] As Stephen Neale observes, "Melodrama . . . puts into crisis the discourses within the domain circumscribed by and defined as the legally established social order, the kind of order instituted at the end of westerns and detective films. Melodrama does not suggest a crisis of that order, but a crisis within it, an 'in house' rearrangement." (Stephen Neale, *Genre* [London: British Film Institute, 1980], 22.)

[13] Except perhaps for the individual professional, who seeks to combine "production and reproduction, economic life and social life"—in short, to fuse his or her work and life—as, for example, Mildred Pierce attempts to do in *Mildred Pierce* (Michael Curtiz, 1945).

[14] Julia Kristeva, *About Chinese Women*, trans. Anita Barrows (New York: Urizen Books, 1977), 14.

atives of real production.[15] Women under patriarchy are excluded as active agents from the economy of desire, of exchange, and reduced to the status of commodities, exchanged between men in a symbolic system according to which the women mediate male desires. All signs, all commodities in patriarchal societies, are exchanged between men, and in patriarchal societies women are themselves among these signs, participating in an essentially male system that denies women their subjectivity. As Irigaray puts it, it is a "hom(m)o-sexual" system, and "Heterosexuality is nothing but the assignment of economic roles: there are producer subjects and agents of exchange (male) on the one hand, productive earth and commodities (female) on the other."[16] According to this system, women very generally tend to represent either motherhood or sexuality—both of which terms are inimical to capitalist production. While mothers in patriarchal society do perform the work of human reproduction, theirs is unacknowledged labor, and woman as signifier of sexuality (of male desire, sexuality as pleasure) is understood to be materially unproductive—indeed, even subversive of masculine aspiration in the public sphere of material production.[17]

As Julia Kristeva observes, woman in the West is excluded from the temporal symbolic order unless she identifies with the father—"the values considered to be masculine (dominance, superego, the endorsed communicative word that institutes stable social exchange)."[18] The separation of "masculine" and "feminine" functions that has been so serviceable to capitalism's operations was already set up in the West by monotheism, which did not have the generation of material wealth as its prime reason, but the more basic one of survival. As Kristeva points out,

[15] For a more extended account of the interrelationship between capitalist society and the individual, and its reflection in private life, see Eli Zaretsky, *Capitalism, the Family, and Personal Life* (New York: Harper and Row, 1972).

[16] Irigaray, *This Sex Which Is Not One*, 192. Irigaray's springboard for her term, *hom(m)o-sexuality*, is Lévi-Strauss' description (in *The Elementary Structures of Kinship* [Boston: Beacon], 1969) of the traffic in women. It designates the structural reality of heterosexuality in its reference to the relation of the heterosexual to male homosocial bonds. Like Lévi-Strauss' kinship structures, Irigaray's representation of how patriarchal societies work describes a structure that turns on repression (the taboo on incest) and which, therefore, excludes actual sex between men (homosexuality).

[17] Later in this study a clarification will be attempted of the identification in our culture of woman with *jouissance*, defined by Lacan as "that which is useless." (Jacques Lacan, *Encore: Le Séminaire XX* [Paris: Seuil, 1975], 10.)

[18] Kristeva, *About Chinese Women*, 37.

Monotheistic unity is sustained by a radical separation of the sexes: indeed, this separation is its prerequisite. For without this gap between the sexes, without this localization of the polymorphic, orgasmic body, laughing and desiring, in the other sex, it would have been impossible, in the symbolic sphere, to isolate the principle of One Law—One, Purifying, Transcendent, Guarantor of the ideal interest of the community. In the sphere of productive relations (at that time inseparably linked to relations of *production*) it would have been impossible to insure the propagation of the race by making it the only acceptable end of *jouissance*.[19]

The Griffith melodramas are still conditioned by the vocabulary of monotheism. But "fate" in most of his films is not yet really understood to have its origins in the separation of the sexes, and only hindsight permits us to call *patriarchal* the laws of "fate" which operate in them. The structuring melodramatic framework here is Christian.

If the family melodrama has (metaphorically or otherwise) come to be a discourse on female subjectivity, it is because all melodramas, all narratives, are essentially dramas of identity, of interpretation. To resort to a psychoanalytic model for a moment to clarify this point: there is no talking about identity without talking about the Other— that which is different. How do we come to know that which we are not? Or, how does one know what one's face looks like, without looking in a mirror? Narratives are interpretations of experience; they are interpretations through that image in the mirror. The melodrama is an attempt to explore the "other" point of view, to give it a chance to speak for itself. But from the phallocentric viewpoint of our patriarchy, the Other (being not-male) is "feminine," and on many levels "otherness" becomes synonymous with notions of the "feminine." From this (masculine) point of view, the "other" point of view is interpreted in the only terms available to it: what we see when we look to the Other, from which a sense of self (identity) can be derived, is that She is "not all."[20] She is lacking that which has a physical correspondence in the penis. The Other, by definition, is castrated; that is the "interpretation" of the evident difference between males and females—the first interpretation from which all others follow in a patriarchal society.

She (the Other) becomes a metaphor for that which we do not understand, a metaphor of absence. The Other is always an image. The

[19] Ibid., 19.

[20] "There is always something in woman as the not-all that eludes discourse." (Lacan, *Encore: Le Séminaire XX*, 34.)

image (in our patriarchy, "woman") is translated, interpreted in the movement of desire itself, as a metaphor. Any attempt, then, to talk about (the) metaphor becomes impossible. As Lacan rather directly says, "Nothing can be said about the woman."[21] But this can also mean, "Nothing can be said *without* the woman" (there being two possible translations from the French of "de la").[22] This, too, is the impossibility at the heart of what the melodrama is "about." It is "about" the Other, because it is about identity, but it is impossible to speak about the Other ("Nothing can be said about the woman"). On the other hand, without the Other, it is impossible to speak at all ("Nothing can be said without the woman")!

All dramatic narrative films, then, with their concern with identity stressed to a greater or lesser degree (in familial-sexual terms), are more or less melodramatic. But the family melodrama, as a type of narrative concerned specifically with the question of identity, is a particularly self-reflexive instance in the Hollywood cinema. The narrative that is about desire is a *mise en abyme*. That the melodrama is, as Stephen Neale suggests, the narrative form that makes desire its subject accounts for melodrama's unsettled status as a term.[23] This prompts some writers to claim that melodrama represents the theatrical impulse itself—"drama in its eternal form; it is the quintessence of drama."[24]

Melodrama is not just narrative with desire as its subject matter; it is in our case Hollywood's fairly consistent way of treating desire and subject identity. Hollywood stands for the " 'common sense,' established social order," even when it produces films that critique that order. To borrow Nick Browne's words regarding Griffith's discourse on the family, Hollywood's "way"—of which the melodramatic discourse is the paradigm—"mirrors the story psychoanalysis gives of the dynamics of desire, law, and identity within the structure of the

---

[21] Ibid., 75.

[22] Larysa Mykyta makes this observation in an article which helped me clarify my ideas for this discussion: "Lacan, Literature and the Look: Women in the Eye of Psychoanalysis," *SubStance* 12, no. 2 [39] (1983): 49–57.

[23] In melodrama, Neale claims, "the disequilibrium inaugurating the narrative movement is specified as the process of desire itself and of the various blockages to its fulfillment within an apparently 'common sense,' established social order." (Neale, *Genre*, 22.)

[24] Eric Bentley, "Melodrama," in *The Life of the Drama* (New York: Atheneum, 1967), 216.

family, which Freud was in the process of formulating, first clinically, then theoretically in the very years the cinema was taking form."[25] Hollywood's way of organizing experience parallels the way of psychoanalysis, whose one true subject is that same family of the family melodrama. That way is to tell stories, in images, and the masterplot—the story from which all others flow and take their model—is Freud's myth of Oedipus.

If the discourse of the family melodrama has been sexualized, it is because we have become more aware that the Law in our culture was founded on sexual difference. All the discourses of the Law—religious, social and sexual—are melodramatic in their binary nature, based at the start on the fact of difference, with the masculine principle privileged. Even *language*, to use the term in its broadest sense, is masculine. We are all inscribed in language, identified by it, and in a patriarchy one's relation to language, if one is male, is as a bearer of language's privileged signifier, the Phallus.[26] It is the positive term of a binary structure. If one is female, one's relation to the symbolic order of language is structured by Lack. The fact that men and women are biologically different seems to have determined all other differences, to have formed the cornerstone, indeed, of our moral universe. All meaning and value in our culture derives from the moral need to distinguish between good and bad, and those terms, bound up inextricably with the difference between men and women, have always been the terms of our moral universe, which it is the melodrama's prime concern to articulate.

[25] Nick Browne, "Griffith's Family Discourse: Griffith and Freud," *Quarterly Review of Film Studies* 6, no. 1 (Winter 1981): 72.

[26] According to Lacan the phallus "is chosen because it is the most tangible element in the real of sexual copulation." (*Ecrits: A Selection*, trans. Alan Sheridan [New York: Norton, 1977], 287.) While the phallus is a signifier, not necessarily a penis, it "is something the symbolic use of which is possible because it can be seen, because it is erect," and "of what cannot be seen, of what is hidden there can be no possible symbolic use." (*Le Séminaire, Livre II* [Paris: Seuil, 1978], 315.)

2. Tragedy, Melodrama, and the "Moral Occult"

As THE Brooks quotation cited earlier suggests, the moral universe articulated by the classical tragedy no longer truly speaks to us, although much of it of course reverberates still in our unconscious. It is the melodramatic—melodrama's way of articulating the moral universe—that in modern times dominates our imagination. The shift from a tragic concept of life to a melodramatic mode of experience received its most decisive impetus roughly two hundred years ago, from, primarily, a collapse of our sense of the Sacred. As aesthetic ideologies that articulate what Brooks calls the "moral occult," tragedy and melodrama share a great deal, but there are significant differences. Tragedy, for our purposes, is part of the formal history of melodrama that predates the cinema; it is a mode that melodrama rejects but does not leave completely behind, just as this study, in a manner, rejects it, through an analysis of melodrama, echoing and responding to Roland Barthes' exhortation:

Tragedy is merely a means of "recovering" human misery, of subsuming and thereby justifying it in the form of a necessity, a wisdom, or a purification: to refuse this recuperation and to investigate the techniques of not treacherously succumbing to it (nothing is more insidious than tragedy) is today a necessary enterprise.[1]

For over two hundred years, in a somewhat circular and sometimes self-defeating fashion, melodrama has engaged in this enterprise;[2] it recognizes, at any rate, that human misery is not inevitable,

[1] Quoted in Alain Robbe—Grillet, *For a New Novel*, trans. Richard Howard (New York: Grove Press, 1965), 49.

[2] Christianity, it should be noted, has been engaged rather longer in this enterprise of refusing tragedy's justification of human misery. Christianity has a *tragic cast* (the narrative includes a crucifixion), but it is, ultimately, optimistic and therefore melodramatic (it includes a resurrection). Susan Sontag points out that the "moral adequacy of the world asserted by Christianity is precisely what tragedy denies. Tragedy says there are disasters which are not fully merited, that there is ultimate injustice in the world. So one might say that the final optimism of the prevailing religious traditions of the West, their will to see meaning in the world, prevented a rebirth of tragedy under

and although it does not always know what to do about it, the melo-drama seeks at least to locate and define the agents of human misery. The melodrama will challenge that suffering, even though it must also eventually find a means, not of justifying, but of coming to terms with it, of questioning its necessity.

The melodramatic discourse is like psychoanalysis, of which, one might say, it is an aesthetic articulation. Brooks has pointed this out:[3] psychoanalysis and melodrama are alike in the way they conceive of conflict, enactment, and cure in a secularized world. The Evil of melodrama is "reworked . . . in the processes of repression," and melodrama's characters correspond to the structure of ego, superego, and id that are the moral terms in psychoanalysis. Furthermore, as the drama of articulation, the melodrama performs the same function as the "talking cure" of psychoanalysis. Like psychoanalysis, how-ever, the melodrama is trapped in its own myth. The shared myth is the myth of Oedipus. It informs us, as Gilles Deleuze and Félix Guat-tari put it, that "if you don't follow the lines of differentiation daddy-mommy-me, and the exclusive alternatives that delineate them, you will fall back into the black night of the undifferentiated."[4] Psycho-analysis and melodrama understand only binary structures. That which lies outside of *difference* is unimaginable, horrible. It is the un-differentiated, first of all, of incest. But as Deleuze and Guattari stress, "Oedipus creates both *the differentiations that it orders and the undifferentiated with which it threatens us.*"[5] As they see it, Oedipus[6] "forces desire to take as its object the differentiated parental persons" but then prohibits the satisfaction of that desire by brandishing the threat of the undifferentiated. We are told to "resolve" Oedipus by internalizing it (or we will "fall into the neurotic night of imaginary identifications"), which, Deleuze and Guattari remark, is like telling us that we can only get out of the labyrinth by reentering it.

Christian auspices—as, in Nietzsche's argument, reason, the fundamentally optimistic spirit of Socrates, killed tragedy in ancient Greece." ("The Death of Tragedy" [1963], reprinted in *Against Interpretation* [New York: Dell Publishing Co., 1966], 137.)

[3] Peter Brooks, *The Melodramatic Imagination: Balzac, Henry James, Melodrama, and the Mode of Excess* (New Haven: Yale University Press, 1976), 201–2.

[4] Gilles Deleuze and Félix Guattari, *Anti-Oedipus*, trans. Robert Hurley, Mark Seem, and Helen R. Lane (Minneapolis: University of Minnesota Press, 1983), 78.

[5] Ibid., 78–79.

[6] The name, Oedipus, refers in Deleuze and Guattari's work to the whole account Freudian psychoanalysis gives of the formation of the subject.

Deleuze and Guattari are concerned with fighting (patriarchal, familial) fascism, which in their own way most family melodramas are also—some more consciously or vigorously than others. However, where Deleuze and Guattari propose what they call schizo-analysis, doing away with both the problem and the solution[7] in order to "reach those regions of the orphan unconscious—indeed 'beyond all law'—where the problem of Oedipus can no longer even be raised,"[8] the melodrama stays with Oedipus and puts its faith in the familial logic of psychoanalysis for the solution to Oedipus. In some sense, the melodrama is resigned to castration.

The melodrama nevertheless does perform some liberating functions. It should be remembered that where the melodrama may be enslaved to the Oedipal account of desire, it incorporates an element of idealization; it speaks more often of love than of desire. While it has been said that the soul of the melodrama is aggressive, erotic, and fetishistic,[9] it is inscribed in a familial discourse, which has the effect of mitigating the dangerousness of desire, even though historically that discourse has collaborated in the repression of so many men and women. As Kristeva's most recent book, *Histoires d'amour*, would suggest, the component of idealization in love, an amorous discourse, might be dangerous, but it is perhaps less dangerous than desire without love. How we love, in the family melodrama, is determined in the psychic spaces created by the family, and the melodrama seeks to articulate its essential nature—to understand those governing laws by which we live (and love).

For an understanding of the melodramatic mode, which implicitly acknowledges the terms of the tragic vision to which it is a response, some remarks of Alain Robbe-Grillet's are worth quoting here. Robbe-Grillet's own response (in his essays, novels and films) is in fact not only to the loss of the tragic vision, but to a loss of faith in the melodramatic vision as well. His is a violent reaction to the inadequacy of the melodramatic response, which he perceives to be insidiously anthropomorphic, fraudulent and self-deluding. In "Nature, Humanism, Tragedy," and "New Novel, New Man," essays

[7] Deleuze and Guattari, *Anti-Oedipus*, 81.

[8] Ibid., 82.

[9] James Leverett, "Old Forms Enter the New American Theater: Shepard, Foreman, Kirby, and Ludlam," *Melodrama*, ed. Daniel Gerould (New York: New York Literary Forum, 1980), 117.

published in 1958 and 1961 respectively, Robbe-Grillet suggests that "we no longer believe in the fixed significations, the ready made meanings which afforded man the old divine order and subsequently the rationalist order of the nineteenth century."[10] Those "fixed significations," of course, form the very foundation of melodramatic belief. Robbe-Grillet rails against them, and one might say that his own enterprise of form is a reaction to melodrama's final capitulation to societal structures that can cause human suffering, and to tragedy's impulse to recuperate human misery—an impulse that produced what he calls the "myths of the nineteenth century." Where tragedy advocates sacrifice and reconciliation, and melodrama protests against evil and demands justice, they share a belief in "fixed significations." That is where Robbe-Grillet believes any effort to refuse human suffering is betrayed. He has suffered the crisis of discovering that the bourgeois class has lost "its justifications and its prerogatives."[11] His disillusionment has been the discovery that "the significations of the world around us are no more than partial, provisional, even contradictory, and always contested."[12] Robbe-Grillet rejects completely the world "of which man was the master," and in which "Balzacian objects were so reassuring," objects that "were chattels, properties, which it was merely a question of possessing, or retaining, or acquiring."[13]

The two World Wars and their aftermath (which includes the threat of global nuclear annihilation) constitute an epistemological crisis in our own time (the context in which we might locate Robbe-Grillet) that is perhaps commensurate with the French Revolution in the late eighteenth century that Peter Brooks identifies as the real and symbolic moment of the nativity of the melodramatic imagination. The catastrophic events of recent history have not destroyed the melodramatic vision, as one might have expected, but they have certainly left marks of self-doubt in the melodramatic form. In order to survive, the melodrama has become sometimes peculiarly self-conscious and ironic. In the modern era of moral ambiguity, the melodramatic imagination has undergone a complex transformation; it still seeks to deny that confidence in the old order has been shaken, but this is not—it

[10] Robbe-Grillet, *For a New Novel*, 141.
[11] Ibid., 140.
[12] Ibid., 141.
[13] Ibid., 140.

cannot be—a simple denial. One need only think of a film like Douglas Sirk's *Written on the Wind* (1956) to recognize immediately that some of the more sophisticated postwar melodramas are consciously implicated in what Jean Baudrillard calls "the characteristic hysteria of our time: the hysteria of production and reproduction of the real,"[14] and that the kind of referentiality we see in the films under discussion in this book belongs, for the most part, to an earlier time, when irony was a simpler thing.[15] Robbe-Grillet picks up where Existentialism left off, and it must be said that his is a lone voice now. The melodramatic imagination has survived because it provides a system, a way of understanding the world, even though the kind of irony and excess that now dominates the address of the film and television melodrama can perhaps no longer so easily be called "progressive."

The melodramatic imagination is profoundly moral; the melodrama does not simply stage a battle between good and evil (with good triumphing), but rather tries to establish that clear notions of good and evil prevail, that there *are* moral imperatives. As it shows a human subject struggling against, or for a place within, the Law, the melodrama seeks to reveal a moral universe in operation, even where it is unable to show good triumphing. The Law might be paternal, familial, social, divine—but the melodrama investigates it, challenges it, in some fashion articulates how it functions, and then in the narrative invariably comes down on the side of it, usually without much conviction. In the best melodramas the "old order" is plainly irrecoverable, but since the form cannot envision a radically new order, the restoration of the "old order" (having been decisively discredited) is regarded ironically. In this manner the melodrama demonstrates that there *is* an operative Law, which is as important as its critique.

The "moral occult" is not merely what we have been calling the imperatives of the Law. Nor is it a metaphysical system. Rather, as Brooks subtly insists, it is

the repository of the fragmentary and desacralized remnants of sacred myth. It bears comparison to unconscious mind, for it is a sphere of being where

[14] Jean Baudrillard, *Simulations*, trans. Paul Foss, Paul Patton and Philip Beitchman (New York: Semiotext[e], Inc. Foreign Agents Series, 1983), 44.

[15] It would take another, different, book to theorize about the contemporary melodrama, which—if one should choose not to follow Baudrillard—one could begin by considering the issues discussed in Barbara Klinger, " 'Cinema/Ideology/Criticism' Revisited: The Progressive Text," *Screen* 25, no. 1 (January–February 1984): 30–44.

our most basic desires and interdictions lie, a realm which in quotidian existence may appear closed off from us, but which we must accede to since it is the realm of meaning and value. The melodramatic mode in large measure exists to locate and articulate the moral occult.[16]

The melodrama seeks to understand how "our most basic desires and interdictions" are held in tension, to know where the desire of the subject stands in relation to the interdiction of the Law. Melodrama's driving impulse is identical to that of genre: to establish a norm, a form, a structure that is recognizable and reproducible. Its reproducibility and commercial viability are the guarantees that it (the generic form) is a legitimate vision of the world. While tragedy and comedy are fairly distinct generic categories implying fairly clear-cut epistemologies, it is melodrama—the form for our time—that reveals the greater complexity (and confusion) of our vision, of our attempt to order experience after the breakdown of the traditional Sacred and its institutions.

As the title of Robert Heilman's book[17] suggests, tragedy and melodrama are two versions of experience. The main difference for our purposes here (as summed up by Michael Walker in a slight reformulation of Heilman's model) is that

where the characters are simply "acting-out" (expressing) ideological projects, tensions or contradictions, then the question of self-awareness does not genuinely arise and the mode is still effectively melodrama. . . . To achieve "full tragic awareness," the characters must in some sense come to understand the nature of the forces which impel them, the choices which confront them. Otherwise they remain characters of melodrama, acting "blindly," to a greater or lesser extent at the mercy of the ideological forces. . . . [T]he self awareness of the tragic character brings with it a greater freedom from the constraints of the ideology (e.g., the freedom of choice), even though the options themselves may be ideologically determined.[18]

So the significant factor in the difference between tragedy and melodrama as versions of experience is *ideology*—the degree of awareness of the part ideology plays in determining destiny. At first it would seem curious, then, that Barthes should excoriate the tragic vision as one that encourages an accommodation to human misery, when, as Walker suggests, the "self-awareness" of the tragic charac-

[16] Brooks, *The Melodramatic Imagination*, 5.

[17] Robert Heilman, *Tragedy and Melodrama: Versions of Experience* (Seattle: University of Washington Press, 1968).

[18] Michael Walker, "Melodrama and the American Cinema," *Movie* 29/30 (Summer 1982): 4–5.

ter "brings with it a greater freedom from the constraints of the ideology." Tragedy's dangerousness, if I interpret Barthes' point correctly, lurks in the fact that it encourages an *identification* with it, in
the name of the self-awareness that Walker refers to. The melodramatic character, at least, uncomplicated by self-awareness, will always know the difference between right and wrong, which in a sense
(the moral sense) makes the battle against wrong easier. If the melodramatic mode is not more "intelligent," it seems more "true." It
seeks to identify evil unequivocally, which makes it more difficult for
human misery to be subsumed in the form of a necessity. While film
characters of course may be melodramatic (i.e., in Heilman's sense,
have inadequate self-awareness), often the film itself will have a
tragic point of view.[19] In Walker's words, "Not in themselves tragic
characters, they nevertheless serve to express the film's tragic view
of the worlds they inhabit."[20] This kind of tragic awareness achieved
by the form during the 1950s and early 1960s represents the melodrama's most impressive and powerful aesthetic accomplishment in
the cinema, before television wrought its changes on the form and
became the next medium where it would flourish and become per-
vaded by a highly complex form of camp.[21]

The film melodrama, as film and as melodrama, has been liberating
for people in their ancient struggle to make sense of themselves and
the world in significant form. Film could articulate the world more
significantly. It molded, "more than any other single force, the opin-
ions, the taste, the language, the dress, the behavior, and even the
physical appearance of a public comprising more than 60 per cent of
the population of the earth,"[22] with more power and immediacy than
any other medium, probably because it engaged in an unprecedented
fashion our most developed sense, sight. The cinema could do all

[19] Walker makes this point (ibid., 24), citing as examples *Rebel Without a Cause, Home from the Hill,* and *Mandingo.*

[20] Ibid., 24.

[21] Cf. Jane Feuer, "Melodrama, Serial Form and Television Today," *Screen* 25, no. 1 (January–February 1984): 4–16; Ien Ang, *Watching Dallas: Soap Opera and the Melodramatic Imagination,* trans. Della Couling (London and New York: Methuen), 1985; and Mark Finch, "Sex and Address in *Dynasty,*" *Screen* 27, no. 6 (November–December 1986): 24–42.

[22] Erwin Panofsky, writing in 1934 on the movie audience, "Style and Medium in the Motion Pictures," reprinted in *Film Theory and Criticism,* ed. Gerald Mast and Marshall Cohen, 2nd ed. (New York: Oxford University Press, 1979), 244.

that the theater and novel and painting could do, and more. Desire, the driving force of all narrative, received through film new impetus, unmediated by the word and made more free by the great ease in filmic discourse of spatiotemporal articulations. The cinema gave a new lease on life to the melodrama, providing it with a unique synthesis of narrative and spectacle for the articulation of a "morally legible universe,"[23] for the demonstration

> that it was still possible to find and to show the operation of basic ethical imperatives, to define, in conflictual opposition, the space of their play. That they can be staged "proves" that they exist.[24]

The film melodrama and its legacy have become the twentieth century's major way of experiencing the world. The melodramatic mode is an ideology of the spectacle,[25] propelled by narrative and powered by emotion. If it can be turned into a story and made legible in images, the experience is legitimate, *real*. Like the Queen of Sheba in King Vidor's *Solomon and Sheba* (1959), we have no faith in the existence of ethical imperatives simply because it is said that they exist. As she approaches Jerusalem, her graven images in tow, Sheba remarks to herself in wonder: *"And all that for a God they don't even see!"* Like her, we put our faith in the image.

[23] Brooks, *The Melodramatic Imagination*, 201.

[24] Ibid., 201.

[25] For the extent to which America lives "by the fabricated iconography of its media," see the films of Robert Altman (especially *Buffalo Bill and the Indians*, 1976); Thomas Elsaesser, "*Nashville*: Putting on the Show" (*Persistence of Vision*, no. 1, Summer 1984); and Jean Baudrillard, *Simulations*, trans. Paul Foss, Paul Patton, and Philip Beitchman (New York: Semiotext[e], Inc. Foreign Agents Series, 1983).

3. Spectacle and Narrative

THE FILM melodrama's image-emphasized origins go back further than silent movies, to the theater of the late seventeenth century when, in France and England at least, there was a ban on the spoken word except in designated "legitimate" theaters.[1] The silence of the early movies thus imitated the popular theater of this earlier time and grew out of the peculiar relationship between narrative and spectacle in what Martin Meisel calls "the new dramaturgy" that emerged from the age of revolutions. In the inherited dramaturgy,

the idea of the play, however peripatetic its course, however contrastive its juxtaposed units, however divided its plots or contrived for the accommodation of turns, remains an unfolding continuum. In the new dramaturgy, the unit is intransitive; it is, in fact, an achieved moment of stasis, a picture.[2]

The new unit is one contrived for effect. It is not a unit of action or passion in which something has to be done or said, suffered or expressed, and in some way justified beyond its intrinsic interest, but a picture, a scene that "goes entirely for what we call *Situation* and *Stage Effect*, by which the greater applause may be obtained, without

[1] "When Louis XIV chartered the Théâtre-Français, otherwise known as the Comédie-Française, his decree provided that under normal circumstances it alone should have the right to perform spoken plays in the city of Paris. This provision begot not only an official stage but a cultural pariahdom governed, theoretically, by the interdiction against dramatic discourse. With the Revolution, the Théâtre-Français surrendered the monopoly it had enjoyed since 1680, which is to say that the boundary line between culture's preserve and the culturally disenfranchised was abruptly erased. In due course Napoleon redrew that line, quarantining theaters associated with *le peuple* inside genres deemed childish or archaic and, on occasion, silencing them altogether lest the vulgar tongue 'contaminate' the mind of France." (Frederick Brown, *Theater and Revolution: The Culture of the French Stage* [New York: The Viking Press, 1980], ix.) In other words, "Under the absolute monarchy, no word could be uttered as theater, no line shown as painting, no note played as music without the king's leave. Theoretically, art sprang from his head and existed as art insofar as it reflected or commemorated him." (Ibid., 33.) For the situation in England, which was similar, see Michael Booth, *Hiss the Villain* (London: Eyre and Spottiswoode, 1964), 18.

[2] Martin Meisel, "Speaking Pictures," *Melodrama*, ed. Daniel Gerould (New York: New York Literary Forum, 1980), 51–52.

the assistance of language, sentiment or character."[3] What is being described here, of course, is not the cinema—not quite, not yet—but what found its logical culmination in the tableau of the theater and tableau vivant of the nineteenth-century parlor.[4] The cinema—its spectacular component, at any rate—sprang from the impulses that produced the tableau vivant, but successfully sought a dialectic between stasis and movement, between spectacle and narrative. The cinema sought to make them both *significant*, although one of these twin components might be emphasized over the other, depending on the film's genre or some other factor, such as the director.[5]

The Hollywood cinema, as melodrama and as an image-based medium, exploits this dramaturgy of which Edward Mayhew's *Stage Effect: or, The Principles which Command Success in the Theater* (1840) is, according to Meisel, one of the best early accounts. When Mayhew writes that the "melo-drama" is "defective in action" and that "To cover their deficiency of action, melo-dramatists give an undue and irregular importance to the scenes and properties of the theater; and their productions abound in 'effects,' without the aid of which the interest evaporates,"[6] he could just as truly have said that interest in a melodrama that is in possession of too much in the way of "effects" and not enough in the way of narrative suspense, will evaporate as fast. The dramatically effective melodrama is sensational, of course, but also excessive in its subject matter and remarkably dependent on narrative suspense. Subject matter is articulated in *situation*;[7] the

[3] These words of Puff, a character in *The Critic* (1799), "put Mayhew's 'Principles Which Command Dramatic Success' in a nutshell." (Ibid., 53.)

[4] This sounds not unlike the early producer-filmmaker Thomas Ince's notion of what a filmmaker ought to know in order to make a good movie: "Primarily the director must know life, but he must know, too, how to project life, not in narrative form, but by selected dramatic moments, each of which builds towards a definite crisis or climax that will bring a burst of emotional response from every audience." (Quoted in David Robinson, *Hollywood in the Twenties* [Cranbury, N.J.: A. S. Barnes, 1968], 47.)

[5] In Vincente Minnelli's musicals, for example, we occasionally see so much emphasis put on spectacle, on *pictures* and *effects*, that a kind of stasis occurs, constant camera movement and movement of characters within the frame notwithstanding. If this happens less often in Minnelli's melodramas, it is due perhaps to the generic demand of the melodrama for a greater emphasis on narrative. Cf. in the chapter on "Address," Laura Mulvey's observation that in the Hollywood cinema male characters drive the narrative (advance the plot) and female characters provide the spectacle; and cf. Stephen Heath's assertion that narrative *ensures* movement.

[6] Quoted by Meisel, "Speaking Pictures," 54.

[7] "From about 1770 to 1870 situation implied a pictorial effect in drama, and effect

charm and distinction of the film melodrama is that these effects, these pictures themselves, speak. In other words, the film melodrama achieves a synthesis of narrative and spectacle; the two become inseparable.

Because the first films were made and screened without the benefit of recorded dialogue, and because their first audiences were vast and heterogeneous—not necessarily literate or all speaking the same language—the cinema drew heavily on melodrama's investment in mise en scène. The movies were made to "speak" without dialogue. As a temporal medium, the narrative requirements of which compressed real time, films learned how to signify as much as possible by means of condensation, displacement, and new codes peculiar to the medium and the form (dramatic, narrative cinema).

The efforts of the film to signify with clarity and force resulted in a dependence on stereotype. Overdetermination at all levels produced what David Bordwell has dubbed "an excessively obvious cinema."[8] The desire to signify, to be understood, in a new medium that was asking us to organize our experience of the world differently, in moving pictures, meant a reliance on a popular tradition, and resulted in the establishment of *genre* in the cinema as quickly and as efficiently as possible. Epistemological tendencies of the preceding two hundred years, such as the dramatization of vision—knowing from seeing, giving rise to the tableau and the tableau vivant—and the notion of life as theater, coincided with a technology and the commercial cinema's industrial requirement of large audiences, to produce the film melodrama, which in its etymology implies a combination of spectacle and narrative.

The music of melodrama, one might at first say, is on the side of spectacle, and the drama refers to its narrative component. But in melodrama, to an unprecedented degree, the picture tells the story. The film melodrama inherited lock, stock and barrel the pictorial theater of the nineteenth century in which figure and ground

---

was likely to mean a strong situation realized pictorially." (Ibid., 54.) By "situation," I presume we still mean something like, the heroine tied to the train tracks, with no help in sight, as the train approaches (i.e., melodramatic mise en scène).

[8] Bordwell is referring, of course, to the Hollywood cinema. It is the title of a chapter in his co-authored book, *The Classical Hollywood Cinema: Film Style and Mode of Production to 1960* (New York: Columbia University Press, 1985).

achieved a sort of parity, and music in the film melodrama functions as ground in this sense. Implicit in the relationship of figure to ground in nineteenth-century theater and in film melodrama is the conviction that environment is important. It is important because it affects and influences characters, because struggles so often are between characters and environment (which invariably includes other characters—the villain, for example), because the environment is out there, conspiring against the sympathetic characters, or because it reflects their inner states.

Meisel suggests that the nineteenth-century theater in fact failed "to resolve the tension between picture and motion and actualize that resolution in an adequate transforming synthesis."[9] That synthesis had to wait for the cinema. Without actually mentioning the cinema, Meisel implies that the "severe tension in the theater of the nineteenth century between picture and motion—between the achievement of a static image, halting (and compressing) time so that the full implications of events and relations can be savored, and the achievement of a total dynamism, in which everything moves and works for its own sake, as wonder and 'effect,' "[10] was realized in the new medium. Tableau filmmaking, we know, predates Griffith and Porter, which lends credence to the thesis that the cinema picked up where the theater left off.[11]

The recent politicization of film theory and criticism (which revealed that every image has political meaning) and the application of psychoanalysis to the study of screen melodrama—the earliest significant outcome of which is briefly summarized in the published results of S.E.F.T.'s Weekend School on Melodrama held in London in March, 1977[12]—suggest that there is a connection between the excess of the melodramatic image (spectacle, mise en scène) and hysteria. Geoffrey Nowell-Smith writes that

[9] Meisel, "Speaking Pictures," 65.

[10] Ibid., 64.

[11] See A. Nicholas Vardac, *Stage to Screen: Theatrical Origins of Early Film: David Garrick to D. W. Griffith* (New York: Da Capo Press, 1987); originally published as *Stage to Screen: Theatrical Method from Garrick to Griffith* (Cambridge: Harvard University Press, 1949).

[12] Griselda Pollock, ed., "Dossier on Melodrama," *Screen* 18, no. 2 (Summer 1977): 105–19.

the undischarged emotion which cannot be accommodated within the action, subordinated as it is to the demands of family/lineage/inheritance, is traditionally expressed in the music and, in the case of film, in certain elements of the mise-en-scène. That is to say, music and mise-en-scène do not just heighten the emotionality of an element of the action: to some extent they substitute for it. The mechanism here is strikingly similar to that of the psychopathology of hysteria. In hysteria (and specifically in what Freud has designated as "conversion hysteria") the energy attached to an idea that has been repressed returns converted into a bodily symptom. The "return of the repressed" takes place, not in conscious discourse, but displaced onto the body of the patient. In the melodrama, where there is always material which cannot be expressed in discourse or in the actions of the characters furthering the designs of the plot, a conversion can take place into the body of the text.[13]

In a sense, then, if the story cannot tell the whole story, the picture(s) will. Griselda Pollock calls for an identification of that repressed, and concludes that it is the displaced feminine.[14] This "feminine," which, according to Pollock, "includes both the feminine position and the foregone phallic sexuality of women," remains outside both patriarchal and bourgeois orders, and is therefore "irrecuperable." The ideological implications of her thesis run throughout this study, but suffice it to remark here that spectacle cannot come last in a poetics of melodrama, as it does in Aristotle's *Poetics* of tragedy.[15]

While all cinema has a large stake in the medium's spectacular component, the melodrama's special investment in mise en scène raises two contradictory issues that are taken up in the following chapter: the notion that men bear the look (that the image is appropriated by *his* gaze), and the notion that the melodramatic image, marked by excesses, subverts the male gaze. The melodramatic image, we might say, is more on the side of the Imaginary, more "fem-

[13] Geoffrey Nowell-Smith, "Minnelli and Melodrama," *Screen* 18, no. 2 (Summer 1977): 117.

[14] Pollock, "Dossier on Melodrama": 113.

[15] I am aware that what we may mean by "spectacle" is not what Aristotle meant by the term. But, as R. S. Crane points out in *The Languages of Criticism and the Structure of Poetry* (Toronto: University of Toronto Press, 1953; reprinted 1970), "The *Poetics* is a statement, or at least an outline sketch, of a science, and as such it deals with principles and causes rather than with conventions or poetic traditions, with the artistic necessities and possibilities of particular forms rather than with accepted rules and models. . . . Poetics, therefore, can never be thought of as something fixed and determined; it must aim, rather, to be a progressive science, always lagging somewhat behind poets but never, if it is to keep alive, remaining indifferent to what new poets are trying to do" (65).

inine" in the sense that it provides "others" in society perhaps with a means to "have some voice in the record of politics and history," a way to "gain entry to social experience,"[16] by "listening; by recognizing the unspoken in speech, even revolutionary speech; by calling attention at all times to whatever remains unsatisfied, repressed, new, eccentric, incomprehensible, disturbing to the *status quo*."[17]

If the family melodrama is a "feminine" form, it is so to the extent that it aspires to *jouissance*.[18] Of course most melodramas are made by men, and they are enjoyed by men as much as by women, but that does not alter anything, for the following pages assert that while there are culturally determined concepts of the "masculine" and of the "feminine," there is only one spectator, who is involved in a polymorphous play of identifications.

Very loosely one might take the feminine to be allied with the Imaginary, or pre-Oedipal, phase of the subject's formation, and the masculine to be on the side of the Symbolic. This distinction proceeds from the observation that in a patriarchal culture the symbolic order is masculine by definition. In representation there is no such thing, however, as pure symbolicity or the purely imaginary; the pre-Oedipal/Imaginary exists alongside the Oedipal/Symbolic. Every film, for example, must hold in tension these two contradictory impulses: the symbolic impulse towards narrative order, closure, etc., and the impulse of the Imaginary that, as we have said, contradicts what the Symbolic stands for. It is towards bliss, the shattering of boundaries, the subversion of the Symbolic, in music, all moments of excess, nonsense, perhaps all emotion itself.[19]

[16] Julia Kristeva, *About Chinese Women*, trans. Anita Barrows (New York: Urizen Books, 1977), 38.

[17] Ibid., 38.

[18] For the best "definition" of this term see Stephen Heath's "Translator's Note" in Roland Barthes, *Image, Music, Text* (New York: Hill and Wang, 1977). Heath notes that "*jouissance* is specifically contrasted to *plaisir* by Barthes in his *Le Plaisir du texte*: on the one hand a pleasure (*plaisir*) linked to cultural enjoyment and identity, to the cultural enjoyment of identity, to a homogenizing movement of the ego; on the other a radically violent pleasure (*jouissance*) which shatters—dissipates, loses—that cultural identity, that ego."

[19] While I assert repeatedly throughout this study that, for a proper understanding of how the film melodrama works, one must appreciate the integral role that music plays in it, I do not analyze this centrally important element of melodramatic address in any great detail. The reader is referred to Carol Flinn's recent article, "The 'Problem'

The melodramatic, then, by way of beginning a definition, is more on the side of the Imaginary than are other modes. Whatever is excessive in the melodrama is precisely so because it is beyond language. It is not recoverable by the driving impulses of the Symbolic to codify. If all of life involves a tension between discipline and desire, work and play—or, to invoke the master terms again, the Symbolic and the Imaginary—then it might be said that the melodrama answers to a desire for more of the Imaginary, for a way out of, or relief from, the excesses of the Symbolic. It may aspire to a purely imaginary realm, but such a thing is not really possible or desirable. In the medium of film the melodrama must bring this aspiration into textual existence through manipulations of sound and image, but as we have said, there is a problem already, with the image.

We should ask first why it is that vision is the privileged sense in our culture. Why do "men" still command the image, the subverting power of its melodramatic excesses notwithstanding? We are returned by this question to the original one of how "men" and "women" emerge from the polymorphously perverse sexuality of every child in the pre-Oedipal phase. Victor Burgin offers an answer:

To deny that biology *determines* psychology is not however to deny that the body *figures*. . . . The body *figures*, is *represented*, in psychic life. In male psychic life these representations turn between the poles of having/not having the phallus. This is so for the female too, but the male has the means of representing the phallus, as an integral part of his body, in the form of the penis. Male desire, in so far as it leaves its trace in the image, is premised on castration anxiety. . . . Man's desire in/for the image is lodged under the sign of *fetishism*. The fetish is that fragment which allays the fetishist's castration anxiety by serving as a reassuring substitute for that which he construes as "missing" from the woman's body. . . . Man's desire is, most fundamentally, in and for that which can be *seen*. If the penis serves as privileged signifier of the phallus, we are told by several writers, it is because it is *visible*.[20]

---

of Femininity in Theories of Film Music," *Screen* 27, no. 6 (November–December 1986): 56–72; and to other articles, such as Noël and Patrick Carroll, "Notes on Movie Music," *Studies in the Literary Imagination* 19, no. 1 (Spring 1986): 73–81; and to my own "Carnal Stereophony: A Reading of *Diva*," *Screen* 25, no. 3 (May–June 1984): 70–77. See also Elisabeth Weis and John Belton, eds., *Film Sound: Theory and Practice* (New York: Columbia University Press, 1985); and, in that excellent anthology, Martin Rubin, "The Voice of Silence: Sound Style in John Stahl's *Back Street*" (277–85).

[20] Victor Burgin, "Man, Desire, Image," in *Desire*, ed. Lisa Appignanesi (London: ICA Publications, 1984), 32–33. All this, of course, comes from Lacan: see n. 26 in "Melodrama and the 'Ways of the World.' "

The suggestion here is that all images are fetish structures, and since, strictly speaking, a woman cannot be a fetishist, how does she "see"? Or rather, under what sign is the woman's desire in/for the image lodged? These questions are considered in the following chapter on the address of film(s) and of the family melodrama in particular.

4. Address

A PROMISE or possibility that melodrama implicitly always holds is "that there may be some other logic. . . . That is, a logic that challenges mastery."[1] When Lacan says, "Just go look at Bernini's statue in Rome, you'll see right away that St. Theresa is coming, there's no doubt about it,"[2] Irigaray asks, "In Rome? So far away? To look? At a statue? Of a saint? Sculpted by a man? What pleasure are we talking about? Whose pleasure?" Irigaray asks these questions because Bernini's statue is not a woman, but a representation—something other than herself. And of her pleasure, her *jouissance*, how is it that we can see it, but not understand it? The same can be said of the film melodrama, the so-called "woman's film." We see it, but what do we see? Can we see what we do not understand? It is possible that in relation to other Hollywood genres the melodrama represents a challenge, and it poses a challenge, certainly, to ask the questions: "Woman's film"?[3] Made by men? What pleasure are we talking about? Whose pleasure?

The questions are implicit throughout this study, and they are the chief subject of this chapter, which addresses the question of address. To whom the family melodrama is addressed and the assumptions on which it is founded are vitally important questions, for the melodrama is a drama of identity, of protest, and of wish-fulfillment. We must thus ask what the melodrama is protesting, what sorts of identities it seeks (for its characters), what its implied utopia is, and how, by its address, it positions the viewer in a play of identifications. We have said that the family melodrama's address is ostensibly

[1] Luce Irigaray, *This Sex Which Is Not One*, trans. Catherine Porter (Ithaca, N.Y.: Cornell University Press, 1985), 90–91.

[2] Jacques Lacan, *Encore: Le Séminaire XX* (Paris: Sueil, 1975), 70.

[3] Although here and elsewhere I appear to suggest that the "woman's film" and the family melodrama are the same thing, I appreciate that they are not. Most of the films in this study, in fact, cannot be called "women's films" at all, but they do share with the "woman's film" a mode of address—an address to culture's "others."

to (traditionally heterosexual) women. But there is evidence that family melodramas appeal as often to (traditionally heterosexual) men, and that in fact film melodramas, unlike romance novels, are most often made by men. Thus, in order to state precisely how these films are understood as "women's films" (in spite of the fact that they appeal to men and are made by men), we need to examine the codes of representation employed in the Hollywood melodrama. Some of these codes are specific to Hollywood, others to the melodrama, and others to modern western civilization generally. This chapter seeks to assess the address of the spectacle, the ideological underpinnings of the film melodrama (some of the assumptions of "realism," for example), and the way in which narrative codes articulate and signify a construction of sexuality.

History/Discourse

If the family melodrama contains both progressive and reactionary impulses, we must ask what is progressive and liberating about the form, and what is reactionary and oppressive about it. Of course, the question immediately produces the next question: for whom is it liberating and for whom (whether they are aware of it or not) is the form oppressive? Is the family melodrama progressive only in its narratives? Or is it progressive also on the level of the cinematic signifier? And how, very specifically, is it reactionary? We ask these questions because some melodramas, for example, have been called "women's films," and it must be ascertained whether that means the form can represent an overtly "feminine" *challenge* to the dominant masculine codes of dramatic, narrative filmmaking, or show where women stand in patriarchal culture (in itself a challenge!), or that the form is covertly one of patriarchal ideology's ways of keeping women in their historical position of subordination to masculine imperatives.

The distinction, then, between *history* and *discourse* is extremely important for this discussion, since it offers a place to begin an investigation of how ideology works—of how it interpellates the subject. Simply understood, discourse and story are both forms of enunciation, but in the discursive mode the source of the enunciation is present, and in the historical (story-fied) form it is suppressed. In a story, one might find a "there," a "then," a "he," "she," or "it," whereas in discourse one is "here, now," and the pronouns are more likely to be "I" and "you."[4]

The cinema, particularly Hollywood cinema, has been examined as a vehicle for ideology, or to use Althusserian terms, as an Ideological State Apparatus.[5] This is to say that certain class positions are expressed by films, but in the story-cinema those positions (which *position* viewers) are not self-conscious in their ideological function, which is to produce and reproduce the individual's relation to the social structure/reality. In other words, it is recognized that film is a powerful medium, and as such cannot be innocent in its address, which will always be in the service of, or will express, one ideology or another. Film's positioning reproduces a relationship to society, and in the "story" mode of classical narrative film this operation of ideology is invisible. Since film theory now is very much concerned with subject identity (what it means to be an "I" or a "you"), and with ideology (the part it plays in the construction of an "I" or a "you"), the terms "story" and "discourse" draw attention to the matter of ideology—the contradictions of which, as we have said, are melodrama's central concern.

In recent developments in the theory of the subject, Marxism and psychoanalysis have been the favored instruments of reading for coming to terms with the construction of identity and uncovering the way ideology works; film theory conceives of its spectator as a "subject" whose "construction" (*before* film viewing) is understood via psychoanalysis (the human subject) and Marxism (the social subject). If films are made *for* viewers—and undeniably they are—to what extent do the films determine the identity of those viewers, and conversely, to what extent do those viewers determine the identity, the nature, structure, mode of address, of the films? The viewer watching a film that is presented as *histoire* (i.e., a mainstream Hollywood film) is not aware of how he or she is being addressed (the address positioning, or inscribing an identity for, the viewer), whereas a viewer watching a film in the discursive mode finds that spectatorship is foregrounded and suspension of disbelief is not so easy.

The curious thing about the story/discourse distinction is that once

[4] Geoffrey Nowell-Smith, "A Note on History/Discourse," *Edinburgh Magazine*, no. 1 (1976): 27.

[5] Louis Althusser, *Lenin and Philosophy and Other Essays*, trans. Ben Brewster (New York and London: Monthly Review Press, 1971), 127–86.

it is recognized with semiotic consciousness that Hollywood cinema is on the side of story (where the avant-garde, say, is not), the distinction becomes useless. A student of film, for example, cannot even "see" a film, any film, as *histoire*, simply because he or she knows how it is constructed *as histoire*. The film then, for that viewer (who "knows about the cinema"), is seen on a discursive plane. Perhaps no film, even for the average viewer—since postmodernist awareness is widespread—is "innocent" anymore, in the way Hollywood melodramas once were. But the "realist" impulse is strong among viewers, and in a dialectical way discursive figures are constantly being appropriated by the historical mode. Everything, even the most bizarre extremities of the avant-garde, is eventually swallowed up, or at least touched, by the impulse that characterizes the story mode—the impulse to naturalize. The melodrama is nothing if it is not a story; the form has been so popular because we love stories. The human subject above all writes experience in narratives, and narratives must naturalize. Where this leaves the history/discourse distinction for viewers—viewers both willing to "believe" the story, and yet imbued in our time with a postmodern sense of irony—is unclear. This study stops short of the supremely ironic Douglas Sirk and Nicholas Ray melodramas of the 1950s and 1960s for this very reason.[6] But for theory, the distinction between *histoire* (the "innocent" melodrama) and *discours* (the ironic melodrama) is one that is still worth making, if only because it can inaugurate a discussion about subject positioning.

The "Masculine" Spectator

On the psychoanalytic level there is really only one spectator, and he/she is "masculine." But to use a term like "masculine" can be dangerous and misleading, unless distinctions are made between masculinity as a *position*, man as a *signifier* in filmic discourse, and men as a *sex* with a dominant status in culture.[7] To describe all spectators

---

[6] Minnelli often belongs with Sirk and Ray and other melodramatists who (in Elsaesser's words) portray the "demise of the affirmative culture." For a discussion of this complex issue of the structure and function of the ironic/pessimistic/progressive text, see Barbara Klinger, " 'Cinema/Ideology/Criticism' Revisited: The Progressive Text," *Screen* 25, no. 1 (January–February 1984): 30–44.

[7] Cf. Griselda Pollock, "Dossier on Melodrama," *Screen* 18, no. 2 (Summer 1977): 109, n. 1.

as masculine is to imply that women can only derive pleasure from films if they identify with a masculine gaze.[8] It suggests also that everything that is not masculine must therefore be "feminine," which can suggest that whatever is repressed in our culture (which in films could result in stylistic deformation) might be described in terms of the "feminine."[9] The terms, rather, should express the relationship between a dominant mode and that which challenges it. There are various expressions of "masculinity" in our culture; as a general notion the term is quite flexible. And it is in this flexible sense of the term—permitting some play at the edges, mixing with some so-called "feminine" qualities, capable of "other" identifications[10]— that I call the film spectator (regardless of sex) "masculine."

Masculinity as a position or philosophical category of course exists, and its effects are perfectly real, but in movie characters masculinity in this distilled sense is figured only in instances, in behavior or aspects of being. Masculinity as a concept, unlike my "masculine spectator," could be characterized in terms of a father's absolute sexual, political, and social control. Thus, "the ultimate social definition of the form of the father's body" is an

imperturbable, unshaken, inflexible, sober-minded, sexless and lifeless, silent, cold, odorous with death, ghastly pale (all blood transfused to the state's disposal), tired but powerful and self-disciplined, disciplining structure. The body of an unmoving father, barricading vast social territory, creates heavy traffic, the traffic which the father will then regulate himself. His lifelessness will regulate life; his sexlessness wants to castrate.[11]

It should be understood, in light of the play of identifications that takes place in the film-watching experience, that masculinity, like

[8] In "Afterthoughts on 'Visual Pleasure and Narrative Cinema' Inspired by *Duel in the Sun*" (*Framework* 15/16/17 [1981]), Laura Mulvey describes this trans-sex identification as a *habit*, a putting on of "borrowed transvestite clothes," which "becomes *second Nature*" (13). For Mulvey, theorizing within Freudian terms that equate activity and masculinity (and that assert that masculinity—a *metaphor*—is at one stage, namely in the phallic phase, ego-syntonic for a woman), the female spectator "temporarily accepts 'masculinization' in memory of her 'active' phase" (15).

[9] Pollock, "Dossier on Melodrama": 109–13.

[10] According to J. Laplanche and J.-B. Pontalis, identification refers to the "psychological process whereby the subject assimilates an aspect, property or attribute of the other and is transformed, wholly or partially, after the model the other provides. It is by means of a series of identifications that the personality is constituted and specified." (*The Language of Psycho-Analysis*, trans. Donald Nicholson-Smith [New York: Norton, 1973], 205.)

[11] Krzysztof Wodiczko, "Public Projections," *October* 38 (Fall, 1986): 6.

femininity, is an attribute of both men and women, and in human beings (film spectators and characters in films) it is rarely manifested in the radical manner described above. The quotation is from an article about public monuments and projections which signify masculinity as a position. But having thus identified masculinity with a "monumental lesson on the patrio-patriarchate,"[12] it should be understood that a discussion of the terms of address in film melodrama is more concerned with men or women as signifiers in filmic discourse, and with men and women as sexes in culture, than with masculinity as a position. In the melodrama we are concerned, ostensibly, with the point of view of the "other" in our (patriarchal) culture, which in most cases is with the "feminine," with feminine concerns. The "feminine" is a notion we might even understand—depending on whether we adhere to the terms of recent psychoanalysis, or follow Deleuze and Guattari—as capable of application to anyone or anything. On the one hand, psychoanalysis tells us that anyone may become a woman in order to have a privileged relationship to *jouissance*:[13] "Everything happens as if 'to become a woman,' 'to be a woman,' opened access to a *jouissance* of the body as feminine *and/or* maternal."[14] On the other hand (Deleuze and Guattari), the "becoming" (woman) refers not to some sort of identification with a Freudian-psychoanalytic notion of femininity (as metaphor), but to "becoming caught up in a process of osmosis (not metaphor) with de-anthropologized and de-identitized entities—women, infants, animals, foreigners, the insane—in order to resist the dominant mode of representation represented by any majority."[15]

Since all of Hollywood cinema is to a greater or lesser degree melodramatic, it becomes necessary to identify the ways in which the melodrama as a genre is singular, to gauge whether, indeed, the melodrama allows the spectator (male or female) special access to a *jouissance* of the body as feminine and/or maternal, and/or catches one up in a process of resistance to the dominant mode of representation.[16] My thesis that the melodrama is more on the side of the

[12] Ibid., 6.

[13] Alice Jardine, "Woman in Limbo: Deleuze and His Br(others)," *SubStance* 44/45 (1984): 51.

[14] Ibid., 51. Jardine is quoting Michèle Montrelay, *L'Ombre et le nom* (Paris: Minuit, 1977), 69.

[15] Ibid., 52.

[16] E. Ann Kaplan asked this question five years ago in a short summary and clarifi-

Imaginary, both in its subject matter and its style (which is to say, also on the level of the cinematic signifier), makes a claim for the genre as one that strikes a unique tension between narrative and spectacle, between, in a loose correspondence, the Symbolic and the Imaginary orders—with masculinity and men commanding the Symbolic, and femininity and women allied with *jouissance* and the Imaginary. The melodrama traffics between modes, between sexualities, between discourses, and the paradoxes of the balance which the successful melodrama achieves are perhaps the form's greatest source of power and fascination.

Suture

If the melodrama spectator is held in a peculiar tension between the Symbolic and the Imaginary, oscillating between regimes of presence and absence, narrative and spectacle, mastery and *jouissance*, how can one account for the allure of this process, and how is the spectator centered, secured, *identified*?

Film theory since World War II has to a great extent been concerned with accounting for the allure of the cinematic image—from André Bazin's notion that the allure of the photographic image has its origins in the desire of the human subject to make resemblances in order to defeat death,[17] to Stephen Heath's thesis that "space becomes place,"[18] in an operation according to which space, dominated by narrative procedures, becomes a site of sense. And where Bazin sought to "preserve the mystery of the human face," out of an unwillingness or inability to probe deeply into the question of what the spectator's relationship with the face is, such later theorists as Christian Metz, Stephen Heath and Laura Mulvey have used semiotics and psychoanalysis to find answers for just such questions.

In his essay "Narrative Space," Heath gives a socio-historical account of how human subjectivity has come to be what it is—of why narrative is necessary in the signifying operations of the cinema. His

cation of several important issues relating to melodrama. See "Theories of Melodrama: A Feminist Perspective," *Women and Performance* 1, no. 1 (1983): 40–48.

[17] Bazin called this desire to make resemblances the "mummy complex," after the ancient Egyptian practice of preserving the bodies of the pharaohs and others who could afford to make such a bid for immortality.

[18] Stephen Heath, "Narrative Space," *Questions of Cinema* (Bloomington: Indiana University Press, 1981), 19–75.

examination of such operations in classical cinema reveals that signifying procedures are dominated by narrative procedures. Invisible editing, for example, is space submitted to narrative. The signifying practice of match-cutting, for example, is made invisible in the service of narrative. It is the movement of narrative that assures us of the position of the subject.

Heath writes about the "imperialism of vision," a way of looking at the world (and therefore, in this culture, of knowing the world) which began in Florence and now rules from Hollywood. The monocular, central perspective painting of the Renaissance, like the photograph (also monocular perspective), produces the spectator as a stable subject. The perspective is an organization of elements aimed at the viewer (me). The painting or photograph provides me with an epistemology, a model of what it is to know. The photograph, centering me as stable subject, produces the illusion that it is I, the subject, who organizes the world out there. Photography demonstrates the "naturalness" of Renaissance perspective by the "fact" that photographs are machine-made and that there appears to be no human intervention in the photograph's tracing of reality. (It is easy to see how Heath might endorse Bazin's "Myth of Total Cinema,"[19] the myth of the constant move towards utopian vision—seeing *and* knowing. However, for Heath this is a cultural symptom, while for Bazin it is a fact of human nature.)

In painting, the perspectival representations are fixed and singular, while in the cinema they are not. The cinema viewing subject is kept secure, however, processed through a series of such perspectival representations. And it is *narrative* which ensures that space will be a site of sense; the subject's position as the point of the world's changing spatial relations is ensured. Heath describes the movement of the cinema as metonymic, running on a perpetual lack (from lack to fulfillment to lack, and so on). There is lack both between frames, in the space that is not recorded as image, and beyond the borders of the frame, in unseen off-screen space. Film, thus, might well de-center us as subjects.

But as subjects we are kept secure because classical Hollywood cinema *uses* that lack (off-screen space) and thereby contains it. Heath

[19] André Bazin, "The Myth of Total Cinema," in *What Is Cinema?*, vol. 1, trans. Hugh Gray (Berkeley: University of California Press, 1967), 17–22.

calls that use of lack *suture*. In its simplest sense, suture refers to stitching the subject into a discourse. In shot counter-shot syntagma it is I (subject) who connect shots A and B. I am between them; I make sense of them. In some sense the point of view in the Hollywood cinema is always mine.[20]

Heath's point about suture is that narrative strategies and functions at the cinematic level do the job of centering as much as narrative on an extra-cinematic level. But his thesis in "Narrative Space" is ultimately a question of convention. "Spaces are born and die like societies; they live, they have a history."[21] What he does, merely, is give a socio-historical account of the way the image is coded, which, for our purposes, suggests that filmic address is a purely culturally-determined process, capable of appropriation by "feminine" imperatives or by the melodrama itself.

Metz's "Subject"

Christian Metz, in a more general way, maintains that the image is coded as analogy.[22] It reenacts an already-completed phase of the subject's formation. While Heath challenges early Metz on the naturalness of the image—claiming that it is the code that produces the subject[23] (or, in other words, that the subject is processed *through* films)—Metz says that one is not formed as a subject by the film. Rather, the subject enters the movie theater seeking to have subjectivity confirmed, for one is an "already constituted ego." Metz's semiotics seeks to transcend both the individual critic and the Bazinian notion that the spectating subject's response to the work of art has a mystical, unanalyzable element.

By a psychoanalysis of the specifically cinematic signifier, Metz attempts to explain the appeal of representations, which leads him to an examination of the spectating subject. Metz argues that in the suc-

---

[20] Much has been written about suture, an overview of which, as it has been discussed in film theory, may be found in Kaja Silverman, "Suture" [Excerpts], *Narrative, Apparatus, Ideology,* ed. Philip Rosen (New York: Columbia University Press, 1986), 219–35. Excerpted from chapter 5 of Kaja Silverman, *The Subject of Semiotics* (New York: Oxford University Press, 1983).

[21] Heath, *Questions of Cinema,* 29.

[22] Christian Metz, *The Imaginary Signifier,* trans. Celia Britton, Annwyl Williams, Ben Brewster, and Alfred Guzzetti (Bloomington: Indiana University Press, 1982).

[23] In Heath's words, *cinema dramatizes vision.*

cessful cinema experience there is identification; there must be identification or the film will not work. This identification of the filmgoer
with what is on the screen takes place, Metz asserts, because all representations are fetish structures. He does not, however, elaborate on
what fetish structures are, in the way Mulvey will. But in his stated
effort to see what contribution Freudian psychoanalysis can make to
knowledge of the cinematic signifier, he describes the *mirror stage* (a
process identified by psychoanalysis), which the child experiences
sometime between the sixth and eighteenth month of its life.

Metz recognizes the integral part that fetishism and voyeurism
play in the film-watching experience, but he feels that one must begin at the mirror stage in order to understand "the desire to see in its
ultimate indivisibility." He differentiates this type of seeing from voyeurism, which is a desire "according to a different system, that of
the primal scene and the keyhole." The Metzian account of the formation of the subject, then, reenacted by the cinema, is the same for
men and women.

The Mirror Stage and Identification

The mirror stage[24] refers to that time when the child first recognizes
itself, from which it develops a sense of self and other. Before this
"moment" the child of course already recognizes the mother, but
does not perceive her as a separate being, for she is, like everything
else in the child's world, perceived as an extension of itself. The moment the child recognizes itself in the mirror (which is only possible
if it simultaneously sees another individual, probably the mother, in
the mirror), the child recognizes that it is an entity in the world, separate from its mother and all other objects. At the mirror stage the
child's motor capabilities are very limited, which has the effect of
making the child's image (in the mirror) seem "superior"—freer, bigger, more coherent and more mobile. This first moment of identification—which paradoxically and simultaneously produces both a
sense of self *and* other (the image)—is one of both jubilation (because
the child imagines the mirror image to be better than actuality) and
loss (because the child senses its "otherness" in the world and its

[24] Jacques Lacan, "The mirror stage as formative of the function of the I as revealed
in psychoanalytic experience," *Ecrits*, trans. Alan Sheridan (New York: Norton, 1977),
1–7.

separation from this perfect image). At this point all relations with others are conceived in terms of identifications. After the mirror phase, castration will always threaten such "self-perfection," prompting the subject to seek the security of an image which it can never again possess. The original image was of the self, and as such the self becomes the object of desire, but it is only through the other, in the image, that the self can in some way be realized. This impossible situation persists to the end of the subject's life.

When Metz says that the cinema runs on an imaginary lack, it is not in a specifically sexual sense of the word (the threat of castration, etc.) that he uses it, as Mulvey, who uses similar terms, does. It is the lack one experiences when facing the mirror/screen image and which is then overcome, circumvented, by the "play of identifications." The cinema, Metz points out, is only *like* a mirror. One cannot say it *is* a mirror. Not only is the fictional signified absent (which puts the cinema on the side of the Imaginary) but, more important perhaps, the body of the spectator is missing (from the screen, that other kind of mirror) because the spectator already has an ego. Strictly speaking, if all identifications after the mirror stage are secondary identifications (Lacan), then cinematic identification would be tertiary. But Metz instead speaks of "primary" cinematic identification as an identification with the camera. This explains why, since there must be identification in the film-watching experience, the image without human figures is still alluring. In scenes of countryside, for example, where am I? I am *all* perception. The film is there for me— a notion similar to Heath's notion of the place of the spectating subject. I am the place where the Imaginary joins the Symbolic. In such a situation, one has pure perception, in which the subject transcends the object. The spectator "*identifies with himself*, with himself as a pure act of perception."[25]

Laura Mulvey and Sexual Difference

While Heath believes that it is the movement of narrative that assures us of the position of the subject, and Metz emphasizes the narcissistic pull of the image (the regimes of absence that put the cinema on the

[25] Metz, *The Imaginary Signifier*, 49.

side of the Imaginary), for Laura Mulvey it is impossible to talk about identification and "the look" without talking about sexuality.

As Mulvey sees it, the unconscious of patriarchal society has structured film form, making it a voyeuristic, scopophilic language of desire, with woman as image and man as bearer of the look. The one who controls the look controls language, and the one who controls language controls the world. Mulvey seeks to question the language in which women are inscribed—the language of the patriarchal order—and in so doing, offers a theory of the spectating subject that is inflected by the recognition of sexual difference.

In "Visual Pleasure and Narrative Cinema,"[26] Mulvey suggests that in patriarchal culture woman can exist "only in relation to castration and cannot transcend it." And it is the image of the castrated woman that gives order and meaning to the (phallocentric) cinema. The spectating subject, then, is always positioned in relation to the phallus as privileged signifier.

If, as Metz and Heath say, the cinema runs on a lack, that lack for Mulvey is specifically the threat of castration which the female's lack of a penis poses. The cinema as fetish object (phallus substitute) circumvents the threat. It is the phallus one's mother never had, the phallus the absence of which is a constant threat to one's corporeal self. The belief of the child is that the mother has been castrated, and the fetish is a defense against castration anxiety.

While Metz sees the Imaginary (corresponding to the mirror phase when the child sees everything as a reflection of self) as more important in the cinema, Mulvey sees the Symbolic (the play of differences that is language) as more important. This is why she puts an emphasis on character identification; it is a form of reassurance. The child enters the Symbolic in order to confirm the child's identity and sense of self.

Like Heath, Mulvey analyzes the cinema in terms of a dialectic of narrative and spectacle, but she feels that narrative in the cinema uses space as a place of action for a *male* ego. The woman, on the other hand, is the privileged object of the spectacle, (1) for the gaze of the spectator in the audience, and (2) for the gaze of a character (usually the male hero) in the film. Moreover, the body of the woman

---

[26] Laura Mulvey, "Visual Pleasure and Narrative Cinema," *Screen* 16, no. 3 (Autumn 1975): 6–18.

gives us a two-dimensional space—it halts the narrative—while the male propels the narrative by his look, his movement through a three-dimensional space.

As Mulvey points out, woman as signifier of castration is not specific to film. What is specific to film is the pleasure of looking. She summarizes the three looks of the cinema: the look of the camera; the look of the spectating subject; and the look between characters within the film. The first two are subordinated to the third, and the third is structured for the identification of the male spectating subject. While this sort of classification of the look is not entirely original,[27] Mulvey's stress on looking as a male prerogative in patriarchal society represents a daring shift of emphasis in Freudian psychology. The issue of sexual difference is now central to any discussion of the spectating subject in the cinema, for the recognition that ours is a patriarchal society has forced contemporary psychoanalysis to attend more closely to the subject's relation to the language of the patriarchy. While Mulvey's crucial recasting of cinematic viewing in terms of sexual difference has been a significant contribution to film studies, she has been criticized for too binary a notion of looking: she makes a distinction between male looking and female "to-be-looked-at-ness." Metz, on the other hand, calls the symbolic order (what Mulvey calls the language of the patriarchy) neither a superstructure nor an infrastructure, but a juxtastructure. Echoing Freud, who destroyed the notion of the unified ego/subject, and Heath, for whom there is no such thing as the unified subject outside the processes that produce it, Metz is attracted to the notion of some "deeper strata" in the cinema that somehow transcend Mulvey's easy opposition.

Heath's project, as I have suggested, is a little different again. He is interested in the address of film—what it means to be an "I" or a

---

[27] Bazin comes closest to locating the position of the spectating subject in his essays on "Theater and Cinema." He establishes the denominator common to the stage and screen as "the viewpoint of the spectator." But before arriving at this point he discusses the three ways of analyzing reality (vis-à-vis editing techniques) and in so doing discusses "the look" which twenty-two years later Laura Mulvey explores further with the tools of psychoanalysis. Bazin lists (1) "the purely logical and descriptive analysis," (2) "a psychological analysis from within the film, namely one that fits the point of view of one of the protagonists in a given situation," and (3) "a psychological analysis from the point of view of spectator interest." These points of view, he says, imply a "psychological heterogeneity," and in so saying, he raises the question of the place and definition of the spectating subject, that site of psychological heterogeneity.

"you." He is interested in the places the film offers the spectator to be an *I*.

Subjectivity and Spectatorship

To reiterate, notions of the spectating subject in post-World War II film theory have generally sprung from an attempt to account for the allure of the cinema. While the *politique des auteurs* posed by François Truffaut (and qualified by Bazin) accepts as a given the notion of a unified subject, the "theory of the subject," as it has come to be called, has functioned as a refusal of the notion of the *auteur* as the unified source of the text—a refusal of the author except as an effect of the text. What we see in film theory from Bazin onwards imitates the kind of change we see in the "moral occult" of the melodrama, from a regard for the Sacred and mysterious and a belief in the unity of the subject (Bazin) towards an increasingly precise analysis of the signifier and a questioning of the unity of the subject (Metz, Heath, Mulvey). While melodrama believes in the unity of the subject, it does so in reaction to the sense that the subject is not unified. Nineteenth-century theatrical melodrama, it must be remembered, was a response to an undermining of the certainties that characterized the coherent universe of the tragedy. Like the operations of suture in the cinema, the melodrama works to create a sense of unity. The power of that sense of unity is *imaginary*, which is to say (as Metz would say), a "perfectly real power."[28]

Moreover, when we consider the family melodrama, or the "woman's film"—the film that is supposedly made for and about the (bourgeois) patriarchy's "other"—in light of recent film theory's politicization of the spectating subject, we find Lacan's assertion to have even more force: "if the libido is only masculine, it is only from that place where she is whole, the dear woman—that is to say, from that place where man sees her, and only from there—that the dear woman can have an unconscious."[29] In short, woman has no unconscious except the one man gives her. The discourses that dominate both the melodrama and film theory have coalesced in psychoanalysis, which suggests that in the end we learn everything about male

---

[28] Metz, *The Imaginary Signifier*, 5.
[29] Quoted in Irigaray, *This Sex Which Is Not One*, 93.

desire from the melodrama, and nothing about female desire. In other words, while "one of the defining generic features of the woman's picture as a textual system is its construction of narratives motivated by female desire and processes of spectator identification governed by female point-of-view,"[30] we find that female desire and female point of view are symptomatic of male desire and point of view. Our poststructuralist perception that nothing escapes writing and that everything is modeled on the structure of language (and the process of its inscription) confirms the rhetorical nature of E. Ann Kaplan's question, "Is the gaze male?"[31] Yes (as Kaplan demonstrates conclusively in her textual readings), of course the gaze is masculine. If language is masculine (and we have asserted that the Hollywood family melodrama is but an " 'in house' rearrangement"[32] under the roof of the language of the patriarchy), then "the gaze"—a metaphor for language—is masculine. The melodramatic discourse, like recent film theory, is always in some sense a discourse on female sexuality—in that sense in which both are concerned with language, and both, finding repeatedly that language is masculine, are returned to questions of femininity.

By questioning the address of the family melodrama in terms made available by psychoanalysis and recent film theory, the whole Western tradition is repeated, but, as Irigaray points out, now the truth of this tradition is brought to light, "a *sexual* truth this time."[33] But to

---

[30] Annette Kuhn, "Women's Genres," *Screen* 25, no. 1 (January–February 1984): 18.

[31] This question is the title of the opening chapter of Kaplan's book, *Women and Film: Both Sides of the Camera* (New York and London: Methuen, 1983). Kaplan's question is clearly a rhetorical/political strategy, a way of addressing certain groups within American feminism at a specific moment. Since Laura Mulvey's famous article on "Visual Pleasure and Narrative Cinema" appeared in *Screen* in 1975, a great deal of fascinating work has been done in the area of theorizing the female spectator. See Bibliography: Flitterman (1978), Gledhill (1978), Doane (1980), Mulvey (1981). Critiques of Mulvey include Willemen (1976), Rodowick (1982a), Kuhn (1982), Walker (1984), and most recently, providing radical challenges to Mulvey's paradigm of spectatorship, Studlar (1984), Koch (1985), and Neale (1986b). Some other significant American contributions in the 1980s to the field of female spectatorship include Doane (1982b, 1983), Modleski (1982, 1984), de Lauretis (1984), and the recent debate in *Cinema Journal* between Linda Williams and E. Ann Kaplan through readings of *Stella Dallas*: Kaplan (1983a), Williams (1984), and Kaplan's response in *Cinema Journal* 24, no. 2 (Winter 1985): 40–43. Some of the theses produced by recent scholarship on female spectatorship are outlined in Hansen (1986) and in Kaplan (1986).

[32] Stephen Neale, *Genre* (London: British Film Institute, 1980), 22.

[33] Irigaray, *This Sex Which Is Not One*, 86.

bring "the truth of this tradition to light" is itself a useful achievement. It is one of the liberating achievements of the family melodrama and of a film theory that can reveal this "truth" in other terms.
And we have observed that in the melodrama, as in sexual pleasure,
there is something which escapes the grasp of discourse. Sexual pleasure, we know,[34] is engulfed in the body of the Other, which is in the
end unattainable, paradoxically thereby "producing" that pleasure.
That "something which escapes the grasp of discourse" might be the
key to a liberation from the shackles of our desire, which is why the
melodrama is drawn to it even though pursuit of it so often seems to
be like trying to see one's own face without the aid of a mirror, or
like trying to catch one's own shadow. For Lacan, certainly, although
the female tells him nothing,[35] there is a possibility for understanding, a possibility for her speech, in *jouissance*, through the interme-
diary of the body's orgasmic pleasure.[36]

While "triumph, despair and protest are the basic emotions of
melodrama, and the art of working each to its highest pitch occasions
the *catharsis* of the form,"[37] the form's ideologically liberating function resides in the *recognition* which occasions the emotion in the
spectator. The spectator recognizes that he or she is not alone in his
or her desire for "some other logic. . . . That is, a logic that challenges mastery."[38] The family melodrama addresses this spectator,
who is too often ignored by other genres and by the world in which
they are produced.

[34] Ibid., 97.
[35] "Le sexe de la femme ne lui dit rien." (Lacan, *Encore: Le Séminaire XX*, 13.)
[36] "par l'intermédiaire de la jouissance du corps." (Ibid., 13.)
[37] James L. Smith, *Melodrama* (London: Methuen, 1973), 9.
[38] Irigaray, *This Sex Which Is Not One*, 90.

5. Genre

THE AFI Catalogue[1] listing feature films made in Hollywood between 1921 and 1930 indicates that almost every film was understood at the time to be a melodrama. Page after page lists melodramas of every sort—rural melodramas, western melodramas, Gothic melodramas, sentimental melodramas, and so on. The American Film Institute took the descriptions of these thousands of films from contemporary press releases and posters. The appearance of the word melodrama in the description/definition of almost every film suggests that an attempt was being made by the industry both to define itself and to develop and consolidate as an industry, which involved reassuring itself and the public on which it was so dependent that films can be differentiated and recognized with ease, classified according to genre. The studio had to know what it was making, and the public needed to know what it was going to see.

The word "melodrama" denoted, or perhaps only connoted, a certain approach to material that became synonymous with the Hollywood formula. This approach had less to do with the notion of specific genres (the western, the crime film), or with basic attractions (sex, character, action, novelty)—which, as James Monaco has noted, "work across the media spectrum without regard to form"[2]—than with consumption. To "go to the movies" was to go to a movie theater in the expectation of seeing the same old basic attractions handled in a certain way. Comprehending all the genres that Hollywood produced is "Hollywood" itself—the Hollywood approach to genre, the Hollywood *formula*, which, as we have observed, is to some extent a function of the industrial context of the American cinema:

Hollywood genre production tended both to foreground convention and stereotypicality in order to gain instant audience recognition of its type—this is a Western, a Gangster, a Woman's Picture, etc.—and to institute a type of

[1] *The American Film Institute Feature Film Catalogue (1921–1930)* (New York: Bowker, 1976).

[2] James Monaco, *American Film Now: The People, the Power, the Money, the Movies* (New York: Oxford University Press, 1979), 12.

aesthetic play among the conventions in order to pose the audience with a question that would keep them coming back—not "what is going to happen next?" to which they would already have the answer, but "how?"[3]

The Hollywood formula most closely resembled what we later came to call the melodrama, after it became apparent that it was pointless to call every film a melodrama. The Hollywood story was told in a linear fashion (flashbacks and parallel action notwithstanding);[4] the line of action was generally straight, and told in an effort to be entertaining and clearly understood—which, of course, encouraged a certain simplification of everything: character, action, moral framework. The narrative tended to center on an individual with whom the audience could identify. This contributed to the advent of the phenomenon of the star, who was an ideal for audience identification and who, as a constant personality from film to film, entrenched the operations of genre, which turn on repetition and ritual. The narrative, primarily for reasons of clarity in a new medium, was structured around a hero and a villain, or more generally and more to the point, around the moral opposites of good and evil. In nearly all Hollywood films, regardless of the genre into which the film might fall, Virtue had to triumph, even if only in a tacked-on coda. This practice was made law in the Production Code of 1934. Generally, active virtue operated in adventure films, westerns, and so on (the films with heroes), and passive virtue dominated in what is generally called the melodrama.

Like the "semiology" which de Saussure foresaw, "of which linguistics would at once be one part and the privileged guide,"[5] melodrama has been consolidated as *a* film genre, but is also the model for *all* film genres. Melodrama is genre's archetype. While there is a genre called the melodrama (what I have been loosely calling the family melodrama), genre in the archetypal sense has no content "until experience has rendered it visible" (Jung). The "archetypal," as Rosemary Gordon elaborates, "is a metapsychological construct

---

[3] Christine Gledhill, "*Klute* 1: A Contemporary Film Noir and Feminist Criticism," in *Women in Film Noir*, ed. E. Ann Kaplan (London: British Film Institute, 1980), 11.

[4] See Eisenstein's thesis in "Dickens, Griffith, and the Film Today," in *Film Form: Essays in Film Theory*, ed. and trans. Jay Leyda (New York: Harcourt Brace Jovanovich, 1949), 195–255, regarding Griffith's montage, which he feels is always linear, and therefore undynamic, regardless of plot convolutions.

[5] Rosalind Coward and John Ellis, *Language and Materialism: Developments in Semiology and the Theory of the Subject* (London: Routledge & Kegan Paul, 1977), 25.

whose function is to subsume under one heading—and to help us recognize—a family link between a number of discrete and observable psychological phenomena and experiences."[6] It is *melodramas* in this sense that make *genre* visible, even though it is commonly understood that the melodrama is merely *a* genre. The paradox, to reiterate, is that the melodrama is already the model, the archetype, for genre itself.

The notion of genre in film goes hand in hand with popular culture and mass production. Genre is not automatically a mass phenomenon, although mass culture has given the term new meaning. In cinema's case the relationship is obvious: films must be mass-produced to reach the largest possible audience in order that the films will be paid for; as a mass phenomenon, the Hollywood cinema depends on a paying audience for its very existence. From this observation it follows that filmmakers will use whatever means are available to them to get people to pay to see their films. Genre is the most obvious of these means. It is a marketing strategy, then, whereas from the point of view of the audience, genre exists as a set of expectations, a "memorial metatext."[7] As Charles Eidsvick, Rick Altman and others have pointed out,[8] genres are not invented as genres, but rather evolve:

Stories beget similar stories. Once enough stories of a kind have become familiar, their conventions become so formulaic as to serve as reference points for further storytelling. Perception is probably always an analogy-making process; thus it is easier to apprehend a story if one has encountered one something like it.[9]

The American cinema is a cinema of entertainment, which quite naturally is why melodrama dominates it. The melodrama is made for the audience that does not want to feel guilt or take responsibility, that prefers to "identify [itself] with angels, and blame everything that goes wrong on devils."[10] It must be remembered that film

[6] Rosemary Gordon, "Desire and Woman: A Jungian Approach," *Desire*, ed. Lisa Appignanesi (London: ICA Publications, 1984), 14.

[7] Jean-Louis Leutrat, quoted in Stephen Neale, *Genre* (London: British Film Institute, 1980), 51.

[8] Rick Altman, "A Semantic/Syntactic Approach to Film Genre," *Cinema Journal* 23, no. 3 (Spring 1984); Charles Eidsvick, *Cineliteracy: Film Among the Arts* (New York: Random House, 1978); Thomas Schatz, *Hollywood Genres: Formulas, Filmmaking and the Studio System* (New York: Random House, 1981).

[9] Eidsvick, *Cineliteracy*, 64.

[10] Eric Bentley, *The Life of the Drama* (New York: Atheneum, 1967), 261.

quickly developed into a mass-utopian form. Film's wish-fulfilling function is first among factors that bring audiences into theaters. Whether or not intended for women (or most women and some men), romance and its vast mythology were brought into the movies. Courtship, marriage and family, as major preoccupations of bourgeois society, found their way into almost every film made, and when they were the main subject of a movie, the movie was (and is) generally and simply called a melodrama. The cinema, like other mass media, has had the effect of making human psychology formulaic. This master-codifying operation is a function of ideology, which in American movies took for its domain that which its audiences would most readily understand and identify with: the family.

The term melodrama, by itself, has crystallized around certain kinds of melodrama (the maternal, the romantic, etc.) and fallen away from many of the other adjective-noun pairs, such as the rural melodrama, the western melodrama, and so on. Melodrama used as a term to indicate a treatment, a formulaic approach, became something of a tautology if the film was made in Hollywood, and so it was dropped, except in those cases where the film dealt primarily with personal relationships, individual identity, and the individual's place within an order that is understood in familial, social or sexual terms.

If the notion of family is conceived of flexibly, the family can be said to represent melodrama's true subject, making the family melodrama a genre, where all other films are only to a greater or lesser degree melodramatic, but do not belong to the genre we call the melodrama. In the (family) melodrama there are nuclear families, surrogate families, pseudo-families, the family of man, couples, or even just individuals (who are unmarried women, fathers, mothers, or whatever). Human identity and human relationships are treated by melodrama *morally* and *emotionally*, and characters are defined in familial terms. Melodrama appeals to the viewer's emotion, not his or her reason or intellect, and tends to put the question of an entry into the symbolic order, or resistance and final capitulation to the Symbolic, at the center of the narrative, treating it somewhat ahistorically and excessively. The melodramatic resonates with the atmosphere of childhood, with the irrational forces of desire, which makes those films that put desire at the heart of the story and treatment melodramatic.

If the family is the melodrama's favorite milieu, it is because there

one finds the most vivid and troublesome contradictions of melodrama's ideological context. Our sense of who we are is determined
first by the familial context, which is why it can generate intense,
primal emotions that are always in some sense in excess of the situations that produce them. To the degree that the melodramatic text
is hysterical, neurotic, or paranoid, so is the family. The family is the
natural breeding-ground for neurosis, for it is the space in which the
first conflicts that form the subject occur. Of course not all melodramas show these conflicts and workings-out in a family, but they occur as if they were, according to the rules of the familial which, incidentally, are now quite subtly understood because of and by
psychoanalysis. With the pervasiveness of the familial as the master-
pattern for how the world of the melodrama turns, it is the hysterical
nature, or should we say emotional treatment, of a story that we call
melodramatic.

Melodramatic direction, then, applied often to films that are not
melodramas per se, is direction that makes emotion its main concern.
In the melodrama emotions (internal states) are exteriorized; the locus of the drama is interior, but these interior states have to be dramatized, to be seen and/or heard. But since any film from any genre
can treat its subject matter excessively or emotionally, and not be a
melodrama, we are returned to the notion of specific conventions of
excess that give melodrama its hallmark.[11] The constant emotional

[11] There is some sliding back and forth here between the words *emotion* and *excess*,
because all emotion generated by the matrix of the familial is in some sense excessive.
Context is everything when it comes to "melodramatic excesses." In *Le Mélodrame hollywoodien* (Paris: Stock, 1985), Jean-Loup Bourget offers a comprehensive list of them
(grouped under "Themes," "Narrative Structures," and "Stylistic [Figures]") as they
have established themselves over time in all the ways through which genres evolve
(repetition, association, etc.): cliché-situations (secrets and confessions, infirmity,
blindness, problematic identity, bastardy, age differences, natural and human catas-
trophes, accidents); social class differences; rituals (marriages, burials, the theme of
substitution of characters, or the principle of reversibility [containing the logic of displacement and delegation]); nature vs. culture (the theme of childhood, wild, or larger-
than-life figures such as Tarzan, Robin Hood, Van Gogh as played by Kirk Douglas in
Minnelli's *Lust for Life*, or Ron Kirby in Sirk's *All That Heaven Allows*, earthly paradise,
imaginary geographies, animals and talismans); flashbacks (circular narratives), sea-
sons (the carnival); happy endings [Bourget uses the American term]; Cinderellas;
cliché-images (women's faces, the woman in the window, gestures, clothes, the check-
ered tablecloth [!], visual stereotypes such as the contrasting images of the great house
and the cottage, architectural symbols such as grand stairways); music; color; camera
movements and montage effects (invisible editing, antitheses), and so on.

core of the drama (with or without a "baroque" outward form) marks melodrama. That emotional core, that familiar but often nevertheless perplexing repertoire of feeling, functions like the latent content of dreams. In dreams, the latent content never really changes, even though the manifest content—generally from the day's residue—does. Direction that takes for its guiding principle the stirring-up of emotion that resonates like latent dream content, is melodramatic, but it will not necessarily result in a melodrama. Melodramatic direction applied to melodramatic subject matter, however, will produce an example of the genre, and what follows are analyses of some characteristic texts of the family melodrama in its evolution as a genre over half a century of the American cinema.

PART TWO

6. D. W. Griffith

1. With one hand Griffith prepares his lovers for their dramatic separation, while with the other he brings in his agent for effecting it. (Vivia Ogden, D. W. Griffith, Richard Barthelmess, Lillian Gish, Burr McIntosh, Lowell Sherman, in *Way Down East*.)

THERE was a time when David Wark Griffith was universally hailed as the greatest director the cinema had ever seen. Indeed, it is still said, but now quite often with the qualification that his genius lay in his being an innovator, in being the single greatest contributor to the development of narrative film. However, "nothing essential," as René Clair said, "has been added to the art of the motion picture since Griffith."[1] How, then, does one account for the decline and eclipse of Griffith's film career in his own lifetime and his virtual disappearance, except as a name and as some sort of frozen cultural edifice (the "Father of the American Cinema")? It can to some extent be explained in terms of Griffith's vision, his view of the world, which has been more recently described as too persistently moral and idealistic in tone, a too high-minded mix of the romantic, sentimental, patriotic and Christian. The themes of Griffith's plots may seem unsophisticated by today's standards, but—and this is the point— their psychological determinations would appear to be deeply ingrained in the unconscious of the American people.

Griffith made melodramas, and while the face of the melodrama has changed, its fundamental characteristics have not. James Agee called Griffith "a great primitive poet, a man capable, as only great primitive artists can be, of intuitively perceiving and perfecting the tremendous magical images that underlie the memory and imagination of entire peoples,"[2] and he was on the right track in not joining the throng of film scholars who revere Griffith today more for his pioneering of film form than for the images he made resonate in the American unconscious.

Griffith himself in all his published writings talked not about film form but about ideas. Technique, for him, was simply a means to an end. It was the content of his films that determined his film technique. The close-up, cross-cutting (parallel action) and the flashback are all, it is true, now part of the basic grammar of film language, but Griffith did not invent many of the techniques for which he is so often credited. Griffith used these innovations to unprecedented effect, however, thus establishing them as the ground rules of film language. The questions to ask—since words like Agee's "magic" are no longer felt to carry in themselves much critical weight—are how that magic works and why Griffith's films are powerful still.

[1] Quoted in James Agee, *Agee on Film*, vol. 1 (New York: Putnam, 1983), 398.
[2] Ibid., 314.

Our Father of the American Cinema is perhaps more aptly named than is often appreciated. When Eisenstein, in one of his more provocative theses on the subject of montage,[3] maintained that Griffith could only give us organic-ness of a general kind, not of an exceptional kind, and that Griffith's parallel montage merely reflected reality instead of constructing it, he was attempting to articulate the important and exciting notion that the American cinema has an identifiable specificity beneath superficial differences of "content." His claim that "the structure that is reflected in the concept of Griffith montage is the structure of bourgeois society. . . . And this society, perceived *only as a contrast between the haves and the have-nots*, is reflected in the consciousness of Griffith no deeper than the image of an intricate race between two parallel lines"[4] is both right and wrong. Eisenstein admired Griffith's work very much, but was perhaps too eager to prove that the Soviet cinema was "neither a poor relative nor an insolvent debtor of his."[5] Eisenstein is correct in describing America as a bourgeois society (in which there are always the haves and the have-nots) and in describing Griffith's montage as a reflection of bourgeois society, but it is drastically reductive to mark bourgeois society's salient feature as a division between haves and have-nots, and to claim that this division is "reflected in the consciousness of Griffith no deeper than the image of an intricate race between two parallel lines." A discussion of melodrama as the mode of representation most suited to the American experience would be more useful, and so in this chapter an attempt will be made to discover, if not why "every article about the cinema ought to talk about Griffith,"[6] then why every article about the film melodrama, and most articles about the American cinema, ought to talk about Griffith.

Melodrama is a complex mode of experience. Two of its chief characteristics can be introduced by way of quoting Griffith himself who, when asked in 1944 by an interviewer from the *Los Angeles Times*, "What is a good picture?" replied, "One that makes the public forget its troubles. Also, a good picture tends to make folks think a little, without letting them suspect that they are being inspired to think. In

---

[3] Sergei Eisenstein, "Dickens, Griffith and the Film Today," *Film Form*, ed. and trans. Jay Leyda (New York: Harcourt Brace, 1949), 195–255.

[4] Ibid., 234.

[5] Ibid., 233.

[6] Jean-Luc Godard, quoted in David Morse, "Aspects of Melodrama," *Monogram* 4 (1972): 16.

one respect, nearly all pictures are good in that they frequently show the triumph of good over evil."[7] Griffith was usually banal in his public statements and writings about film, but his response is absolutely on target here so far as his own films are concerned. The suggestion that the triumph of good over evil is an ingredient of every good film (or that every film is good because it shows the triumph of good over evil) is an indication of the melodramatic nature of Griffith's imagination.

There is little doubt that the American Civil War deeply impressed young David Wark Griffith, and it is not surprising that, coming from the recently defeated South, with his imagination already molded by the binary, oppositional nature of the conflict between North and South, carrying with him a strong sense of loss and betrayal and of his family having seen better times, Griffith should have found in the melodramatic mode of representation an already organized and satisfactory way of coping with the world, of "uncovering, demonstrating, and making operative the essential moral universe in a post-sacred era."[8]

As in the Balzacian world to which Robbe-Grillet refers in "New Novel, New Man,"[9] objects in the Griffith world are reassuring, and one's way of knowing this world is a question of possessing, retaining, or acquiring them. The significations of the world around Griffith's characters are not partial, provisional or contradictory—precisely because the melodramatic mode insists on it. In the melodramatic mode villains are recognizable as such (Lennox Sanderson in *Way Down East*, with his cigarette, too-suave manner and sneering asides; Battling Burrows in *Broken Blossoms*, with his crumpled ear, ill-fitting clothes and swagger; the Vestal Virgins of Uplift in *The Mother and the Law*, in their dark, severe clothing—to name a few) and Virtue is invariably represented by a passive feminine protagonist or a suffering or impotent male. Lillian Gish is the archetypal Griffith heroine—a virginal waif who is as beautiful as she is vulnerable. The melodrama asserts that there is a moral universe, that there is good and bad, right and wrong, and most melodramas will strive

[7] Quoted by Eisenstein, *Film Form*, 206.

[8] Peter Brooks, *The Melodramatic Imagination: Balzac, Henry James, Melodrama, and the Mode of Excess* (New Haven: Yale University Press, 1976), 15.

[9] Alain Robbe-Grillet, *For a New Novel*, trans. Richard Howard (New York: Grove Press, 1965), 133–42.

to produce a happy ending, even if that happy ending must come out of a hat after Virtue has been under siege for nine-tenths of the film. The moral center of the melodrama can be found in the staging, however contrived, of the triumph of good over evil, even if, as in *Broken Blossoms*, Virtue's reward is posthumous.

The other point worth discussing in Griffith's response to the *Los Angeles Times* reporter is his assertion that "a good picture tends to make folks think a little, without letting them suspect that they are being inspired to think." The way to do this, of course, is to make the drama turn on situations they are sure to identify with, on questions of family, private property and marriage, and to locate it in the home and/or small town. Large or complex ideological conflicts are represented metaphorically in "understandable" family situations (the most common metaphor of class struggle in the melodramatic scenario being the threat of rape to the figure of virtue). As Thomas Elsaesser has observed, "popular culture has . . . resolutely refused to understand social change in other than private contexts and emotional terms."[10]

Film is a popular medium and Griffith understood well the difference between his "sausages" (as he called his run-of-the-mill melodramas) and the films which he hoped would live up to his conception of himself as a great talent, being aware that "solvency was primarily based on popular successes." But when Griffith said that "the cinema camera is the agent of Democracy. It levels barriers between races and classes,"[11] he spoke truer than perhaps he realized. He once said, "We've found a universal language—a power that can make men brothers and end war forever," but he cultivated the manners and pretensions of a Southern aristocrat, and his *The Birth of a Nation* (1915) quite possibly fortified barriers between races and between North and South as much as it helped to remove them. Griffith's aristocratic personal style can be seen as a function of the paradoxical threat he felt his involvement with the cinema represented. His films, after all, are an expression of solidarity with the American bourgeoisie and working classes. Indeed, Griffith's camera as an agent of Democracy seeking to level barriers between classes was

[10] Thomas Elsaesser, "Tales of Sound and Fury: Observations on the Family Melodrama," *Monogram* 4 (1972): 4.

[11] D. W. Griffith, "Motion Pictures: The Miracle of Modern Photography," *The Mentor* 9, no. 6 (July 1, 1921): 3.

really only a camera seeking to unite the middle classes against all the forces that threatened to besiege them. His camera succeeded in helping to popularize and homogenize American culture generally because it is in the nature of the commercial cinema to do so.[12] Griffith's sense that his personal noble heritage was snatched from him forced him to ally himself with the very groups which also threatened him: the poor, the disenfranchised, the helpless and the vulnerable. Elsaesser's description of the melodrama as recording "the struggle of a morally and emotionally emancipated bourgeois consciousness against the remnants of feudalism"[13] is as much an accurate profile of America in the early twentieth century as it is a description of the class conflict within Griffith himself. Griffith had never wanted to go into the cinema, preferring to cultivate his aristocratic pretensions and his dream of becoming a great literary man, and he was at first ashamed to sign his full name to the one-reelers he made at the Biograph Studios. The "feudalism" of melodrama's original context was the *ancien régime*; its counterpart in the twentieth century, represented explicitly or metaphorically again and again in Griffith's films, is big capital and the urban industrial complex.

For a clearer understanding of the special relationship between melodrama and the cinema, and of Griffith's place in the development of the American film melodrama, it must be remembered first of all that Griffith's cinema is a silent cinema. This fact, and the fact that the American cinema's antecedents are nineteenth-century painting and the theater and literature of Victorian melodrama, explain much—especially perhaps the mise en scène of the Griffith film. In the silent cinema signification is achieved most expressively in the human body and the mise en scène. When (writing about the melodramatic imagination and literature) Brooks notes that "everything appears to bear the stamp of meaning,"[14] it is easy to recognize that this should be true of almost all silent cinema. Everything *must* bear the stamp of meaning, since characters cannot speak (except in intertitles) and meanings normally conveyed by speech can generally

---

[12] As a mass medium that Griffith helped to make respectable enough for the middle and upper-middle classes to participate in, the cinema for several decades became the great uniting influence on American culture—as the title and thesis of Robert Sklar's *Movie-Made America* propose.

[13] Elsaesser, "Tales of Sound and Fury," 3.

[14] Brooks, *The Melodramatic Imagination*, 10.

be evoked only through mise en scène and mute gesture, or through music.

The development of the cinema as a system of signs with which audiences became increasingly familiar resulted in the overwhelming predominance of the genre film in the American cinema—of the genre film as the American cinema's most characteristic film. The generic character of the American cinema and the establishment of a syntax and of a naturalized and yet hyper-signifying mise en scène owes its well-launched beginnings to D. W. Griffith, for part of Griffith's genius lay in his ability to signify with certainty, "poetry" and fullness. Griffith assigned to the cinematic image a *significance* which in literature by that time had been taken to an extreme by Henry James (to use Brooks' example). Brooks describes this operation of the melodramatic imagination as "the postulation of a signified in excess of the possibilities of the signifier, which in turn produced an excessive signifier, making large but unsubstantiable claims on meaning."[15] However, it is not "unsubstantiable claims on meaning" that might prompt a viewer nowadays to call Griffith's cinema "melodramatic" (in the pejorative sense). The excess of the melodramatic mode of representation is not what dates Griffith's work; it is the content. No longer, for example, do we recognize as a familiar figure the virgin waif who can be fooled into a false marriage by a wealthy, wolfish landowner, nor does the law now allow—if it ever did—the snatching of a baby from a mother on flimsy grounds of neglectfulness. This question of what will date and what remains constant, this matter of the generic signifier, is discussed by Stephen Neale in *Genre* using, in his chapter on genre and sexuality, a lengthy quotation from Jim Kitses' *Horizons West*.[16] The point Neale makes is worth reiterating for the light it sheds on mise en scène in melodrama and the locus of power (the functioning of the Law) in melodrama. It also refers to what is relatively constant in genre—to what Rick Altman in melodrama's case would call its semantic dimension—which should help to explain why every article about the film melodrama should talk about the Griffith melodrama, even though the modern melodrama might seem to be significantly different from the Griffith melodrama.

---

[15] Ibid., 199.
[16] Jim Kitses, *Horizons West* (Bloomington: Indiana University Press, 1969).

Jim Kitses describes the western in terms of a shifting ideological play of antinomies (the wilderness/civilization, the individual/the community, freedom/restriction) which Neale notes "finds a particular focus in the body of the male hero."[17] What Kitses calls a "philosophical dialectic" is realized in concrete images. The antinomies Kitses lists

articulate the space of the functioning of what is defined in genre as the Law, and the space which is defined as outside it, as Other. The body of the hero is situated within a series of other bodies (those of Indians, outlaws, townspeople, farmers, and so on) across which this opposition is marked, hence the importance of codes of dress, comportment, movement, adornment, etc. It is marked also across a spatial economy whose polar instances are natural landscapes on the one hand and the township/homestead on the other. Here again, the body of the hero is located dynamically at the point of their intersection, oscillating between them. . . . The drama of the western, in its concern to explore various modes of inscription of the Law on the human body, and in its obsession with definitions of masculinity, involves the location of the body of the hero as the object par excellence of its spectacle.[18]

Griffith melodramas constantly show the failure of femininity in dealing with the world. The protagonist of the melodrama does not prevail, as the male hero of the western does in the sense that the masculine is affirmed. The suffering body of the hero(ine) becomes a privileged site for the inscription of the Law; what we see is the *other* side, the *other* point of view, and not surprisingly it is the body of a woman that is the object *par excellence* of the Griffith melodrama's spectacle. Inasmuch as the Law is masculine, the melodrama takes the feminine, the "castrated," for its point of view, which inevitably thereby reinforces notions of the masculine and in the final analysis affirms the viability of the masculine point of view. Like the western, then, the (family) melodrama is also obsessed with gendered identity, but its concern with Otherness returns it always to notions of masculinity.

In the family melodrama, whether the protagonist is male or female, the outcome is essentially one of failure—the failure to act and to prevail. The happy endings of many melodramas seem to be tacked on, for they cannot erase the lavishly demonstrated failure of the feminine which precedes them. The Law is literalized in *The*

[17] Stephen Neale, *Genre* (London: British Film Institute, 1980), 58.
[18] Ibid., 59.

Mother and the Law in the policeman and the prison, but it is really the factory owner Jenkins, the maker of the law of legalities, sitting above institutional law, who incarnates the patriarchal function in the social sphere. In *Way Down East* the prime agents of the Law are Lennox Sanderson and Squire Bartlett, who represent a system that divides the world into those who have and those who have not. In *Broken Blossoms* the familial law of the Father prevails in a harsh form, in the agent of an actual father, Battling Burrows.

Griffith usually made family melodramas, whether the emphasis in them was on the social, the romantic, or the historical-spectacular. In the three films under discussion in this chapter we are given a window on that moment in American culture when, in Ann Douglas' words, "America lost its male-dominated theological tradition without gaining a comprehensive feminism or an adequately modernized religious sensibility."[19] *Way Down East*, *The Mother and the Law*, and *Broken Blossoms* signify an attempt to shift from Christian justification to something more modern: a moral order which is inflected by a social and a psychoanalytic consciousness.

In the films of D. W. Griffith we see a nineteenth-century world giving way to the twentieth century. Griffith relies heavily on several conventions of nineteenth-century theatrical melodrama in the face of—perhaps because of—an increased awareness of the extent to which America's "traditional Sacred" was breaking down. Industrial capitalism was profoundly transforming the face of America during the first decades of the twentieth century when Griffith was making films, and his films provide some of the best examples in the cinema of melodrama's response to a rapidly changing world, for melodrama will not permit the admission of confusion, and always attempts to make sense of things.

In *Way Down East* Griffith sticks fairly close to melodrama's theatrical, dramatic precedents and retains the nineteenth-century flavor of the play on which his film is based, but we see how in fact he mixes several discourses, and, in particular, how he attempts to couch social problems in religious analogies. Made during a great wave of the woman's suffrage movement, *Way Down East* understands Anna Moore's story to some extent in social and psychological

---

[19] Ann Douglas, *The Feminization of American Culture* (New York: Avon Books, 1977), 13.

terms, but only dimly. The film tells the story of a young woman betrayed, sentenced, crucified and resurrected, and shows a family, the Bartletts, in transition from domination by an Old Testament patriarch towards a less harsh, New Testament rule by love—a rule administered by the mother.[20]

In *The Mother and the Law* Griffith breaks free of certain theatrical constraints and also takes on some of the complex issues of life in the big twentieth-century American city. The largely rural locale of *Way Down East* is abandoned and the rural-urban opposition gives way to a more sustained confrontation with urban problems such as poverty, crime and unemployment, although it retreats always into personal terms. The film grapples with what it calls the "fate" or "destiny" of its characters, in terms that are more modern than "fate" or "destiny" would suggest—through mise en scène, primarily.

Broken Blossoms is a self-reflexive instance in Griffith's work that shows the melodramatic form to be aware of itself and takes an interesting step forward for melodrama's expressive possibilities. Melodrama's obsession with family is stripped to its sources in *Broken Blossoms*, and sexual desire is revealed to be the bedrock of familial interaction, even though the film does not—as later melodramas (by Vidor, by Minnelli) often do—understand itself psychoanalytically. The unpredictable violence of Battling Burrows, which results in Lucy's murder, is still seen as irrational. To a remarkable extent desire, repressed in the narrative system, is displaced into masochistic, inward-turning formal structures, and on the level of the story, it implodes in the suicide of the film's male protagonist.

In the excitement of the finale of each of the three films, what is lost sight of is that there is no genuine resolution of the films' social and psychic contradictions. This ideological failure in fact reflects those contradictions, which it was Eisenstein's project, in another kind of cinema, to "make manifest." It provides, thereby, a critique of what Robbe-Grillet calls "the myths of the nineteenth century." Those myths would have us believe, as Griffith did and as the melodramatic mode asserts, that in art and life there are systems of signi-

[20] In her autobiography, Lillian Gish writes that Griffith told Billy Bitzer, the photographer, "not to concentrate so much attention on [her] but to concentrate on photographing Brucie to advantage. 'She's the mother,' he would say, 'and I want her to look lovely.' " (*Lillian Gish: The Movies, Mr. Griffith, and Me* [Englewood Cliffs, N.J.: Prentice-Hall, 1969], 230.)

fication which are whole, with a purpose, and those wholes are closed systems in which nothing is extraneous and of which multiple readings are limited. Griffith as a melodramatist recognized the need for change but could not in his fictions resolve the trouble he exposed. He could *see*, and could show and tell with genius what he saw, but, as with his film technique, he was not truly an innovator— he could not sketch a viable new order. He manipulated nostalgia, resorting to sentimentality and melodrama, which would seem to be the trademarks of the consumer culture that dominates America today and which Griffith stood on the threshold of eighty years ago.

THE VICTORIAN HERITAGE: *Way Down East*

Way Down East is a classic melodrama in that the major components of melodrama, both syntactic and semantic, are represented, scarcely modified from their nineteenth-century theatrical origins.[21] The story itself is fundamentally melodramatic in its concentration on the tribulations of a victim. It is the Law of patriarchal society which defines this victim, and by extension, society, along the axes of oppressors and oppressed, masculine and feminine, rural and urban, desire and morality, upper and lower classes. This is a Christian discourse, one which stops short of real social or psychoanalytic self-awareness. To the extent that the film does possess insight of a sort we would now read in psychoanalytic terms, we can see this, perhaps, in the acting style of the main characters, the psychological realism of Griffith's editing style, and his use of close-ups. But, for all that, the villain is a villain in this film, and Griffith is content for the most part to imply that the world would be a better place if only it did not have nasty, spiteful, or selfish people in it.

An upper-class, villainous rake lures a poor, rural virgin into a

---

[21] A discussion of some of the changes Griffith made to *Way Down East* in his adaptation of the play for the screen can be found in Sarah Kozloff, "Where Wessex Meets New England: Griffith's *Way Down East* and Hardy," *Film/Literature Quarterly* 13, no. 1 (Spring 1985): 35–41. See also Stanley Kauffmann, *Living Images: Film Comment and Criticism* (New York: Harper and Row, 1975), 285–89. Although the film was made after *The Mother and the Law* and *Broken Blossoms*, I put it before these other two because it is more old-fashioned. As Lillian Gish writes in her autobiography, "We all thought privately that Mr. Griffith had lost his mind. *Way Down East* was a horse-and-buggy melodrama, familiar on the rural circuit for more than twenty years. We didn't believe it would ever succeed." (Gish, *Lillian Gish*, 229.)

2. David rescues Anna from the ice floe and the storm, to restore her to her rightful place within the family structure. (Richard Barthelmess and Lillian Gish in *Way Down East*.)

mock marriage and then deserts her. She gives birth to a child who dies, and she is forced to find work as a servant on a farm. There the farmer's son falls in love with her, but even as he is declaring his love for her, her past life is being detailed to the farmer by the village gossip. She is banished from the house and in suicidal despair runs into a violent snowstorm. After a frantic search, the farmer's son finds her collapsed on an ice floe that is rapidly making its way toward a waterfall. He saves her without a moment to spare, and when she recovers, the farmer asks her forgiveness. She forgives him and all those by whom she has suffered, and she and the farmer's son marry.

By the time the film reaches the point at which the Squire banishes Anna Moore from his house and she flings herself into the cold night, it is of course quite clear that it is not the Squire who is the villain. He is a patriarch who is merely doing his job. One of the biggest differences between the Victorian melodrama (whose heritage we see in this eminently Victorian film) and later melodramas of the kind made by Vidor and Minnelli is this: the Victorian melodrama believes in the Father, and later melodramas cannot. The Squire may not be much of a *character*, but what he stands for stands firm. Once we get to Minnelli's *Some Came Running* and *Home from the Hill*, for example, we find that actual fathers cannot measure up to the impossible standards of the patriarchy. While *Way Down East* appears to turn on a series of coincidences and hazards of fate, there is the unifying theme, driven by ideological imperatives, of the loss and restoration of the Father.

As a story from the victim's point of view, *Way Down East* begins with an image of impoverishment (the shots of Anna and her mother, two poor and unprotected women) and ends on an image of phallic restoration. The heroine is resurrected, after betrayal and crucifixion, to join a holy family that potentially bestows on her the only state of grace that patriarchy usually grants a woman—legitimate motherhood. The difficulty for men (or the impossibility for women) of living up to patriarchal society's ideal order[22] is the very stuff of melodrama, and in telling a story of a blameless young woman's extraordinarily unfortunate experiences, *Way Down East* registers an ambivalent protest against this melodramatic truth. Villainy's identity, its origins and causes, are always the most interesting thing about the melodrama, but melodramas are often not very clear about what the villain really is. To be more precise, melodramas at the time of *Way Down East* are not aware of the complex interrelatedness of misfortune's myriad causes. *Way Down East* still has a classic villain of the kind found in nineteenth-century stage melodramas, but the casual way in which he is dismissed at the end of the film once he has served his dramatic purpose proves that even Griffith realizes that the human villain is not the true cause of everything that goes

[22] Geoffrey Nowell-Smith, "Minnelli and Melodrama," *Screen* 18, no. 2 (1977): 116.

wrong in Anna Moore's world. There are other causes, not so easy to define. The following analysis of *Way Down East* attempts to identify some of those causes.

The opening shot of Anna Moore and her mother clearly articulates the repression and powerlessness of the feminine situation with which the melodrama is so often concerned. In the center of the frame, seated, immobile, surrounded by objects in such a way that there is no suggestion of life beyond the frame, the two women convey the paralysis of their condition with tiny hand movements (necessitating the close-ups that follow this shot). This incomplete family is without a father or other figure of patriarchal authority or beneficial provision. This absence reads immediately as a loss, for we learn that the Moores are very poor, and there appears to be nothing that they can do about it—because they are women, and as the interior of the living room tells us, because they are respectable. However, they have been talking about their dilemma, for the mother, after a clearly visible moment of calculation, says with a careful balance of casualness and design: "After all, you know, the Tremonts are our own very near kin—even if they are rich." Grasping immediately her mother's implication, Anna retorts: "Oh, Mother, I hate to ask them for money!" But she soon relents, persuaded, like Tess of the d'Urbervilles, that some good may come of it. She has only charm, youth, and feminine beauty—a combination of assets that is more powerful than she realizes.[23]

In fact, Anna's charm, summed up as a specific form of sexual desirability (at times indistinguishable from her vulnerability), will be a central factor in her destiny. When in the final shots of the film we see her married to David Bartlett, she is happy and her marriage to him is understood to be her reward. But, of course, her identity is still constructed in terms of men, male action, and castration; her union with David restores and perpetuates her female passivity and dependence. David has succeeded in confirming patriarchal principles by defying his father and *acting*—to save Anna from the ice floe.

But David is not the central character of *Way Down East* from whose point of view we see most of the action. The final shot of the whole film is actually of a kiss between Anna and David's mother, orches-

[23] James L. Smith describes a Victorian melodramatic stage heroine "whose helpless perfections attract disaster like a magnet." (James L. Smith, *Melodrama* [London: Methuen, 1973], 21.) Anna Moore is just such a heroine.

trated by David himself who, with an arm around his mother and an arm around his wife, brings them together and looks on with visible pleasure. In this gesture Griffith's moral universe is clarified. It is the Mother—her (New Testament) love and sanction—who matters, and the emphasis in the Oedipal drama (reenacted by every melodrama) is here on the mother-son relation. It is in this sense that Griffith's melodrama is essentially a male Oedipal fantasy. The son's pleasure at seeing his mother kiss his wife, and his wife kiss his mother, simultaneously deflects and realizes vicariously, through identification, his Oedipal desire. What is more, the shot seals Anna's solidarity with the feminine lot right there under the patriarchal gaze. Mrs. Bartlett was once a young bride, and now Anna is a Mrs. Bartlett.

David's mother is presented as the most positive image of moral stability in *Way Down East*. Mrs. Bartlett not only persuades her harshly paternal husband to employ Anna, but restrains him when he reacts violently to the news of Anna's past life. She is herself properly shocked to learn that Anna once had a child, but she is forgiving, and is at least distressed when Anna is ordered out of the house. She is Christian to the letter and is generally associated with love and nourishment (the kitchen, the butter churn). But we should note that Mrs. Bartlett lives only for and through her husband. She is very clearly identified as a good wife and mother.

While Griffith blatantly endorses the "ideal of one man for one woman," his film demonstrates the cruel injustice to women not so much of a masculine polygamous instinct, as one title puts it, but of an ideal which permits no other place, no other role, for women who do not fall as if by magic into the arms of the perfect man. The film melodrama at this time can only identify woman as virgin, mother, or prostitute, and we know that so long as Anna remains an unmarried woman, until we see her in a wedding dress standing at David Bartlett's side, she will be prey to all sorts of disasters directly or indirectly related to her femaleness. Even landscape and weather will persecute her.

The title which opens the sequence in which Anna is forced to take up residence in Belden after she gives birth to her doomed child is indicative of the fundamental contradictoriness of the melodrama's ideological endeavor: "Maternity—woman's Gethsemane." On the one hand (in the figure of Mrs. Bartlett) Griffith elevates motherhood as woman's *raison d'être*, and yet here in a flash of protest calls it woman's betrayal. Under patriarchal Law motherhood is held to be sacred, but any falling away from the ideal patriarchal pattern of things (which endorses motherhood in very specific terms) results in disaster. Griffith laments the disasters he represents, but can only recommend a more careful adherence to the patriarchy. This adherence can only *contain* contradiction, at a price that overwhelmingly must be paid by women. The very title of his earlier film, *The Mother and the Law*, is expressive of the paternal metaphor that resonates in Griffith's cinema. Melodrama articulates the subject's relation to the Father, as the title of that film so aptly suggests. The Mother and the Law (women and men, women *versus* men) are in conflict with each other, and by turns these polarities are represented favorably and unfavorably. If, as in *The Mother and the Law*, the hero and heroine are married, then it is the authority of the institution, rather than the authority of the father/husband, that is opposed. But in any event the Father is quite overtly the reason for the melodramatic narrative. If motherhood is the only safe place for a woman under patriarchy, the mother's role also expresses all the differences that make the Law intelligible in the first place. The law of the Father spawns narrative out of differences between the Mother (as metaphor, or literally) and the Law (as metaphor, or literally). Death of the Father, Roland Barthes writes, would

deprive literature of many of its pleasures. If there is no longer a Father, why tell stories? Doesn't every narrative lead back to Oedipus? Isn't storytelling always a way of searching for one's origin, speaking one's conflicts with the Law, entering into the dialectic of tenderness and hatred?[24]

When, in the boarding house at Belden, Anna is "stricken with this terrible fear for her baby's soul," she decides to baptize "the child without a name" herself, "in the name of the Father and of the Son— and of the Holy Ghost." It is a cruel irony, of course, that she baptizes her child *in the name of the Father*, since it is a father, and the Father as a metaphor (the Name-of-the-Father), that have wrought this hideous misery for her. When she is evicted by the landlady, Anna takes to the road, and the title calls it "The pilgrimage. Upon her back the age old cross." The age-old cross? Is it the fact of her femaleness? The fact of her being an unmarried mother? In any

[24] Roland Barthes, *The Pleasure of the Text*, trans. Richard Miller (New York: Hill and Wang, 1975), 47.

event, the "name of the Father"—which implies her castration and all its effects—is her cross.

However, the narrative's definition of Anna in terms of male desire and paternal Law does not represent a condition that is peculiar to her as a character. All of the women in the film, in one way or another, share this identification. When Anna first meets her Tremont cousins she is the object of suspicion and jealousy quite obviously because she is prettier than they. At the "Great Tremont Ball" Emma's daughters dress Anna in a dowdy outfit, but "solely to pique the sisters, of whom she is not over-fond, the aunt makes different arrangements for Anna." The aunt can afford to, for she quite obviously has no stake in the game of attracting male attention. She wears glasses, dresses plainly, carries a walking stick and has been described with melodramatic simplicity as "eccentric, but enormously rich." After the aunt has re-outfitted her, Anna immediately becomes the center of attraction and becomes so popular with the men (and unfortunately for her, especially Lennox Sanderson) that "Cousin Emma hurries Anna off to bed—perhaps in fear of her own daughters being outshone." These women have wealth and social status and beauty, but they are reduced to scheming, jealous rivalry by the fact that they are not married.

One of the functions of the ball is to provide a legitimate opportunity for the showing off of women, and so it is not surprising that upon meeting her at this erotically charged event Sanderson should place Anna in an imaginary tableau vivant, as Elaine of Astolat. The tableau vivant, as Jean-François Lyotard has described it (with reference to Klossowski's fantasmatic), is "the near perfect simulacrum of fantasy in all its paradoxical intensity." The perverse pleasure to be derived from the tableau vivant can be achieved because "the object, the victim, the prostitute, takes the pose, offering his or her self as a detached region, but *at the same time giving way and humiliating this whole person.*"[25]

This representation (of Anna as Elaine of Astolat) within representation (the film) momentarily refers to the imaginary nature of the cinematic signifier and is emblematic of the principle of desire upon which the film, and film itself, turns. Lillian Gish is by turns fetishized and abused (all of it making her a *representation*—a fetish struc-

[25] Jean-François Lyotard, "Acinema," *Wide Angle* 2, no. 3 (1978): 58.

ture) for the pleasure that such evocation and circumvention of castration anxiety affords the viewer.[26] While it has been said that the melodrama represents the other (than masculine) point of view, it must be noted that Anna's sufferings are often actually seen from a "masculine" point of view. We see close-ups of Sanderson playing cards with his male friends, of Sanderson puffing on his cigarette, close-ups of his shifty eyes ever on the lookout for opportunities for sensual diversion, shots of Sanderson looking, and then of what he is looking at. In other words, he is central, as are his desires. Anna is innocent of every design on her virtue, while we the audience are acutely aware of every tiny sign that betrays the villain's real intentions. This forces on us a complicity of sorts with him. And when Anna is surprised by Sanderson's sudden moves at his apartment, we see *her* frightened face, not because it is her consciousness that we share, but because it is what Sanderson sees. Naturally, virtue is dull, and displays of fright and spectacles of flight offer sadistic pleasures for the viewer under the pretext of showing how beastly the villain can be. While his example of shocking behavior ostensibly arouses our condemnation and indignation, its real function is to relegate the heroine to secondary status while the film's primary focus remains the male.

On the other hand, we are more encouraged to share Anna's fantasy to marry David, than David's to marry Anna. The question is, will she get David, not whether David will get her. Whether or not they marry is entirely up to him, particularly since her "shameful" past should render her altogether unmarriageable. Even the first title of the film ("Today woman brought up from childhood to expect ONE CONSTANT MATE. . . .") launches the narrative from her point of view. While the marriage between David and Anna provides the resolution of the Oedipus complex (David in his turn becomes the Father, and thus the cycle is completed and the narrative closed) it is achieved as much in order to repress our hero's fundamentally

---

[26] The sexuality of the Gish heroine is by no means a simple thing. The spectator may feel, as the villain in G. H. MacDermott's *Driven from Home* (1871) says of the heroine in that play, that "her very virtues incense me with a sensuous desire to possess her." (Quoted in Smith, *Melodrama*, 22.) She does not simply signify heterosexual male desire (as if that were a simple thing), but might, for example, also strike a pedophilic chord in the spectator. As the incarnation of the *idea* of good that so animates the melodrama, the virgin heroine can evoke a complex array of feelings in the spectator—nostalgia, narcissism, tenderness, and . . . sadism.

polygamous nature—as a title gives us to understand is the male condition—as to contain our heroine's sexuality at last by conferring on her the identity of legitimate (past and future) mother. The point is that female sexuality is dangerous, and the marriage that can contain it, while a male invention, implies the end of polygamy for the husband. The premise in Griffith's opening title is that women are not polygamous by nature, and theirs is a superior condition, but "because not yet has the man animal reached this high standard," the woman today "suffers more than at any point in the history of mankind." The whole film's general point of view, then, is a feminine one, but it is a point of view that is assumed by a masculine narrator. The film offers a man's version of the female experience (the film's origins in a play written by a woman notwithstanding).

As in *The Mother and the Law*, Griffith's method of disclosing information in *Way Down East* develops a point of view that becomes identifiably masculine, although as Anna's story, the film unfolds in a way that emphasizes the theme of threat to the heroine. It is *her* destiny that determines the omniscient narrator's choices. We see what threatens Anna, although she herself does not usually appreciate what danger she is in. Griffith has Anna encounter the villain first, and only later do we meet David (Richard Barthelmess), whom the conventions of the form lead us to expect will save her.

Appropriately enough, Anna meets the villain at a bridge party at the Tremonts' city house, already a slightly sinister place for the likes of her. The house is initially shown from the street, behind its high, spiked fence. Anna must first gain entry through the extremely high outer doors (the verticality of which is emphasized by the masked sides of the frame)[27] and then through some wrought-iron gates that open into the hallway which accommodates a dramatic, sweeping staircase. All this contrasts with the impoverished pastoral of the opening scenes. Sanderson's apartment, to which he is able to lure the unsuspecting Anna, also has unusually high ceilings. "The dashing Lennox Sanderson, who depends for his living upon a rich father," spies on Anna from a doorway until she becomes aware of him and involuntarily retreats a step.

---

[27] This verticality of course is suggestive of phallic power and impregnability. High doorways and ceilings suggest that giants reside within or that the residents are rich enough to afford expensive, "useless" spaces that serve only to create effects of an aggrandizing sort.

As one of the three basic types of men in the film, Sanderson, and the mise en scène by which he is to some extent defined, is markedly different from young David Bartlett, who is first seen standing by a well, stroking a pigeon, his mother and father nearby, forming a familial tableau of pastoral order and serenity. As in *The Mother and the Law*, the rural scene is romanticized and the urban place is associated with evils. This alternation structures the entire film. The Bartlett family is introduced thus:

— a farmhouse with cows in the foreground
— a close-up of the foliage of a tree
— another close-up of the foliage of a tree
— a close-up of fledglings in a nest
— chicks being covered by a blanket for warmth
— a long-shot of the Bartlett family outdoors, seated, with David
standing at the well, and chickens in the foreground.

The title that introduces David in close-up establishes him as everything that Lennox Sanderson is not: "David Bartlett, though of plain stock, has been tutored by poets and visions as wide as the world." He is ordinary but has aspirations toward something transcendent; this makes him singular, exemplary—that is to say, perfect for the ideal(ized) woman.

As a son still under the stern rule of the patriarch, David, like Anna, must achieve, by film's end, a stable identity within the Oedipal context which defines him, just as the Dear One and the Boy in *The Mother and the Law* cannot live with their fathers forever, and just as Lucy in *Broken Blossoms* must escape Battling Burrows. David does not want to marry the girl of his parents' choice, and until Anna appears on the scene, he is caught in an uncomfortable bind between his mother's love and the prospect of marrying Kate. Twice during the film David and his mother kiss tenderly, a sign of their strong bond: when David picks up the butter churn for his mother and they enter the house arm in arm, while the Squire looks on (!), and again during the barn dance after the two of them have danced alone with everyone standing around them, applauding rhythmically. This second kiss is even more tender than the first. Griffith frames them in close-up, with David's head turned to partially block the kiss from view, as if this love between mother and son is felt by Griffith at some unconscious level to be losing its simplicity; this is what gives the film its peculiar tensions, its utterly moral stance which is fraught with perverse implications.

Griffith introduces his main characters and main themes in a simple, alternating manner, characteristic of the Griffith structure. Since the villain provides the melodrama with its motor power,[28] Griffith introduces him quite some time before we see how he and the hero will cross paths. To establish a link between the two worlds that must sooner or later collide, a modern melodrama would probably seek a more plausible, or at least disguised, way than Griffith chooses to link Anna, David, and Sanderson. By the melodramatic means of an unlikely coincidence and shot juxtaposition, the ring with which Sanderson is to marry Anna falls to the carpeted floor during their marriage "ceremony" at precisely the moment that "far away it happens that David Bartlett is dreaming a troubled dream." Long before Anna and David meet, Griffith's melodramatic vision insists that the world is a unified coherent place and that there is such a thing as an ultimately benevolent destiny which always has the last word—even in melodramas of defeat. Fate or God's will, bolstered by Biblically inflected intertitles, makes this claim. Because David is a nice young man and Anna is a nice young woman, they must come together. It is an affirmation that there is a moral universe still, and that the forces of good are everywhere struggling to combat the forces of evil. The melodramatist seeks to be assured that the significations of the world are not, in Robbe-Grillet's words, "partial, provisional," or "contradictory and always contested,"[29] even when he or she must be forced to recognize that they are.

I have described in a previous chapter how the tableau crystallizes the way melodramatic mise en scène signifies, and if one bears in mind the fact that the term mise en scène comes from theater, one can from time to time see quite clearly in Way Down East how much the film owes to the Victorian image. Even though by 1920 the "Victorian era" was for most intents and purposes over, Griffith managed in a modern medium to preserve uncannily, but with great success, much of the cinema's Victorian heritage. Indeed, the essential drama of Way Down East is depicted in a Victorian mode: in the "stagey" mise en scène of the shot in which Squire Bartlett orders Anna from

---

[28] Smith, Melodrama, 20.
[29] Robbe-Grillet, For a New Novel, 141.

3. When her past becomes known, Anna is banished from the hearth and the family table, and sent into the storm. (Burr McIntosh, Kate Bruce, Vivia Ogden, Lowell Sherman, Lillian Gish, Mary Hay, Creighton Hale, George Neville, Richard Barthelmess, Edgar Nelson.)

his house. This also bespeaks the film's stage-play antecedents: posters for the play show precisely this "scene"—characters frozen emblematically in mid-gesture.[30] For all its frenzy of emotion, it is a moment of stasis. It literally *holds* the action in the manner of nineteenth-century narrative painting.[31] Almost every character in the film appears in the shot grouped along the same focal plane behind the long table, with Squire Bartlett on the left, David on the right, and Anna in the middle. She is alone on this side of the table facing the door which the Squire's dramatic pointing gesture indicates is off-screen to the left. The Squire's legs are set firmly astride; Anna's head is bowed. Mrs. Bartlett clutches at the Squire's sleeve in an attempt to restrain him without seriously challenging his authority. The image is weighted with the Squire, Mrs. Bartlett, Martha Perkins (who

[30] I am grateful to Sandy Flitterman-Lewis for telling me about the poster.

[31] Cf. Martin Meisel, *Realizations: Narrative, Pictorial, and Theatrical Arts in Nineteenth-Century England* (Princeton, N.J.: Princeton University Press, 1983).

betrayed Anna to the Squire), and Lennox Sanderson on the left, and the others (Kate, the Professor, the Constable, David Bartlett, and Hi Holler) on the right. The table clearly divides the scene along its axis into a visible organization of Law and Other. Alone on the carpet in front of the table, Anna stands accused in a theater of middle-class morality, prejudice and hypocrisy. David is not on this "jury," but his position at the bottom of the table and his being the only one seated (neither on the near nor the far side of the table) puts the onus of resolution on him. He shatters a plate, and moves to defy his father. What David will do, of course, is rescue and (with his father's blessing) marry Anna: it is the only possible resolution, and it is a male one. He becomes a husband to a mother, and a re-phallicization of the order which restores Anna to her "proper" position as wife/ mother is at last achieved.

The logic of the film's coding as a melodramatic narrative can be understood from a position that sees all of Western civilization as built on the irreducible fact of sexual difference, with the phallus as original, privileged signifier, and woman relegated to a negative status defined by lack. Not only does melodrama tell us that there is no desire without the phallus;[32] it recognizes that society, as Julia Kristeva has written, "is a complex organism, [and] that its ethic is determined perhaps above all by its family structure, and that it thus depends directly on the economy of the sexual difference."[33]

Way Down East, then, ends on the image of the married couple, as if this marriage were the whole point of the story. In some sense, as we have seen, it is. While the cinema's early family melodramas had various emphases, it was their romantic element that reached into almost every movie made in Hollywood and that seemed to say something enduring about our society. It was the romantic element of the family melodrama that in the end shifted the genre towards a strongly psychoanalytic understanding of itself. Whether the film ends on the coming together of a couple, or on the unification of a family of some sort, or on the defeat of this effort, the bedrock impli-

---

[32] Pam Cook, "Masculinity in Crisis?" *Screen* 23, no. 3–4 (September–October, 1982): "But, as the sister of tragedy, melodrama, tells us, there is no desire without the phallus (think of the endings of *Written on the Wind* and *All That Heaven Allows*, where the heroines are caught in the consequences of their desire to overthrow the phallus) and though we may take it up we can only do so at the expense of male castration" (46).

[33] Julia Kristeva, *About Chinese Women*, trans. Anita Barrows (New York: Urizen Books, 1977), 200.

cation is the same: the world can only be understood in binary structures, in which the male-female difference is the privileged binarism.
If the emotional core of early melodramas is the constant and catastrophic threat of the fall of the heroine,[34] it is because the heroine
embodies virtue. And "as virtue was personified in the heroine so
was the threat to it presented in physical, specifically sexual,
terms."[35] Julia Kristeva reminds us in her book about Chinese women
that our modern societies are not "simply patrilinear, or 'class-struc-
tured,' or capitalist-monopolist," but governed by "a monotheism
whose essence is best expressed in the Bible: the paternal Word sustained by a fight to the finish between the two races (men/women)."
A radical separation of the sexes—"castration, if you like"—is "the
support of monotheism and the source of its eroticism."[36] And so it
is with the Griffith melodrama, in which Kristeva's words curiously
echo Eisenstein's: "And this society, perceived *only as a contrast between the haves and the have-nots*, is reflected in the consciousness of
Griffith no deeper than the image of an intricate race between two
parallel lines."[37]

Kristeva's drawing of a link between monotheism and castration is
consistent with the pattern of melodrama's evolution from what I
have been calling an essentially Christian discourse towards the psychoanalytic discourse that dominates the form now. In keeping with
the Christian imagination, of which we have observed the melodramatic imagination is a somewhat secularized variation, *Way Down
East* tells a story in which characters perform archetypal functions,
and the terms—not just in the intertitles—are fate, forgiveness, sacrifice, punishment and retribution, expulsion, recognition, mercy, reward, and salvation. As an expression of Christian, social, and psychoanalytic logic, the film stands at that complex moment in
American history when the Christian moral universe was being replaced—first by a sense of how class and social conditions determine
destiny, and later by the Freudian mythology.[38]

---

[34] David Grimstead, *Melodrama Unveiled: Theater and Culture 1800–1850* (Chicago: University of Chicago Press, 1968), 175.

[35] Ibid., 175.

[36] Kristeva, *About Chinese Women*, 22–23.

[37] Eisenstein, *Film Form*, 234.

[38] This shift in the moral occult of the melodrama began in the theater before the advent of the cinema, as David Grimstead has observed: "The melodrama also avoided moral ambiguity by making sin wholly a product of character rather than of situation

THE LOOM OF FATE: *The Mother and the Law*

The Mother and the Law was made immediately after *The Birth of a Nation*, but after the great success of the latter, Griffith decided that his tale of hard times in the big city was too small to follow his national saga, and so he decided to develop *The Mother and the Law* into something larger. The result was *Intolerance*, a four-story epic that was dominated by the original film (as the modern story) and by a visually stunning and expensively produced story Griffith called *The Fall of Babylon*. In August 1919, however, realizing perhaps that *The Mother and the Law* was too good a film to be lost in the often-confusing, financially unsuccessful larger work, Griffith decided to release *The Mother and the Law* as a separate film—three full years after *Intolerance* was first screened.

Starting with its title, *The Mother and the Law* describes rather well not only Griffith's main concerns (themes which we find throughout Griffith's work), but the general concerns of the family melodrama itself. The themes are primarily of social consciousness: the bad outcome of immorality, the evils of alcohol, the poor hero or orphan succeeding, the breakup and restitution of the family, good versus evil, rich versus poor, capitalists versus workers, the salvation of love, and, of course, the grand theme which is meant to unify the film—intolerance.

The theme of intolerance is only intermittently addressed in *The Mother and the Law*, but it underlies everything, for the term is almost as abstract as "fate." The story is told essentially from the victims' point of view (metaphorically, and literally, the Mother's), not from an attitude demonstrated by the oppressors (the Law of the film's title, the law of the Father). Griffith, for the most part on the side of Victorian morality, endorses the authority of the father, but not of the non-life-generating institution, the Jenkins Foundation. The Ves-

---

or society. Circumstances were sometimes used to explain why an essentially good man had done bad things, but generally one's moral stance was cause rather than caused. Beginning in the late 1830's a few plays suggested familial upbringing as reason for a character's faults, and by the 1850's some, most notably *Uncle Tom's Cabin*, tentatively gave a social rather than personal explanation of evil. The growing tendency toward 'realism' in the melodrama of the late nineteenth century reflected largely an increasing willingness to see man's character not as a moral abstraction but as a complex product of a particular personal and social environment." (Grimstead, *Melodrama Unveiled*, 222.)

4. Agents of the Law restrain the Dear One, while her husband is taken off to prison. (Mae Marsh in *The Mother and the Law*.)

tal Virgins of Uplift, as he calls the zealous reformers, have no right to prescribe behavior, and the antagonisms that exist between the private institution (the family) and public institutions generate the conflicts in the film, suggesting that if all families were in harmony, the world would be in harmony, or that the world should be structured on the model of the happy home of the united family.

A title that appears fairly early in the film announces that "the Loom of Fate weaves Death for the Boy's Father." Fate, it seems, is the capitalist Jenkins, for the shot of the dying father is intercut with a shot of Jenkins at his desk—which in fact is the same image with which the film begins. When the father dies, the Boy (Bobby Harron) goes to the nearby city where he meets the Friendless One (Miriam Cooper). The Dear One (Mae Marsh) and her father also go to the city, and "Fate lead[s] them all to the same district." Fate, in *The Mother and the Law*, is what Griffith called intolerance—the intolerant Jenkins, his sister, and the Vestal Virgins of Uplift. Fate is that which opposes the family: social injustice, misguided reform. Fate, as Sergei

Eisenstein (another kind of melodramatist) would have described it, is capitalism—the economic system that is founded on class differences which fuel class conflict and produce oppressors like Jenkins.

When the Boy enters the city he is immediately "caught in the meshes of an environment too strong to escape," and the Friendless One is befriended by a "musketeer." Fate and environment are synonymous in the sense that fate is merely another word for what happens, and the agency of what happens is associated with Jenkins, who is identified as not only capitalistic, but hypocritically so—an intolerant reformer. We are meant to understand that in some way men like Jenkins are responsible for the urban industrial complex in which the displaced rural proletariat, in the absence of a support system of family and community, are propelled during hard times towards crime.

The opening long shot of Jenkins alone at his desk is followed by the title, "My own way of thinking, eating and drinking is the only way." This constitutes a direct hit for the theme of intolerance, but the image of Jenkins at his desk, isolated in the center of a large room, soon comes to represent all capitalist oppressors. In the following shot Jenkins' spinster sister is shown at a sumptuous party she is giving. The juxtaposition of this shot of the sister, set apart from her dancing guests, and the previous shot of her brother alone at his desk, suggests that something is not quite right about this incomplete family. They have no parents, spouses, or children, and involuntarily one understands their bachelor-/spinsterhood to be an unwholesome thing. If halfway through the film one recalls these opening shots, it becomes more apparent that the misfortunes that the Boy and the Dear One suffer (such as the loss of their baby) are in some sense due, according to the logic of the melodramatic narration, to this brother and sister, and to the Vestal Virgins of Uplift. They are embittered and soured; they have resisted, or defied, or escaped, through one circumstance or another, the familial destiny of a correct bourgeois fate, they have not married and had children, and this failure of obligation is a source of evil.[39]

In the scenes that introduce Jenkins' middle-aged sister we are shown how Miss Jenkins senses that she is excluded from the privileges of youth and marriage. She gazes at herself in a mirror and sees

[39] This notion was first suggested to me by John Belton.

her truth: she is too old for romance or to have a family of her own; she has no other person to return her gaze. A shot of melodramatic horror on her face is juxtaposed with a happy scene (exterior shot) of the Dear One jumping about with youthful vitality. The Dear One enjoys, with her father, geese and chickens, "a fair measure of happiness and contentment," but this happiness of course will be threatened, and the Dear One's feminine destiny in a bourgeois era will push her towards other kinds of happiness—the love of a young man, and the pleasures of motherhood and family. Is it "fate" that "of course" will threaten the Dear One's happiness? The intertitles often say so, but the mise en scène and editing structures tell a different story. The juxtaposition of the shots of Miss Jenkins and the Dear One underscores the fact of the Dear One's vitality and prettiness; what the two shots have to do with each other cannot immediately be determined, but putting them together heightens the effect of each.

This pattern of oppositions, opposites, and complements is maintained throughout the film. The Boy is clearly the Dear One's complementary counterpart, just as he is set in some kind of opposition to Jenkins. The factory owner, alone in a large room, is the Law which the Boy must oppose or become. He must become a man and a Father, without becoming an oppressive embodiment of capitalistic, masculine prerogative like Jenkins. The Boy enjoys the community of his fellow workers but is also, along with them, oppressed like a brother among brothers, under the rule of a harsh patriarch. The boy is whatever a boy is: not yet realized (i.e., not fully masculine), still in some sense feminine, still overtly subject to the law of the Father. The melodramatic blurring of the larger issues with the more private, family-scale configurations begins, as we can see, as soon as the film starts, and in spite of the filmmaker's attempt to write a narrative essay on the theme of intolerance, we get a series of short-term causalities to add to an accumulating list that should in sum explain why the Mother of this story has a bad experience of the Law.

When the Boy is introduced into the narrative (leaving the house where he lives with his father to go to work in the Jenkins factory), his appearance and surroundings contrast vividly with the Jenkins-Miss Jenkins pair. As "the Boy" he has a part to play in a story designed by fate. This naming of characters, in the most literal sense the basis of identity, is melodrama's way of clearly defining who has what moral status. The melodramatist's function as a storyteller is to present a coherent world that, for all its complexity, is knowable and legible. For example, because the Mae Marsh character is called the Dear One, we will know more or less what to expect from her. She will also be, we presume, the mother of the film's title, and since she is at the beginning a virgin, her treacherous passage from virginity to motherhood (avoiding that other area of feminine definition under patriarchy—prostitution) will no doubt constitute the narrative.

If we know, then, what the Mother is (and—as metaphor—it includes the Boy, and by extension, the working masses), what is the Law? The Vestal Virgins of Uplift, certainly, are a major tentacle of the Law's Hydra head. The Law, as I think the film means the metaphor to be understood, is a matter of interdiction and prohibition. It is *masculinity* as I describe it in chapter 3: it wants to castrate. This is why Griffith grotesquely masculinizes his representatives of the Law. The Vestal Virgins are three grim-looking, mannish women dressed in black. "We must have laws to make people good," they insist. We have seen no shots of people who would seem to require laws to make them good, but this shot of the Vestal Virgins is followed by a festive, jolly scene of factory workers (and the Dear One) dancing in the local dance hall. It is this scene the Vestal Virgins wish to destroy. Inserted is a shot of Miss Jenkins receiving a check from her brother for the cause of Moral Uplift. Outside the dance hall Jenkins is surprised and annoyed to discover that his workers are within, when they should be in bed getting a good night's rest before the day's work in the factory. As Kristeva defines the symbolic function (language—for our purposes, another metaphor for the Law): "a system of signs . . . whose goal is to accredit social communication as exchange purified of pleasure. . . . We are speaking, then, of a training process, an inhibition."[40] In other words, the sexuality of the working classes must be subordinated to the demands of capitalism.

The rich are represented as idle (Miss Jenkins "entertains"), as unhappy (Miss Jenkins) or embittered (the Vestal Virgins), and as essentially indifferent (*viz.* Jenkins) to the real needs of the poor. Industrial society requires of its factory workers an inhumane discipline which, quite wrongly, it is thought by the factory owners, leisure activities undermine. Representations of injustice are heaped up, but the

[40] Kristeva, *About Chinese Women*, 30–31.

melodramatic conviction that there *is* justice in the world does its work: the rich are unhappy, lonely, and so forth *because* they are rich, while ordinary "folks" know how to have fun, because they have more direct access to life's flows of desire and sources of affect.

The question of desire is at the heart of *The Mother and the Law*'s causes and effects. Energy is perverted into repressive economies, and—when equated with money—can be used against itself or drawn by other people for their own oppressive, damaging purposes. For example, when the expenditures for the crusade for Moral Uplift begin to strain the resources of the Jenkins Foundation, and Jenkins orders a wage cut for his factory workers, a strike follows. Griffith quickens the tempo by intercutting shots of onlookers, the militia, the strikers, and the Dear One rushing frantically to and fro. A tableau of "Hungry Ones" waiting to take the strikers' places provides a somber image of the misery Jenkins' action has caused. Jenkins orders the wage cut by telephone (signifying his alienation from the flows of desire with which the working classes are associated—or, indeed, which they signify) and once again he is shown at his desk, isolated in space, far from the riotous mob.

Although it is fate that brings the Boy and the Dear One to the same city at the same time, it is not only fate that brings them together. Griffith acknowledges that the Dear One's sexual awakening is inevitable, and so, perhaps, it is some kind of fate after all: the Dear One consciously makes herself (sexually) attractive to men. *The Mother and the Law* as a melodrama requires the Dear One (the mother) to be as far as possible beyond reproach, which is why the narrative includes the Friendless One (who presumably has become a prostitute for the musketeer) to represent the less morally good woman in the story.

Through the visual metaphor of the "Hopeful Geranium"—the inspiration, the good example, of nature—the Dear One's hopes and dreams are suggested, but fate puts evil lures everywhere. Just behind her potted plant is the window from which the Dear One notices how much attention the provocative walk of an attractive young woman commands on the street, and she resolves to learn the walk herself. With furtive, guilty glances at a statuette of the Virgin Mary, the Dear One ties a sash about her knees and practices her walk. In a typical move from the cosmic level of Fate to the mundane level of "everyday human beings" Griffith has the Boy meet the Dear One as a result of this new walk of hers. It is the workings of a fate that decrees that the Good will inevitably find the Good or, as we see later, that the virtue in each character (the Boy, the Dear One) will overcome any stirrings of vice in the other. With his bowler set rakishly at the back of his head and with his hand in his pocket, he claims her: "Say kid, you're gonna be my chicken." She is delighted and disturbed, but her father, the source of legitimate authority, makes it plain that she has done wrong and must pray to the Virgin Mary to be forgiven. The father's effort to keep his daughter's desire in check almost kills him. He clutches at his heart and appears to be thoroughly fatigued by his paternal responsibility to repress her sexuality. An element of suspense is introduced: will he die before she is safely handed over to another man (a husband)?

When she "persists with her new walk to win admiration," a man follows her into the building where she lives, and the Boy follows shortly thereafter. A fight between the Boy and the stranger ensues and "the lady fair watches the knights battling for her lily-white hand." Consistent with the chivalric code of courtly love to which the intertitle refers, Griffith later shows the Boy reproaching the Dear One for continuing her sexy walk after they are married. It may have been appropriate as a means to attract the Boy's attention, but ceases to be appropriate now that she is his wife. We understand that their marriage represents a small victory for the forces of Good in that the threat of rape to our heroine is for the meantime shelved. Before they marry, however, with Freudian logic, the Dear One's father dies. And again the shot of the dead father and the sobbing child is followed by a shot of Jenkins at his desk—from which, it is implied, he is able to cause such things to happen.

The shot of Jenkins is a preparation for the introduction of another threat, the Committee of Seventeen, who report that they have cleaned up the city; there is no more drinking, dancing, or prostitution. Griffith's nastiest stab at one sector of his intolerant detractors[41] ("When women cease to attract men, they turn to reform as a second choice") describes an operation of melodrama itself—the translation

---

[41] Not everyone who saw *The Birth of a Nation* had unmitigated praise for it, and Griffith seems to have been surprised and hurt by the more vigorous protests against the film. He not only published a 45–page pamphlet entitled "The Rise and Fall of Free Speech in America," but consciously sought to answer his detractors in film—with *Intolerance.*

of private matters into public consequences, and the drawing of local, private significance from public action. Griffith goes on to show that Prohibition (of the sale of alcohol) results in the proliferation of private stills and that prostitution flourishes in spite of efforts to curb it. He offers as an institution of real love and charity the Salvation Army, but as with his images of the ideal family, the image of the succoring Salvation Army nurse is static and depressing.

If the marriage of the Boy and the Dear One looked like this, of course there would be no movie. After the Boy and the Dear One are married, the first thing the Boy does is leave the apartment, and his wife is left sweeping the floor. The tone of the shot is positive, which implies that Griffith thought, as no doubt most men of his time did, that the *idea* of marriage, the fact of being married, is itself enough for a woman, who will perform domestic chores with gratitude and enthusiasm in return for the protection that her husband will provide. The responsibility the melodrama assumes in representing such domestic arrangements is considerable, because implicit in the genre as a form articulated within mainstream ideology is an assumption that this is the way things should be. The suggestion that a man's role is and should be an active one, necessitating forays into the outside world, and that a woman's place is in the home, cannot in all fairness be harshly criticized in a film made in 1915; more important should be the observation that *The Mother and the Law* at least attempts to articulate a moral framework, an order of things, that will keep human suffering to a minimum.[42] *The Mother and the Law* locates the sources and agents of misery not directly in sexual difference and society's ways of handling it (which results in power imbalances between men and women) but in bad people like Jenkins, in women like the Vestal Virgins who have lost out in the system the melodrama advocates (marriage, family, etc.) and who, therefore, spoil it for the rest. The melodrama attempts to provide a way to live in the world as it is; it does not advocate doing away with the Father (for, what then?), but only, perhaps, the overthrow of the Father, to replace the Father with a better one.

---

[42] Only later, in some of the *noir* melodramas of the 1940s (a "genre" that generally eschews the "happy ending"), is the melodrama's commitment to the monogamous married relation and to the redeeming qualities of love severely challenged and undermined.

A logical tracing-back to the real sources of misery represented in the narrative results only in confusions and impossibilities. If *The Mother and the Law* is explicitly a critique of capitalism, but can only offer that critique in personal terms, it is because, as we have said, as a melodrama it cannot envision a radically different order of things.[43] If heterosexuality is really the impossible problem, is homosexuality an answer, as Deleuze and Guattari suggest?[44] Is sexuality itself the problem, as Foucault and Heath imply? Or, as Dorothy Dinnerstein asserts, is it the fact that we are all raised by mothers? When the Boy is framed in a street robbery and sent off to the "sometimes House of Intolerance," he is once again forced to "flounder helplessly in the nets of fate." The implicit reasoning is no more sophisticated than this: if Jenkins had not ordered a cut in wages, the Boy, by a series of fateful happenings, would not now be in prison. Griffith draws connections between Fate, environment and intolerance with melodramatic facility, to produce an equation in which the urban environment is intolerant owing to the intolerance and hypocrisy of the capitalist.

But we see how narrative causality *is* the very effort to explain why things go wrong. Jenkins ordered a cut in wages because the Jenkins Foundation was running short on funds because Miss Jenkins and her soured spinster friends were too zealous in their efforts to stop everybody else from having any fun because *they* weren't having any fun because they are not married because . . . they are not attractive to men.

[43] Some melodramas are driven by ideological contradiction to make (or rather, almost make) the conscious and political choice to abandon bourgeois ideology. *Our Daily Bread*, for example, makes the choice that *The Crowd* almost makes. A film like *The Battleship Potemkin*, of course, is another thing altogether; it comes after the revolution. The American family melodrama seeks a way out of this impasse by resorting to the logic of psychoanalysis.

[44] It should be observed, since I mention homosexuality and Deleuze and Guattari in the same sentence, that they develop a rather eccentric notion of homosexuality which is not at all Freudian. For Deleuze and Guattari, homosexuality is synonymous with their notion of *le devenir femme*, which is to say, a becoming minority, opposing the fascism of the majority. For an introduction to this notion, see Gilles Deleuze and Claire Parnet, *Dialogues* (Paris: Flammarion, 1977); Félix Guattari, "Becoming a Woman" [sic], *Molecular Revolution: Psychiatry and Politics*, trans. Rosemary Sheed (Harmondsworth, Middlesex: Penguin Books, 1984), 233–35; and George Stambolian, "A Liberation of Desire: An Interview with Félix Guattari," *Homosexualities and French Literature* (Ithaca: Cornell University Press, 1979), 56–69.

5. In a classic last-minute rescue, the Boy (Robert Harron)
is saved by the Governor's pardon.

The film makes shifts from sexual and familial causality to more
abstract social machinery, which grinds up individual desire. The
way in which issues are externalized and obfuscated is most spectac-
ularly obvious in the conclusion to the film (the Death Watch and
chase sequence that follows the Boy's conviction for murder). While
the film benefits structurally from this final burst of energy that rises
to a peak of emotion when the Boy is saved, seconds before hanging,
Eisenstein is right, after all: Griffith's "montage" appears to be "a
copy of his dualistic picture of the world, running in two parallel
lines of poor and rich towards some hypothetical 'reconciliation'

where . . . the parallel lines would cross, that is, in that infinity, just as inaccessible as that 'reconciliation.' "[45]

The chase/last-minute rescue is not only pure Griffith but pure melodrama, juxtaposing, as it does, two scenes each of which heightens to maximum effect the emotional possibilities of the other. The Boy's slow, despairing preparation for his death by hanging is pierced again and again by shots of the racing car. The cruel injustice of his position is returned to repeatedly, and inevitably the viewer's concern for the Boy's plight is aroused by his or her participation in the race for the Boy's salvation. Good is racing to overcome Evil: it is a struggle to affirm the necessary belief that this is not an indifferent universe—in spite of the demonstration by the greater part of the film to the contrary. God may be dead or useless (the priest can do nothing to save the Boy), but Good *must* prevail in the melodramatic universe, since nihilistic despair or cynicism are among the few alternatives to the loss of the tragic vision, which as Barthes has observed is "merely a means of 'recovering' human misery, of subsuming and thereby justifying it in the form of a necessity, a wisdom, or a purification."[46] Melodrama, wherever it can, refuses this kind of recuperation of human misery.

The film ends on the first real kiss between the Boy and the Dear One. It is as if Griffith was charmed by the coy, skittish sexuality expressed in the hesitant near-kiss, perfected later by Lillian Gish in *True Heart Susie* (1919). The kiss between the Boy and the Dear One *is* the resolution of this melodrama of separation. The entire film has worked towards this union of the ideally good young man and woman whom adversity, mostly in the form of social evils arising from the urban-industrial phenomenon, has kept apart. The heterosexual union, in its monogamous, married form, is posited as the bedrock of social, sexual and psychological stability. However, one might wonder briefly, now that the melodramatics are over, of what their married life will consist. In effect, the end of the melodrama marks the resumption (if the film had a life beyond the last shot, as it were) perhaps of tragic consciousness. In this film social evils and inequities constitute the backdrop for an Oedipal drama which itself to some extent provides a metaphorical version of the workings of

[45] Eisenstein, *Film Form*, 235.
[46] Barthes, quoted in Robbe-Grillet, *For a New Novel*, 49.

bourgeois-capitalist society. The final shot of *The Mother and the Law* represents no real victory. The battle to save the Boy from hanging has been won, but has the war? Jenkins still owns the factory, and social conditions remain unchanged. The Boy and the Dear One have been reunited, but they have lost a great deal (a child, at the very least). At best, they have been returned to Square One. As in *Way Down East* and in *Broken Blossoms*, the protagonists' misfortunes in *The Mother and the Law* can only be presented as a lesson for the audience. How else, in a film of good fathers and bad Fathers, to overcome the fact that it is the good fathers who die?[47]

"The Tragic Dead End of Victorian American Culture": *Broken Blossoms*

A persistent element in the films of D. W. Griffith is a highly repressed sexual concern, most frequently condensed, displaced, or varied in a configuration of the family. The pseudo-family, surrogate family, "natural" or "unnatural" family, as a central motif in so many Griffith films, provides a hermeneutic thread, a code of explanation for the strange tensions with which Griffith's melodramatic style and plots are often charged. More specifically, the relations among family members, the breakup and restitution of a family unit, Griffith's perplexing notions of femininity and masculinity, and the difficulties surrounding the question of where or how love and sexual desire meet and differ, tend to characterize the Griffith film, and *Broken Blossoms* in particular.

Several of Griffith's obsessions that appear, like the recurrent latent content of ever-changing dreams, are present in *Broken Blossoms*. The film differs markedly, in appearance and pace, from anything Griffith had made to date, and yet the familiar subtext of incestuous, repressed desire is intensely present, and the film's syntagmatic structure (a certain symmetry, a parenthetical way of disclosing information and using titles, the use of establishing shots followed by

---

[47] As Susan Sontag has written, "In the world envisaged by Judaism and Christianity, there are no free-standing arbitrary events. All events are part of the plan of a just, good, providential deity; every crucifixion must be topped by a resurrection. Every disaster or calamity must be seen either as leading to a greater good or else as just and adequate punishment fully merited by the sufferer." ("The Death of Tragedy," 1963; reprinted in *Against Interpretation* [New York: Dell Publishing Co., 1966], 137.)

medium shots, etc.) is not unlike the structure of previous films—reaching, perhaps, the dead-end of a certain familiar logic. It is a pessimistic, heartbreaking tale of poverty, prejudice, fear, and tenderness that is almost classical in its tragic purity. *Broken Blossoms* is a tragic melodrama that streamlines the Griffith discourse on the family into a kind of stark, sublime simplicity, and yet the film is rather different from the others Griffith made: there are only three main characters; the action is simple; it was shot almost entirely inside a studio (which creates a unity of "look" and thereby of place); and there is an overpowering sense of inevitability in the narrative's slow but steady movement towards death.

This tragic sense derives, finally, from the death of Lucy and the suicide of the Yellow Man, but in the first intertitle we suspect that Griffith is attempting in advance to recuperate for melodrama some tragic effect of his "tale":

We may believe there are no Battling Burrows striking the helpless with brutal whip—but do we not ourselves use the whip of unkind words and deeds? So, perhaps, Battling may even carry a message of warning.

It is a melodramatic necessity that even when Virtue is not seen to prevail over Evil, she will find her reward somehow—either in the afterlife, or in the example her tale provides the reader/viewer.

Above all, as a drama of impossible desires, *Broken Blossoms* can only end in death (or impossible frustration). Photographed by Henrik Sartov, the film presents as a dominant value the beautiful, the pictorial, the tableau, the exquisite face, rather than the unfolding and resolution of a narrative. It is a style characterized by shallow focus and soft, radiant close-ups of faces. Describing the film's effect on the audience at the film's premiere, Karl Brown (who assisted in photographing the film) senses that it has operated "through something as mysterious as instinct itself." Brown, like Griffith, only half understood the sources of *Broken Blossoms'* power:

For the abysmal brute has always existed, and Battling Burrows was not Donald Crisp but an archetype of ignorant power exulting in cruelty for cruelty's sake. Lillian Gish was not a poor cringing slavey after all but a creature of exquisite beauty thrown by some unknowable fate into the grip of a monster.[48]

[48] Karl Brown, *Adventures with D. W. Griffith* (New York: Da Capo Press, 1973), 241.

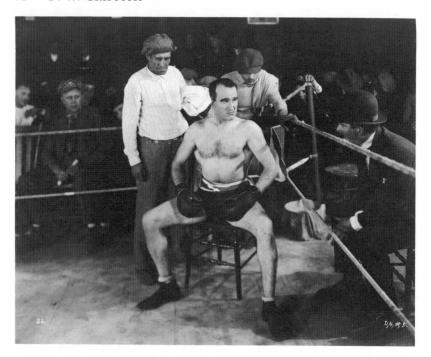

6. Battling Burrows, one of the "sons of turmoil and strife." (Donald Crisp in *Broken Blossoms*.)

That there is such a thing as "cruelty for cruelty's sake" is a melo-dramatic notion. The truth lies somewhere in Burrows' being "an ar-chetype of ignorant power" and Lucy's being "an exquisite beauty." What happens need not be described in terms of "unknowable fate," but in terms of the sexual desirability of exquisite feminine beauty.

By insisting that *Broken Blossoms* is a fantasy, Brown unwittingly encourages a psychoanalytic reading of its "archetypical beings out of the long inherited memory of the human race."[49] When he writes that "No such people as we saw on the screen were alive in the work-aday world of today or any other day,"[50] he is admiring the power of melodramatic convention to strike at the heart of truthful resonances. The film's characters are two-dimensional—they are not realistic—and the film's power derives from a knot of repressed desires that is typical of melodrama, even though it attempts to disguise its well-

[49] Ibid., 241.
[50] Ibid., 241.

springs of emotional affect under the cover of "art." The "long-inher-ited memory of the human race" connotes seething sexual forces which besieged pre-civilized man and which have been repressed in the name of civilization into "love" in its various forms, of which the Yellow Man's love for Lucy is one and Battling Burrows' abuse of his daughter is a perversion.

The characters are "misty," as Brown and Griffith suggest, because they are not *psychological* characters of the sort we see developed in the nineteenth-century novel. Lucy, the Yellow Man, and Battling Burrows are, as I have suggested, two-dimensional, melodramatic characters, which is to say they are archetypes. "The principle char-acteristic of archetypal phenomena," Rosemary Gordon has written, "is that they are powerful, stark, absolute, fascinating, have an all-or-nothing quality and so conjure up a fairy-tale world."[51] If Brown understands *Broken Blossoms* to be a "parable in poetry," the question is, what is the lesson to be learned? And why is it a "tale," and what is the "warning"? Brown calls the film a vision, and the characters "creatures of a poetic imagination that had at very long last found its outlet in its own way in its own terms." Griffith is very clearly iden-tified as a mythmaker, and this film, Brown implies, is the most clearly articulated representation of Griffith's sensibility at this time. But Griffith saw *Broken Blossoms* as different from his previous works. The film was conceived, made, and marketed as an "art film."[52]

With the opening title the emphasis is on the static image and the story's simplicity (in the sense that it is a tale): "It is a tale of temple bells sounding at sunset before the image of Buddha. It is a tale of love and lovers: it is a tale of tears." It is, of course, rather an unusual love story, if one accepts Griffith's description of the tale as one of "love and lovers," for it is a love story only for the Yellow Man. The title's evocation of ethereality and timelessness is followed by a shot that suggests precisely that—a Chinese port at sunset with ships drifting slowly on the river. The same shot closes the film, thus add-

---

[51] Rosemary Gordon, "Desire and Woman: A Jungian Approach," *Desire*, ed. Lisa Appignanesi (London: ICA Publications, 1984), 14.

[52] See Dudley Andrew, "Broken Blossoms: The Vulnerable Text and the Marketing of Masochism," *Film in the Aura of Art* (Princeton: Princeton University Press, 1984), 16–27; Vance Kepley, "Griffith's *Broken Blossoms* and the Problem of Historical Specific-ity," *Quarterly Review of Film Studies* 3 (1978): 37–48; and Arthur Lennig, "*Broken Blos-soms*, D. W. Griffith, and the Making of an Unconventional Masterpiece," *Film Journal* 2 (Fall-Winter 1978): 2–9.

ing to the film's quality as a tale. Although Lillian Gish's status as a Griffith heroine was well-established by 1919 (the year *Broken Blossoms* was completed and premiered) she shares the center of the film with Richard Barthelmess who, as Cheng Huan, the Yellow Man, both inaugurates and closes the narrative.

The story begins in China, in a brightly-lit, bustling city street. That we already know this to be a tale of tears, of broken blossoms, fills the opening shots of smiling children, well-dressed Chinese going about their business, sunshine "and skylarking American sailors" (images of prosperity, vitality and order) with a faint sense of foreboding. The destruction of this image is the end towards which the narrative will move. The shots of a Buddhist monk striking a gong and the closing shot (which is also the opening shot) of the ships at sunset, exist in a special timelessness. The narrative, in effect, ends with a reenactment of the Yellow Man's futile attempt to stop brutality (he arrives too late and himself employs violence rather than philosophy), and with the destruction of his shrine and his suicide.

We see the Yellow Man preparing for his journey to London where he hopes to take his "glorious message of peace to the barbarous Anglo-Saxons, sons of turmoil and strife." Griffith's use of "sons" suggests that we are all sons (brothers)—even Chinese and Englishmen. It is the beginning of the comparison between the Yellow Man and Battling Burrows as sons, as men who are different and yet, in at least that respect, the same, brought into melodrama's familial orbit.

The Yellow Man's mission to bring peace to the Western world, like his attempt to intercede between two quarrelling sailors in the prologue, fails. After a shot of the Yellow Man departing his native city in a rickshaw, the China chapter is closed by the familiar shot of the port at sunset. We then see a shot of Limehouse (London) some years later. The Yellow Man's youthful dreams have, needless to say, "come to wreck against the sordid realities of life." In a kind of refuge from those "sordid realities" the moral man becomes the aesthetic man. He is known locally simply as a "Chink storekeeper" but he buys and sells beautiful objects, and the shrine he later builds around Lucy represents his ultimate aesthetic gesture. The Yellow Man's immersion in an aesthetic world (and afternoons in the local opium den) when his desire is thwarted is an expression of what melodrama itself as an aesthetic ideology must do. Melodrama must always find an aesthetic, textual solution to ideological contradiction, and in *Broken Blossoms* it reveals its own operation (*as* a melodrama, a symbolic field in which the basic positionality of the film and viewer is charted), both on a formal level and in its very subject matter and story. As D. N. Rodowick has written,

Between ideology and the textual modes in which it is worked, there is an uneven quality, an incompleteness, a distance between the aesthetic "solution" and the determinate condition which ideology has placed on the articulation of the "problem." Therefore, what ideology cannot admit appears as contradiction within the work of the text, and what the text cannot resolve it must displace and attempt to work out at another level, or within another problematic.[53]

The Yellow Man leads an aesthetic life, finding it easier to locate beauty and order in objects than in people, and easier to live in the ghetto with the simpler imperatives of small business and sensual pleasure, than to deal with the moral strife of the larger world (offered only in the metonymy of the fighting sailors, and referred to in the "sordid realities" intertitle). The text must sidestep the vague, larger problem of why Anglo-Saxons are "sons of turmoil and strife," and attempt to work it out in the more local problem of Lucy and Battling Burrows. Of course, there is no working that one out either (Griffith's vision and discourse being pre-psychoanalytic) and it ends in violence and suicide, with Griffith having displaced into signifiers of "art" much of what the text cannot resolve.

What we do have, though, is the text itself, which shows "the operation of basic ethical imperatives."[54] The text defines "in conflictual opposition, the space of their play." In Peter Brooks' words,

That they can be staged "proves" that they exist: the melodramatic mode not only uses these imperatives but consciously assumes the role of bringing them into dramatized and textual—provisional—existence.[55]

No one is expected to like Battling Burrows, but how to challenge him is a problem. Where the Yellow Man's initial efforts to persuade the West, by moralizing and preaching, that violence is not the answer to difference are shown to fail, his cult of the beautiful is an implicit alternative. Griffith offers the film itself as an aesthetic ex-

[53] D. N. Rodowick, "Madness, Authority, and Ideology in the Domestic Melodrama of the 1950's," *The Velvet Light Trap* 19 (1982): 40.

[54] Brooks, *The Melodramatic Imagination*, 201.

[55] Ibid., 201.

ample, a means of coping with some of the worst effects of the Law (the Battling Burrowses). In effect, *Broken Blossoms* offers fetishism over sadism, which is no real progress, for it is a response still from within the very system that understands the world in terms of castration, which we know produces the violence of Battling Burrows. The question becomes not how to challenge or overthrow patriarchal culture or how to subvert the aggressive thrust of capitalism, but on what to stake the integration of otherness in patriarchal culture. Griffith offers a kind of Christian passivity, a tragic acceptance, which he then, with the innate optimism of the melodramatic imagination, tries to counter by stressing that he is telling a "tale," from which we might learn not to make the mistakes his characters make. It is the Christian optimism of the "resurrection" that follows the "crucifixion."

By arguing in "The Death of Tragedy" that Christian values are inimical to the pessimistic vision of tragedy ("every crucifixion must be topped by a resurrection"), Susan Sontag lends support to the observation that Christianity is melodramatic in structure and intent.[56] *The Mother and the Law*, to illustrate the point I wish to make for *Broken Blossoms*, is not a tragic melodrama, because the Boy is saved from hanging. The tragic melodrama, on the other hand, includes the crucifixion (and a resurrection). *Broken Blossoms* is certainly tragic (Lucy and the Yellow Man both die), but it is not a tragedy. We cannot truly say of *Broken Blossoms*, as Susan Sontag says of tragedy, that it is "a vision of nihilism, a heroic or ennobling vision of nihilism."[57] It is melodramatic, for the reasons I identify; it is a melodrama because it manages to include in its structure a sense of resurrection.[58]

The claustrophobic sense of fate and of life as theater evoked in *Broken Blossoms*—entrapping the characters in a predetermined drama—is to some extent achieved by showing the main characters in relatively unpopulated mises en scène, in parenthetically arranged shots. For example, we see the Yellow Man leaning against a wall—

---

[56] Sontag, *Against Interpretation*, 132–39.

[57] Ibid., 136.

[58] Cf. Steve Neale, "Melodrama and Tears," *Screen* 27, no. 6 (November–December 1986), for a compelling discussion of melodramas with "unhappy" endings. Neale argues that an "unhappy" ending "can function as a means of *postponing* rather than *destroying* the possibility of fulfillment of a wish. An 'unhappy' ending may function as a means of satisfying a wish to have the wish unfulfilled—in order that it can be preserved and re-stated rather than abandoned altogether" (21).

contemplative, alone—and the London street (unlike the Chinese street of the opening shots) is almost deserted and resembles a theater set. What follows is either a reverie from the Yellow Man's point of view, or simply Griffith's way of presenting information. The shots of the opium den which represents the "broken bits of his life in his new home," and a brief shot of temple bells in China, are followed by the shot (which began the sequence) of the Yellow Man leaning against the wall. Even this structure is contained within a larger syntagmatic structure which ends with a shot of boats drifting down the Thames—corresponding thus with the entire first section of the film that ends with the shot of ships drifting into a Chinese port at sunset. This parenthetical style is appropriate for the film, giving it a sense of enclosure, as a portrait is framed. It is a self-reflexive style which corresponds to the inwardly-turned personalities of the Yellow Man and Lucy, and the introverted, "failed" resolution of the story's conflicts, of which the Yellow Man's suicide is the most emblematic image.

When Battling Burrows is introduced, exactly the same arrangement of shots is used: an establishing shot of the waterfront followed by a shot of Burrows drinking at a table in his house, a medium shot of the boxing ring where he recently defeated the "Limehouse Tiger" (a flashback within the larger unit), back to Burrows at the table (a girlfriend walks in, talks to Burrows and leaves) and then back to the shot of the waterfront.

The introduction of Lucy follows the same pattern, beginning and ending with an establishing shot of the waterfront, and the second shot corresponding with the second-to-last shot of Lucy sitting on a coil of rope in a reverie. Between these parenthetical shots Lucy's situation and options (or rather, her lack of options) are presented. A married acquaintance (in a shot of a large family of grubby children, a toiling, skinny mother, a father) has told Lucy, "Whatever you do, dearie, don't get married." The image of married life Griffith offers of course tells us why Lucy should not marry. What are Lucy's alternatives if, "warned as strongly by the ladies of the street against their profession," she is to escape the misery and squalor of her lot? There is no alternative. This tale, ordered even on the level of the cinematic by the logic of identical syntagms within syntagms, ends in death. But precisely because it is a tale, Lucy represents more than simply one of those who are "weaker than the rest—butt of uncouth wit or ill temper." She is an archetype. She is the girl-child. She is female.

Lucy is the illegitimate, fifteen year-old daughter of Battling Burrows. Her "bruised little body may be seen creeping around the docks of Limehouse," one of the horrific, sentimental titles tells us, "when not serving as a punching bag to relieve the Battler's pent-up brutishness," and Griffith's first example of Burrows' sadism is particularly alarming in that Burrows is not shown beating Lucy in a blind rage, but taunting the terrified girl with threats of violence, and pursuing her around the table with a whip in his hand. Intercut with "Don't whip me—don't!" and "Please Daddy—don't" are long-held shots of Lucy's pathetic, beautiful, tearstained face, and the sneering Burrows with his twisted mouth and crumpled ear. Unlike the Yellow Man's loose-fitting clothes and shoes which are more like slippers than footwear for London streets, Burrows' clothes are tight and constricting; his shoes are huge, hard boots, to emphasize his size and power.

Burrows actually throws a spoon at Lucy when her back is turned, and giggles like a miscreant child. His repressed, incestuous desire for his daughter, the "weaker object," indeed finds its release in a most unfortunate way. His profession as a boxer (the kind of boxer that would "gloat" over an opponent's defeat) underscores the fact that Burrows is no normal figure of masculinity. It is a false move on Griffith's part, I think, to show (earlier) the girlfriend paying Burrows a visit, unless of course she is not a girlfriend but a prostitute, for it gives Burrows a "normal" sexual identity which he does not really have. Burrows' problem is fundamentally one of self-definition through violent domination of both men and women, which we are given to understand is an extreme case of what afflicts Western man generally. Even with the very first shot of Lucy on the dock we are given an image of masculinity of which Lucy's femininity is the radical opposite. Standing rigid, erect, is a tall sailor smoking a pipe (a phallic signifier in the service of an eminently masculine activity), while the frail, tiny Lucy, two feet away from him, stares vacantly in the opposite direction. By the melodramatic method of drawing the inference of universal significance from the particular, Griffith associates Western man with rigidity, imperialistic power, violence, and ugliness.

When we see the Yellow Man again he is being approached by two missionaries, one of whom is about to depart for China. (What irony!

They are his inverted doubles; he came to Limehouse as a missionary himself.) One of the men hands him a booklet and a close-up reveals its title to be HELL. The Yellow Man falteringly says, "I—I wish him luck." The suggestion is that Western imperialistic zeal, borne of patriarchal ideology, is undesirable, but Eastern philosophy (less clearly defined, but presented in the androgynous figure of the Yellow Man) is powerless to challenge its threat. The West has the upper hand—not only does it have the published word (the pamphlet) but it is organized (there are two missionaries versus one Yellow Man).

The underside of the West's (London's) power and prosperity is terrible cruelty (Burrows), suffering and poverty (Lucy). We see Lucy unearthing something from beneath a flagstone of the kitchen floor. It is her most prized possession—a strip of ribbon left to her by her mother. After stroking her cheek with it she puts the ribbon in her hair and goes into the street looking for tinfoil which she might be able to sell for a few pennies. The terms of Lucy's physical existence and the reach of her aspirations are drastically circumscribed—incredibly so—but believable on melodrama's terms.

The shot in which we see Lucy and the Yellow Man in the same frame for the first time is important for the film. Lucy is first seen walking around in front of the Yellow Man's shop looking for foil. "The Yellow Man watched Lucy often. The beauty which all Limehouse missed smote him to the heart." Then follows a shot of Lucy peeling a piece of foil from a strip of paper. Behind her, in his shop, the Yellow Man is staring at Lucy through the shop window. Lucy is a beautiful image, seen through glass, framed and unattainable. It is the beginning of the Yellow Man's fetishization of her. He keeps her always at a distance, in a disavowal of knowledge, as a defense. Burrows' response to the threat she represents is sadistic; his desire is to tear the loved object apart, whereas the Yellow Man's response is fetishistic. His drive, which is also ours and Griffiths', is to see (to *not* see, really), to make of Lucy a representation. It is a stroke of genius that Lucy is shown being seen by the Yellow Man through a frame; it is a shot that reawakens a primitive sense of the cinema.

Poor Lucy turns and looks at a doll in the shop window, just as the Yellow Man is looking through the same window at Lucy who is herself a doll. It is a complex, affecting moment, for Lucy has no mother, no siblings, no friends, no one to return her gaze.[59]

[59] In returning an image of a doll, the shop window indeed functions like a kind of

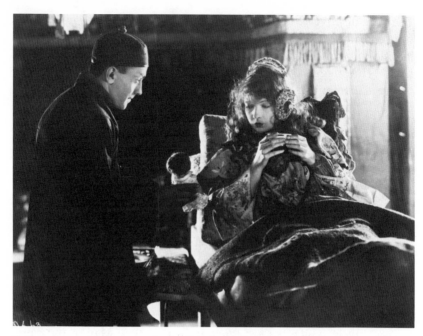

7. Forming a strange pseudo-family, the Yellow Man presents Lucy with the doll she had wanted. (Richard Barthelmess, Lillian Gish.)

While Lucy is framed in shots that are presumably from the Yellow Man's point of view—presumably, because the distance between the camera, the Yellow Man, and Lucy does not correspond exactly with the distance between the camera and Gish—it is, to the viewer who is equidistant with the Yellow Man from Lucy in the medium long-shot of the two, Richard Barthelmess' beautiful face that is framed by the mullions of the shop window. Here, as elsewhere in the film, we are encouraged to fetishize Barthelmess, just as the Yellow Man fetishizes Lucy.

The title describes Lucy as "this child with tear-aged face," and certainly her wish to have a doll would suggest that she is still a child. Yet Lucy is obviously not merely a child, and later when the Yellow Man gives her a doll she becomes a kind of mother in a strange, pseudo-family, with the Yellow Man as oblative father and husband. She arouses a sadistic impulse in her father and a worship-

mirror. After all, a doll—*pupa-ae*, L.—is what Lucy would see if she looked into the pupil of her own eye.

ping impulse in the Yellow Man, proving that she must be reckoned with as a sexual presence, passive and etherealized though she is. Buried in the comparison between Burrows and the Yellow Man is a sense of desire's contradictions and some of lust's violent dialectic. Griffith knows, and yet does not know, that Lucy signifies the desire of the other. The kind of effect she has on the Yellow Man is well described, in spite of its sentimental, flowery obliquity, by the title: "The spirit of beauty breaks her blossoms all about his chamber." Griffith's means of achieving thematic unity and narrative coherence—in this instance flowing, flowering from the title of the film, linking intertitle and image with a central metaphor—are effective. Lucy crosses the street and tries to buy a flower with the foil she has collected. Cut to Burrows being reproached by his manager for drinking, and Burrows' response in the floral metaphor, thereby characterizing his oppositional role vis-à-vis Lucy: "Wot yer expect me to do? Pick violets?"

The manager's protest against Burrows' dissipation sends Burrows home in a rage, and he beats Lucy senseless while (Griffith's famous instinct for suspense comes into play here) the Yellow Man is wandering about outside their hovel. Burrows marches off to prepare for a fight, while the Yellow Man, we discover later, went to his den for "tea and noodles" and a "whiff of the lillied pipe." Griffith makes vivid the contrast between what Burrows does with his time and what the Yellow Man does with his, by telling us what they are both doing while Lucy, "after dim aeons . . . struggles dumbly, blindly from her house of suffering."

When Lucy stumbles into the Yellow Man's shop and he finds her curled up on the floor, unconscious, the scene functions like a dream wish-fulfillment, a fantasy. He has the vulnerable girl-child all to himself. She simply appeared, like a windfall, and he rubs his eyes in disbelief. He fetches a bowl of water. It is an archetypal fantasy— bathing the wounds of one's helpless, dependent object of desire. The Yellow Man's ecstasy cannot be adequately expressed: "Oh lily flowers and plum blossoms! Oh silver streams and dim-starred skies!" With clasped hands he kneels before Lucy and almost kisses her. He carries her up to his room and lays her on his bed and prepares the room "as for a princess." He offers her "a magical robe treasured from an olden day," and when she begins to put it on he swoons with pleasure.

Lucy is transformed by the Yellow Man's adoration, and with "blue and yellow silk caressing white skin, her beauty so long hidden shines out like a poem." For the first time in her life—through love— she is beginning to achieve a positive identity. He crowns her with a garland and, to signal this "first time," she smiles. He offers her incense and flowers. "Her dreams, her prattle, her bird-like ways, her sweet self—are all his own." This title describes one of the two ideal Griffith women (the more athletic, balletic Carol Dempster being the other type of ideal woman). She is a sweet, birdlike creature who dreams and prattles inconsequentially, is an object, a possession that walks and talks, but is no threat and does not, ultimately, have to be taken seriously as an equal. When Lucy caresses the Yellow Man's smooth cheek and asks, "What makes you so good to me, Chinky?" one wonders indeed, particularly at her asking. The ideal (virtuous) woman must, somehow, be sexually innocent.

The sexual undercurrents of *Broken Blossoms* are constantly being pressured to the surface by the narrative. They build in a confusion of desires expressed as jealousies and hatreds, and in figures of repression. It is desire that links intercut scenes of tenderness and violence. When Burrows is told by a spy where Lucy is, "he discovers parental rights. A Chink after his kid! He'll learn him!" The taboo against miscegenation lurking in the wings of this film is brought out into the open with this title. Burrows' fear of the Chink is at least as great as his fear of his daughter: "Above all, Battling hates those not born in the same great country as himself." It is a familiar plea from Griffith for a brotherhood that will transcend national boundaries.

Griffith, nevertheless, shares the fear of difference that Burrows and the Yellow Man both have. We see in the shots of an increasing intimacy between the Yellow Man and Lucy an extreme close-up of the Yellow Man's face hovering in front of the camera (in the place of Lucy's face), which represents the high point of a crisis (it coincides with Burrows' victory in the ring), and we see Lucy drawing away from the Yellow Man in wonder tinged with fear. He diverts his impulse to embrace her and kisses her robe instead: "His love remains a pure and holy thing."

When Burrows comes to fetch Lucy, the Yellow Man is not at home, and the expected scene of terrible destruction follows, with Lucy crouching in terror on the floor and Burrows smashing everything in sight, screaming, "You! With a dirty Chink!" Outside, "the cloaking river mist" corresponds with the blind confusion of accelerating tragedy. In semidarkness Burrows drags Lucy through the streets to the hovel where they live, and there he flings her onto the bed. But Lucy manages to wrest free of his grip and seeks refuge in the closet. Intercut with shots of the Yellow Man's distress (his face distorted with anguish, his collapse on the floor of his devastated shrine) are shots of Lucy going mad with fear in the closet, as Battling—in a symbolic rape—hacks through the door with an axe.

The Yellow Man picks up a gun and runs through the misty streets. Burrows drags Lucy through the smashed door of the closet and beats her to death. When the Yellow Man enters the room and finds her, Burrows is in the next room. Burrows comes through and stands before him; he cannot believe that the Yellow Man is really a threat, but as he reaches for an axe on the floor, the Yellow Man pulls out the gun and shoots Burrows, who parodies a few punches before dropping dead. It comes as a shock that the gentle Yellow Man is capable of such violence, committed with such resolution, and that he uses a gun, for it is a weapon so much associated with the West and the phallicism that he rejects. He picks up Lucy's dead body and carries it back to his shop and there lays her body on the altar, covers her with the richly brocaded garment, and places some flowers beside her. He smokes a pipe, reads from a small book in solemn ritual, and looks up to the statue of Buddha. "As he smiles goodbye to White Blossom, all the tears of the ages rush over his heart," and in a final dramatic gesture he stabs himself. Following a shot of the police entering the Yellow Man's shop downstairs is the familiar shot of a Chinese gong being sounded, and the film ends on the image with which it began: ships drifting on a Chinese river at sunset.

The pattern of a family unit (Burrows and Lucy) which is disrupted (when Lucy runs away from home) only to be reformed (first when she enters the Yellow Man's shop and becomes his object of worship, and then when Burrows drags Lucy back home) is present in many of Griffith's films, but this film presents us with no positive or ideal image of the family or substitute configuration. The "love and lovers" of Broken Blossoms are tinged with the bizarre in that Lucy and the Yellow Man are inevitably an unstable, sterile unit. Not only is miscegenation in the Griffith world a taboo, but Lucy is fetishized rather than loved. And she herself is presented as too innocent to do more than graciously acknowledge the Yellow Man's worship of her.

Marriage, for the working classes at least, is bondage and drudgery, and prostitution is not even considered seriously as an alternative for Lucy. The only women with an acknowledged sexual identity are the prostitutes, and the only "legitimate" love is the kind the Yellow Man has for Lucy—a so-called "pure and holy thing." Burrows, for his part, is an image of perverted masculinity, while the beautiful, androgynous Yellow Man, powerless as he is to challenge the Law, is presented as the only attractive alternative to the "barbarous An-glo-Saxon sons of turmoil and strife."

The film plays out what Ann Douglas has called "the tragic dead end of Victorian American culture."[60] The Victorian sexual ethos is an impossibility, a stalemate, which is reflected in the film's very structure and look—long takes, tableaux, soft focus, pictorial values, an inward-turned symmetry. Racial difference is presented as the largest single obstacle to happiness in *Broken Blossoms*, but the specificity of it is irrelevant, for every kind of difference that is represented—religious, aesthetic, economic, sexual—immediately refers to another kind, showing them all to be interrelated. The religious and social discourses in earlier Griffith films can here no longer be supported without some recognition of what has come to be called the unconscious, and of the complexities and potential violence of desire. The stark nature of the film's paralyzing obsession with difference reaches a kind of limit with *Broken Blossoms*, bringing even narrative to a near-standstill. Of course, the film has a story, and suspense, but the frenzy of the scene in which Burrows hacks his way into the closet and then beats Lucy to death is extreme to the point of madness, and the melodrama cannot for long simply conclude that this is a mad world. The family melodrama from here on will return to explore other sources and explanations of villainy, of why there is suffering in the world. Economic conditions, always a significant issue in the fates of Griffith characters, will return to the family melodrama in the films of King Vidor, where we see a more complex treatment of social class and a more lucid understanding of the dialectic between class and sex.

[60] Douglas, *The Feminization of American Culture*, 305.

7. King Vidor

8. King Vidor (center) in conversation with Jennifer Jones on the set of *Ruby Gentry*.

IN THE melodrama there must always be someone or something to blame, to struggle against; otherwise it has the complex fatality of tragedy or comedy. As Griffith's world of virtuous maidens and un-equivocally evil villains was eclipsed by the modern age, and as America started truly to become a mass society, our moral universe inevitably became more complex and it became less possible to lay the blame for life's contradictions, reversals, unhappinesses and in-equities on a few sharply defined figures of villainy.

World War I, it might be said, marks symbolically the collapse of what Laura Mulvey has called a "coherent culture of oppression,"[1] which, rather than clearing the way for a new age without oppres-sion, had the effect of creating new anxieties. The old villains did not simply die; they slipped into the shadows. Life of course still had its problems, but now it was harder to lay the blame for those problems at someone's feet. Villainy—being no longer an upper-class rake (Lennox Sanderson in *Way Down East*), an intolerant factory owner (Jenkins in *The Mother and the Law*), or an inexplicably cruel father (Battling Burrows in *Broken Blossoms*)—becomes hard to *figure*.

The post-Griffith melodrama confirmed that villainy was being re-cast in ideological terms. As Vidor told Richard Schickel,

I don't think I've ever had a villain in my films. I can't remember one real villain, you know. It's the straw man we set up to knock him down—and we don't need that. We don't need to symbolize or to construct one just to knock him over—kill him, you know. Life is enough of a battle in itself.[2]

True, indeed. Vidor does not kill his villains, because he knows they cannot be killed. Unlike Griffith, whose vision remained mid-Victo-rian to the end, and whose filmmaking days were over by 1931, Vi-dor moved with the times and made successful melodramas for forty years. During those years—1919 to 1959—the face of the melodrama changed almost beyond recognition, but Vidor's remarks on villainy and his observation that life is enough of a battle as it is, reveal what has remained constant—in the Vidorian melodrama, at least.

While there are few cloak-and-dagger villains in Vidor's cinema, the films unquestionably are marked by struggle, suffering, conflict and difficulty. The difference (between Vidor and, say, Griffith) is that Vidor understands with greater sophistication, and is more suc-

---

[1] Laura Mulvey, "Notes on Sirk and Melodrama," *Movie* 25 (Winter 1977–78): 53.
[2] Richard Schickel, *The Men Who Made the Movies* (New York: Atheneum, 1975), 159.

cessful in exposing, the structural reality of the American class system. Despite the unattractive truths that they sometimes reveal about the class system in America, however, Vidor's films are driven by an optimism—an optimism that has nothing to do with happy endings. His leading characters often have great energy and determination. They are vital, animated by intense desires, motivated invariably by a passionate personal integrity. It is a Christian universe, still, but not a preachy one or an Old Testament one. Rather, Vidor seems to understand well the tremendous difficulty of repressing desire, and the paradox that desire can increase in proportion to the size of the obstacle to its satisfaction. There is a peculiar honesty in Vidor's approach to questions of desire, a special regard, for example, for the body, which we find so little of in America's Puritan heritage. Vidor's uses of music, color, and movement are a frank acknowledgment of earthly pleasures, a visceral celebration. Life is a battle, but it is all we have, which means it must be celebrated, lived, enjoyed.

In his own words, Vidor believes "in the motion picture that carries a message to humanity," and "the picture that will help humanity to free itself from the shackles of fear and suffering that have so long bound it with iron chains."[3] These would be, as one can see, the chief tenets in any manifesto of the melodrama. The Vidor hero(ine) *wants more*, and although he or she will meet with tremendous odds, Vidor's underlying optimism, and his belief that his characters have a right to happiness, here on earth, makes him particularly American. It is the optimism of the melodramatic imagination, the imagination that knows how much suffering there is in the world. Late in his life Vidor said,

I think it's a beautiful world; I'm interested in everything that's happened. I can only be terribly optimistic about it, and terribly appreciative about it. . . . I don't believe in life being bad. . . . I don't believe in a bad world.[4]

Vidor "can only be" optimistic because the melodramatic imagination is not interested in compromises and muddling through, and the "bad world" of the alternative would be too bad to endure.

Vidor admired Griffith tremendously, and consciously strove to emulate him. Like Griffith, Vidor understood that harmony is always

---

[3] These are the first two (of six) tenets Vidor published as his "Creed and Pledge" in the January 1920 issue of *Variety*.

[4] Schickel, *The Men Who Made the Movies*, 160.

a fragile, provisional state, always menaced. Like Griffith, too, Vidor was expert at creating metaphorical geographies: Manhattan in *The Crowd* and *The Fountainhead* (1949), the steelworks in *An American Romance* (1944), the desert in *Duel in the Sun* (1946), Loyalton and its flame-spouting factories in *Beyond the Forest* (1949), the swamp in *Hallelujah* (1929) and *Ruby Gentry*; and at supplying conviction to his antinomies: Millhampton versus New York in *Stella Dallas*, Judaism versus Paganism in *Solomon and Sheba* (1959).

When it comes to his melodramas Vidor conforms to the principle that the more unattainable a thing is the more desirable it becomes. Vidor knows that in order to represent an extreme of emotion, of desire, he must erect barriers that are to the measure of the exceptional aspirations, will, and energy of his (often otherwise ordinary) characters, and he succeeds in drawing the connection between a character's desire and a personal issue of identity. It is a matter of life and death, for example, that Rosa Moline get to Chicago in *Beyond the Forest*, for Rosa believes that there she will be able to realize herself at last. All struggles, while made concrete in external ways, are made to seem primal and impossible in a violent, contrastive manner. As Alain Carbonnier has observed, the most beautiful love scenes in Vidor's films are those in which the lovers tear at each other, the most extraordinary action scenes are those in which man wrestles with hostile elements; in each case there is a struggle, *body to body*.[5]

While not considered a director of "women's films," Vidor is attracted, especially after World War II, to the energies of women. In his films, women rebel against men, who have taken it upon themselves to impose the Law. In the postwar films there is distinctly a masculinization of the heroine and an eroticization of violence.[6] Vidor's melodramas represent, after all, a masculine point of view. Like Griffith before him and Minnelli after him, Vidor often sympathizes

[5] Alain Carbonnier, "King Vidor, ou l'ambivalence du désir," *Cinéma 82* 288 (December 1982): 32.

[6] Michael Henry, "Le Blé, l'acier et la dynamite," *Positif* 163 (November 1974): 43. The most obvious example of the masculinized heroine after Pearl Chavez in *Duel in the Sun*, and Ruby Gentry, is Dominique Francon (Patricia Neal) in *The Fountainhead*. She takes it as her right to look at Howard Roarke (Gary Cooper) while he cuts marble at the quarry, but orders him not to look at her. She is tall and has a deep voice, she rides horses, brandishes whips, has money, and through her newspaper column exercises the power of the Word.

with the underdog, but, unlike Griffith, he is acutely aware of his responsibility not to erect "straw" villains. If a simple notion of villainy evaporates with Griffith, what is it that still binds humanity in "shackles of fear and suffering"? Vidor understands that in a post-Christian era we are still bound by an essentially Christian morality, a Christian ambivalence towards desire, although we are beset by the same old problems and are always trying new approaches to solving them. Vidor presents, for example, different accounts of the American class system—from the idealized, flexible system in *An American Romance*, to the ossified, cruel, unbending structure in *Ruby Gentry*; he treats racism in *Duel in the Sun*, and in all the melodramas, grapples with the paradoxes of desire.

There is a moment in *Solomon and Sheba* when Solomon, who has been invited by the Queen of Sheba to dine with her, deliberates about whether or not to go. He looks at a small lamp on the table and draws a parallel between Sheba and its flame:

At times a man feels drawn towards the dangers that confront him, even at the risk of his own destruction, like a moth approaches a flame. . . . I could put it out in one second. . . . Such a little flame . . . yet unrestrained it could destroy all of Jerusalem. . . . But perhaps without it, there would be darkness.

And so it is with desire generally in Vidor's films. It is dangerous, but it is necessary, and there is no point in trying simply to repress it.

Solomon and Sheba is a fitting last feature film for Vidor,[7] in that it is a dramatization of the ancient origins of our Judeo-Christian culture. Solomon represents, and is the literal embodiment of, Judaic law. Like Sheba, Solomon is both a person and a State (in her case the conflation is more absolute—she bears the same name as her country) and therefore his every action bears the responsibility of the Law. He represents the law of the Old Testament, and she represents desire, which until now he has been able to deal with only through repression. Solomon's famous wisdom is to see that "perhaps without it, there would be darkness." A little Sheban sexuality, in other words, is necessary to lighten the dour face of Judaic law. Hers is an

---

[7] As a friend of mine puts it, *Solomon and Sheba* has a "terminally bad reputation." If it is not a very good film, it is in many respects, nevertheless, eminently Vidorian, just as Minnelli's last film (*A Matter of Time*, 1976) is often listed in guides to movies on TV as a "BOMB," and yet is unmistakably—and for many, magnificently—Minnellian.

ancient nation that has always been ruled by women; his nation is founded on absolute allegiance to the Father, to patriarchal principles. Sheba, then, stands for all women and the feminine principle; Solomon stands for all men, and the masculine principle.

"Truly, the way of a woman is beyond our understanding," the Pharaoh says to Sheba; and Vidor has his heroine reply, "The way of a woman is simple, my lord. It is always to follow the way of a man." This, presumably, is her wisdom. She is in a man's country, and so while she is there she will "follow the way of a man," in order to get what she wants. At home, in the land of Sheba, she can presumably do as Shebans do—that is, be herself, a woman. All the paradoxes of our (which is to say, Vidor's) Christianity, now secular and expressed in other terms, are presented in *Solomon and Sheba*. Solomon has democratic ideas, which are a threat to the Pharaoh and to Sheba, and yet his religion is monotheistic, patriarchal, autocratic. The pluralism of Sheba's many gods must be subordinated to Solomon's one God, if they are to share the same bed. The genius of Solomon's maneuver is that while he posits a single, transcendental God, he is himself (like his father before him) so identified with that God—although as Sheba observes, one cannot even see Him—that he becomes God's voice.

Sheba becomes frustrated because she feels she is dealing with something intangible (and she is—it is a moral force). She wants to seduce Solomon, to bring things to a human level, a level where she has some power to act. It is the melodramatic operation par excellence, this putting of abstract or moral terms into concrete, visible, human terms. She prays to her God of Love: "Make me the most desirable of women! Make my lips sweet as honey, my skin soft and fragrant like the petals of a flower. Give him to me! I want him at my feet!" Moral authority cannot be established merely by assertion (like Adonijah simply calling himself the king, before his father is dead) and so its validity must be established in other terms. There must be an appearance of sanction by nature. This is where melodramatic logic begins. Nature has made men and women different, and everything else in this system is founded on that difference, which is why Sheba begins there. The melodrama may not understand heterosexual attraction, but it starts there and ends there: it is a truth. However, Vidor strives to figure out why men and women are attracted to each other, and his effort begins with the recognition that there are women who are as capable as any man. If Solomon tells Sheba that he has always known that "behind those lovely eyes is the brain of a very clever woman," Vidor knows it, too, of all his female protagonists. He recognizes their beauty, and celebrates it, and if they are not very clever (as, for example, Stella Dallas is not) they do have something else.

They have passion. Like the men, they will fight for what is right or deservedly theirs, and they may even show "a little imagination." These last words are Tring's advice to Clemency in Vidor's *Cynara* (1932). Clemency's husband Jim (played by Ronald Coleman) has had an affair (reluctantly, and after much persuasion by Tring and various unusual circumstances) while Clemency was in Venice. The affair turns out badly (the young woman commits suicide) and Clemency at first is stonily unforgiving. The judge tells Jim modestly that he ought to have exercised "more restraint," but the verdict, all the same, requires Jim to emigrate. Before Jim leaves on his ship for South Africa, Tring rushes to urge Clemency to exercise a little imagination. She does, and the last shot of the film shows Jim and Clemency sailing off together.

Tring's words speak for Vidor. If one is to help reduce the suffering and pain in the world, one must bring some passion to this life, and a little imagination. As one of the great filmmakers who started in the cinema when there were few rules, Vidor (like Griffith) had to rely on sound instincts to guide him; he had to know truly why he was making a film in the first place. Although Vidor has never been especially interested in storytelling per se, he has usually been committed to the generation of extreme emotion, which we know is the heart of the melodrama. He made *Hallelujah*, for example, because the "sincerity and fervor of [the Negroes'] religious expression intrigued [him], as did the honest simplicity of their sexual drives. In many instances the intermingling of these two activities seemed to offer strikingly dramatic content."[8]

In *Hallelujah* there is a great deal of dancing and someone is always singing or playing music. While Zeke looks up at the clouds, in the conviction that "there ain't no more pain, there ain't no more sorrow, and there ain't no more grief up there with the Lord," Vidor's characters come more and more to look for paradise on earth, and they

[8] King Vidor, *A Tree Is a Tree* (New York: Harcourt Brace, 1952), 175.

will fight for it if they have to. Zeke is tempted by a woman, and if she is the wrong woman it is because, as she sobs during her dying moments, "I've never known what I wanted!" Identifying what one wants is not always easy. Often, it is impossible. Rosa Moline in *Beyond the Forest* believes, rightly or wrongly, that she *must* get to Chicago (a possible goal), Pearl Chavez in *Duel in the Sun* wants Lewt's passion and Jesse's gentle understanding in the same person (impossible), Ruby and Boake in *Ruby Gentry* want what is "sweet and wild and crazy" and also to be accepted by the "respectable" citizens of Braddock (impossible), Stella Dallas would like ideally to "keep" her daughter *and* see her married to Richard Grosvenor III (impossible), and so on.

In *The Crowd* we see a character who strains for subjectivity in a system that would have him only maintain the social order according to his designated, containing identities (husband, father, worker in a capitalist economy) without rocking the boat or seeking to change anything in the system that denies him control over his own life. In the other two films discussed in this chapter, however, *Stella Dallas* and *Ruby Gentry*, we see the beginnings of protest, and the ways in which two different types of woman try to combat the Law that oppresses them.

As a melodrama *The Crowd* is unusual in at least one important respect: it shows a man—an ordinary man—struggling for survival in an ordinary world shared by millions of men just like him. John Sims' struggle in relation to the Law puts him in a traditionally feminine position, and yet in his representative function he must preserve the masculine principle. The more clear-cut issues of a woman's oppression in a man's world are not examined in *The Crowd*. Rather, the dialectical relation of production and reproduction is exposed in a story of ordinary aspiration confronted first by soul-destroying labor and then by unemployment. John Sims' problems cannot be resolved within the family, nor can he adjust to the fact that in his relation to the forces that control production (New York City—the offices in the skyscrapers, the bosses, etc.) he is truly just "one of the crowd." He must abandon the individualist ideology he was brought up on and now stake his identity on this abstract notion that on his own he is nothing. With no clearly identifiable villain in the film, *The Crowd* threatens to pull the rug out from beneath even melodrama's traditional supports—a rock-firm belief in the *idea* of good and evil and a demonstration of justice prevailing, with class positions set forth clearly. *The Crowd*, curiously enough, is a melodrama that resists being one. John Sims' position in society is not collapsed into some analogical Oedipal structure, and in carefully preserving his "Mr. Anyman" status Vidor shows in the example of John Sims how in mass society we are all—men and women alike—subject to the Law, how we are all castrated by our own system.

In *Stella Dallas* Vidor gives full play to the special status of motherhood in the family melodrama. Motherhood in *Stella Dallas* becomes a pleasure for Stella, rather than a means of removing her from the circulations of patriarchal exchanges and making her do the work of reproduction for that system of relations between men. Stella Dallas achieves a subjectivity outside of the "hom(m)o-sexual" system of exchanges, and she is punished for it. The film is typical of family melodrama in deriving its pathos from the representation of a thwarted struggle for subjectivity and a triumph for the patriarchy at a tremendous, but apparently necessary, "justifiable" cost to a woman.

Ruby Gentry shows a different kind of woman entirely, engaged in the same struggle, with gender and social class against her. Ruby's various, contradictory efforts to achieve some satisfactory identity—through traditionally "feminine," means (masquerade[9] and presenting herself as a phallic mirror/mirage) and at other times by taking "masculine" control—reveal a basic truth of the melodrama: that while a man may succeed in achieving a satisfactory place within the phallocratic, bourgeois-capitalist order, a woman never does. Ruby Gentry is doomed by her love of a man. Love, so often a woman's chosen means to self-fulfillment in melodrama, is a problem for Ruby, since masochism and self-effacement are not her style. We see in *Ruby Gentry* some of the Oedipal dynamics that go by the name of "love," and the bitter outcome of its logic taken to an extreme conclusion.

Vidor has claimed that the principal theme in his important films

---

[9] Masquerade: "An alienated or false version of femininity arising from the woman's awareness of the man's desire for her to be his other, the masquerade permits woman to experience desire not in her own right but as a man's desire situates her." (Luce Irigaray, "Notes on Selected Terms," *This Sex Which Is Not One*, trans. Catherine Porter [Ithaca, N.Y.: Cornell University Press, 1985], 220.)

has always been man's search for truth.[10] In his melodramas, that search, we find, is intimately tied up with personal identity, which at first is inscribed dominantly in economic (and, as always in the family melodrama, familial) terms, but later increasingly in terms of social class and of sexuality, which are found to be dialectically linked.

MELODRAMA AND IDENTITY IN MASS SOCIETY: *The Crowd*

The Crowd is problematic as a melodrama. Vidor puts an ordinary man at its narrative center, and yet treats his story in a way that makes it difficult to identify causes—or rather, identifies causes that are too complex for the melodrama to comprehend. In melodramas "fate" can intervene in fantastic ways, but a moral truth is always asserted, a sense of justice, of right and wrong, is established, and a casting of blame is always achieved. In *The Crowd* it is John Sims' identity which is at stake, his place in the symbolic order and mass society, and as "Mr. Anyman" (which is what Vidor calls him),[11] his example seeks to offer us an invigorating lesson and a comforting reflection of ourselves.

But John Sims runs into so much bad luck, and luck is not felt by the film to answer satisfactorily as a cause. Quite clearly, in the second half of *The Crowd*, a pattern of misfortune runs through the lives of the film's main characters. John's wife, Mary, at one point out of sheer frustration calls her husband a bluff and a quitter, but we know the accusation to be unfair. He in fact keeps his job at the insurance company for more than five years, and tries as hard as any man to make a go of things. He is an amiable, good-looking, average fellow, and there is no particular reason for him not to succeed in life. He is one of the crowd, but like any of us, cannot afford to perceive himself as such. Who or what, one then needs to know, is to blame when John finds himself unemployed, or when his child is killed, or when his wife threatens to leave him? Melodrama always seeks answers to questions like these.

To show the failure of feminine effort is one thing, but to show a man's failure and not to identify satisfactorily the reasons for his fail-

---

[10] Bernard Cohn, "Entretien avec King Vidor," *Positif* 161 (September 1974): 21–22.
[11] Clive Denton, "King Vidor: Texas Poet," *The Hollywood Professionals* 5 (New York: Barnes, 1976): 7.

ure disturbs the semantic field on which melodrama is charted; no explanation for unfortunate reversals in the lives of the characters can be given, no villain properly identified. Nevertheless, it is precisely because he seeks to get at the truth of causes that Vidor wherever possible resists melodramatic structures. *The Crowd*, on the one hand, seeks to create what Barthes calls "a singular theater" of "mediocrity," and on the other hand to give (back) the common man (John Sims) the dignity that mass society denies him. Barthes asks,

Why do some people, including myself, enjoy in certain novels, biographies, and historical works the representation of the "daily life" of an epoch, of a character? Why this curiosity about petty details: schedules, habits, meals, lodging, clothing, etc.? Is it the hallucinatory relish of "reality" (the very materiality of *"that once existed"*)? And is it not the fantasy itself which invokes the "detail," the tiny private scene, in which I can easily take my place? Are there, in short, "minor hysterics" (these very readers) who receive bliss from a singular theater: not one of grandeur but one of mediocrity (might there not be dreams, fantasies of mediocrity)?[12]

The clue to this fantasy (probably as with any fantasy, any theater) is the phrase, "in which I can easily take my place." That is our, and John Sims', desire—to take his place (in the crowd)—and it is that which perhaps most of all marks the film as a melodrama. "The crowd," however, is a metaphor, and for this reason the film lacks the usual thrust of dramatic narrative. The film is essentially a description of the universal process of entering the symbolic order. It is offered as a story of an ordinary life, and in its chronological linearity reads as a description in the traditional sense of the term, for which reason, precisely, the text is ideal for examining the signification of social and psychic determinations. As Geoffrey Nowell-Smith observes, "the 'subject positions' implied by the melodrama are those of bourgeois art in a bourgeois epoch, while the 'represented object' is that of the Oedipal drama."[13] Yet Vidor seems in *The Crowd* to resist representing an Oedipal drama, and it is a mass society, not a nineteenth-century bourgeois society, into which John Sims is born. Vidor strives to make his film's represented object (a man's life) repre-

---

[12] Roland Barthes, *The Pleasure of the Text*, trans. Richard Miller (New York: Hill and Wang, 1975), 53.

[13] In "Minnelli and Melodrama" Geoffrey Nowell-Smith points out correctly that melodrama as artistic representation, (*any* artistic representation, for that matter) "does not 'reflect' or 'describe' social and psychic determinations. Rather, it *signifies* them." (*Screen* 18, no, 2 [Summer 1977]: 114.)

sentative—in a special effort of "realism," not "melodrama." The film's style is famous precisely because of the unique results that Vidor achieves in his attempt to blend MGM production values, expressionism, and in-the-street documentary realism, but the film cannot avoid being, in the end, a melodrama. There are melodramatic excesses, such as the violent death of the Sims' little girl, and the depiction of the office John Sims works in at the insurance company; the film on the whole is faithful to one of melodrama's main sources of affect: the fates of ordinary human beings who live and suffer as we all do.

The Crowd, examined here as an example of the post-religious melodramatic discourse, is still, however, pre-psychoanalytic. Melodrama's middle period is perhaps the most difficult for the form, because it must come to terms somehow with the fact of social pressures that create problems that cannot necessarily be resolved within the family or be recuperated by psychoanalytic logic. Economic realities determine John Sims' destiny, yet how can melodrama provide relief or avoid being depressing in the face of this awareness that an ordinary man can be defeated by conditions that are widespread and are beyond his power to control or circumvent? The villain, no longer personified, has grown to the measure of the world's largest industrial city, New York; but it is not even so simple as that, because New York is, as one title indicates, home to seven million people. It is the world, and cannot function therefore as the force of evil in any implicit struggles between good and evil in the lives of New Yorkers.[14]

Ultimately, in the family melodrama, it is the patriarchy, or more generally, the Law, that is the villain, but since there is no organized life, no society without Law, melodramas tend to fasten onto the Law's more repressive structures to articulate villainy (usually in displaced, personified form). In *The Crowd* there is no ferocious, mean boss at John Sims' office, no unscrupulous, wily fellow-worker competing with him for a promotion, no Great Depression (yet), no psy-

[14] In *Our Daily Bread*, the sequel to *The Crowd* that he made ten years later, Vidor does seem to suggest that there is no way out of this dilemma, for he removes John and Mary Sims from the city. They leave New York, where it has become impossible to make a living, and set up a communal farm with other men and women who have been defeated by Depression-era urban existence.

chological flaw in John's character, no wife whom it was for one reason or another a mistake to marry.

John Sims' life is like anybody else's, and the disturbing question (since we identify with the protagonist) is why, since he plays by all the rules of the game and has all the bourgeois virtues of the average man, can he not "get ahead'? "Get ahead" of what? The crowd? It is only a figure of speech, since every member of the crowd must "get ahead" in order just to keep up and have a place within the economy or feel, within the confines of the milieu that the family provides, that his sense of individual worth is being maintained. Ellen Seiter, in her article "Men, Sex and Money in Recent Family Melodramas,"[15] indicates that there has been a trend in melodramas made in the 1970s and 1980s to "specify the class of their characters as upper middle class, members of a professional elite, intellectual and culturally high-brow" in large part out of a realist impulse to confront contemporary economic distress and situate the family within it. Middle- and working-class families currently suffer more from economic than from psychological difficulties, but "the assignment of blame, the investigation of guilt and the cure for such [economic] suffering would, of necessity, involve a world larger than the nuclear family."[16]

This difficulty in what Seiter calls "locating the cause of turmoil and designating scapegoats" is the same one experienced in *The Crowd*. Vidor's film, however, does offer by example some palliative suggestions on how to live in this world and where to look for sources of affect and emotional reward: in the redeeming power of love (between John and Mary, as lovers, and later as husband and wife); in the pleasure that children provide and in the hope they represent for a better future; and quite markedly in the distraction of commercial entertainments (Coney Island, the theater).

The ambivalent status of mass entertainment in modern society is broached in *The Crowd*, but more fully explored by Vidor ten years later in *Stella Dallas*. Is the resort to consumer entertainments an answer or an escape, a central necessity of modern life or an evasion of responsibilities? "Going to the movies," we know, can be psychologically beneficial, even if it does not actually solve any of our economic problems. The film industry itself, certainly, has recognized the vital

---

[15] Ellen Seiter, "Men, Sex and Money in Recent Family Melodramas," *The Journal of the University Film and Video Association* 35, no. 1 (Winter 1983): 17–27.

[16] Ibid., 19.

importance to the human subject of the Imaginary, and historically the industry has flourished most during economically hard times— that is to say, when the operations of the public sphere and the Symbolic have been undermined. *The Crowd* shows this most directly in its last scene, in which the Sims family goes to the theater. It is a question, quite simply, of morale. Melodramas are meant to be good for morale, just as the domestic sphere is charged with the task of maintaining morale, providing on the side of the Imaginary what the symbolic order and public sphere exclude.

Andrew Bergman, writing about Hollywood movies of the thirties, claims that "the movies made a central contribution towards educating Americans in the fact that wrongs could be set right within their existing institutions" and that, to borrow Franklin Roosevelt's words (from a statement he made in 1936 that had nothing specifically to do with the movies), they were "against revolution," and "waged war against those conditions which make revolutions—against those resentments and inequalities which bred them."[17] Americans did not attempt to remedy wrongs by advocating the overthrow of their institutions. The melodrama, however, is animated by both this conservative impulse *and* revolutionary impulses. The form attempts to remedy wrongs within existing institutions, but it often shows instances of rebellion (as opposed to revolution) or some sort of return by the main characters to the Imaginary.

While New York City is in an overarching sense the cause of the Sims' problems, it cannot be identified as such (at least not until *Our Daily Bread*). The city is represented in heroic, energetic terms, but of course all those magnificent skyscrapers are offices in which people work, and we see the price office workers must pay for that famous skyline. The division between work and play in the life of the professional is blurred. John Sims is not a professional; he is a wage laborer, and as such does not combine his work and his life in one happy continuum in the way the professional endeavors to. For him, his family life and his leisure time must make up for what his job cannot give: an emotional life and the pleasures of friendly human intercourse.

[17] Andrew Bergman, *We're in the Money: Depression America and Its Films* (New York: Harper & Row, 1972), 167.

John Sims' experience in the big city makes him a modern man, in whom the gap between aspiration or life as it is meant to be, and life as it in fact is, registers in a lifelong pattern of self-alienation and sense of having or being "never quite enough." Poor John keeps trying gamely to cheer his wife or to mitigate his feelings of insufficiency with references to the day when his ship will come in. Every member of the crowd—that metaphor for modern society—is castrated (to use the psychoanalytic metaphor), is marked by the Law which, ironically, the crowd itself represents.

Nevertheless, a notion of family persists, and so does the recognition of the central importance of affect in human life. This recognition marks *The Crowd* as a melodrama, and the movie attempts to locate the wellsprings of desire and to celebrate them while offering a critique of mass society. That critique is generally offered in the movie in an ironic register. The very first shot, for example, is of a modest, contemporary house, squeezed between others, and the bustling street in front of it which the camera tilts down to as this title inaugurates the narrative:

—but what was a little thing like the Declaration of Independence compared to the great event happening in the Sims household?

John Sims is born in 1900—at the dawn not just of a new century but of a new age. He is compared with George Washington and Abraham Lincoln. He will, as his exultant father proclaims, be someone the world is going to hear from.[18] This newborn infant has so much to live up to! The mantle of patriarchal responsibility already sounds too heavy even for an exceptional man, and the allusions to Washington and Lincoln refer to a past of heroic individualism (exaggerated by time and hagiography) to which, only twenty-eight years into the twentieth century (the year *The Crowd* was made), it is sensed we shall never again return. A few shots later, when the boy is twelve, one of his friends asks him what he wants to be when he grows up. The other boys in the group express the wish to be this or that, but the reply of young John Sims, our exemplary child, is: "My Dad says *I'm* going to be somebody big." His identity is determined by his father and the patriarchy—not by him, if such a thing is possible.

The question or dominant hermeneutic code inaugurated is

---

[18] With the advent of the talkies we do at least hear his voice in *Our Daily Bread*.

whether indeed John Sims will, as his Dad says, be "somebody big." Of characters in the melodrama we know (as Nowell-Smith puts it) that "in their struggle for the achievement of social and sexual demands, men may sometimes win through, women never."[19]

"Masculinity" (denoted by Washington, Lincoln, "somebody the world's going to hear from," somebody like John Sims' Dad, and later, Mary's brothers) is what John Sims must struggle to achieve. As Nowell-Smith observes, a woman's failure to be male is, in the terms of the argument, understandable, but a man's failure to be male (if he is to preserve his masculine dignity) is a problem towards which the melodrama as a genre is especially attracted.

When John Sims' father dies, Vidor shows the boy in a high-angle shot slowly mounting an endless staircase that seems to grow bigger as he tries to reach the summit where a nurse is exhorting him to "be brave now, little man. . . . like your father would want you to be." When as a young man he reaches New York—the city that represents in the social-symbolic sphere the same challenge his father does in the familial—he is told, "You've gotta be good in that town if you want to beat the crowd."

The film's most consistent metaphor is "beating the crowd," but at the very least John must find his place *within* the crowd or risk not gaining an identity at all, let alone an identity to the measure of a Washington or a Lincoln. The montage-hymn to New York City in all its phallic and swarming splendor near the beginning of the film represents the masculine principle; the very skyscrapers themselves are tumescent icons in brick and stone that stand as "proof" of the system's vitality and success. Since John Sims cannot become a building, or at least is not likely to, how can he measure up? The camera cranes up and into a randomly chosen window in a skyscraper to reveal what most of New York is made up of. Inside the building, in a mammoth office filled with hundreds of clerks at their desks, the camera continues on its track and comes to rest on John Sims somewhere in the middle at desk number 137. John is perusing a newspaper advertisement that commands him to use his "genius" to come up with an advertising slogan. This would seem to be the film's answer to the

[19] Nowell-Smith, "Minnelli and Melodrama," 116.

problems it stirs up: every man, although he may be like every other man in every significant respect, has a potential quotient of "genius."

John's untapped "genius" will turn out to be for advertising slogans.[20] But John does not recognize this for quite some time, and his unspectacular life proceeds happily enough, sustained by his love for Mary and hers for him. Heterosexual love even in its minor-key vicissitudes supplies the Hollywood melodrama inexhaustibly, and *The Crowd* is no exception, giving us delightful scenes of their courtship and early life together which, as far as they go, keep the movie moving. However, Vidor does not, it seems, want *The Crowd* to be a love story as such. John's attraction to Mary is conventional, and there is no lengthy courtship. John is not identified as a lover, and *The Crowd* is not a romantic melodrama, but a family melodrama in which the emphasis is on social factors, on aspects of mass society and consumer culture. He is attracted by an advertisement for furniture that promises that the advertiser will supply the furniture if the reader will supply the girl. The conception of home and marriage which the advertisement signifies and to which John is attracted gives the lie to how love is shaped by ideology and entangled in consumerism—a problem which Vidor explores in greater depth in *Stella Dallas*.

We see again the role of the media in mass culture when John and Mary arrive at Niagara Falls on their honeymoon: Mary strikes a variety of poses for John's camera. It is a subtle play by Vidor on the extent to which courtship and love subsist in the images of courtship

---

[20] In his *Culture as History: The Transformation of American Society in the Twentieth Century* (New York: Pantheon Books, 1984), Warren I. Susman devotes a third of a chapter to Bruce Barton, a "cultural hero" and one of the "most prominent men of his time." Barton founded one of the most important advertising agencies and "shap[ed] the development of the advertising business—so crucial itself in shaping the new mass society of the period—in significant ways." Barton in a sense "rewrote the American primer on success in a way that most effectively served the middle class of the 1920s. This revision provided a necessary kind of secular religion, a special vision of piety essential to the nation's transformation into a modern industrial mass society. His version of the success story helped ease the transition from an older, more producer-centered system with its traditional value structure to the newer, more consumer-centered system with its changed value structure. Barton's inspirational writings (and in a way this includes his brilliant advertising copy) found a way of bridging the gap between the demands of a Calvinistic producer ethic with its emphasis on hard work, self-denial, savings and the new, increasing demands of a hedonistic consumer ethic: spend, enjoy, use up." John Sims, we can see, is caught somewhere in this transition, during an economically difficult period.

and love—in their realization, their acting out. That desire is tied to representation is of course something these lovers do not know; they believe, as John tells Mary, that their love "will never stop. It's like these falls." Like a refrain throughout the movie John tells Mary, "You're the most beautiful girl in all the world." This is, nevertheless, love at its least examined level in Vidor, which is consistent with this study's thesis that desire and subjectivity are generally still relatively uncomplex matters in the melodramas of the teens and twenties. What is sought is a better understanding of the social-economic world, not the psycho-sexual world still to come or the theologically-fated world of the recent past.

Success in *The Crowd* is measured largely in terms of having a good job and bringing home the bacon; Mary's ugly family (mother and two brothers) harps on these themes constantly. The behavior of characters and the turns of events are explained often not in terms of "fate," "destiny," or the imperatives and transgression of Christian morality (as in Griffith's world), or in terms of a roiling unconscious or "return of the repressed" (as in later Vidor and in Minnelli) but, astoundingly, in terms of the influence of the mass media and economic factors understood vaguely to be tied to the industrial-capital complex. It is a newspaper advertisement, claiming "One of these model homes is located near you," that prompts John to find a home, and the catalyst in their decision to have a child is an advertisement ("Time to re-tire") of a small child holding up a car tire.

Although John is attracted by the mass media, he fears "the crowd" that threatens his sense of individual identity. Even on his arrival in New York at the age of twenty-one, when he is on the threshold of the adult world in which one is responsible for one's own life, John is defined as an individual—a subject apart from the world—but already also as merely one in a crowd: he becomes "one of seven million that believe New York depends on them." And when the fellow passenger on the boat carrying John to Manhattan remarks that you have to be good in New York if you want to beat the crowd, John replies, "Maybe . . . but all I want is an opportunity." His reply, ordinary as it is, resonates with the hope (of America, the land of opportunity) that must deny the fact of mass society. All the John Simses of the world make up what Harold Rosenberg called "the herd of independent minds." Or if those minds are not so very independent, John Sims can perhaps be better understood by

Philip Wylie's paradoxical observation that "what makes common man worthy of note is his occasional, individual rise *above* the commonplace."[21]

Within the confines of their tiny apartment and as long as John is employed, working at the Atlas Insurance Company, the Simses are happy enough. He strums on his ukulele and sings,

> Wife and I are happy
> And everything is swell;
> It's heavenly inside our flat
> But outside it is El!

The El(evated train) that thunders past their window at short intervals represents the inhospitable outside world that cannot be wished away but which can be tolerated. So long as John is employed there will be a turkey to roast at Christmas, the folding bed in their apartment will retreat with a gentle kick, the cistern will function, and it will not bother them that the bathroom door does not close properly.

But from the outside, where the El and the office are, comes Mary's family on a Christmas visit. They do not in themselves represent a threat, so much as they are a sign of forces that are hostile to the Sims' idyll, for they penetrate that happy space, judge John Sims, and find him lacking. To ease the awkward strain of their visit, Mary persuades John to show her mother and brothers his new "broken arm" trick. The broken-arm trick unconsciously speaks of their castrating effect on him. Exactly why they dislike him is not clear; their disapproval may be no more than a melodramatic device to introduce the shift in John's fortunes, or it can be read as an unconscious display of jealousy in a familial tug for Mary's love, which this mother and these brothers will not accept Mary now offers also to a husband. The trick fails utterly to amuse them, and Mary's mother crushes John with a demand to know if he has received a raise at work yet. "No . . . but everybody tells me my prospects are good," he replies lamely.

In melodrama we are often offered scenes of how others see a character, and through identification we experience the injustice of every misperception. Mary's family sees none of John's charm, energy or good humor; they see only an ordinary man whom they believe to be

---

[21] Philip Wylie, *Generation of Vipers* (New York: Rinehart, 1942; reprint ed., New York: Giant Cardinal, 1959), 94.

unambitious and rather childish. When during their visit John goes at Mary's suggestion to borrow some liquor from Bert, one of Bert's girlfriends offers another view of him entirely: "Oh, Gee Baby! How did the angels ever let *you* leave Heaven?" This modern girl who no doubt believes in the "winning image" and that nothing succeeds like the appearance of success, presses herself into his arms, leads him in a dance, and remarks, "Gee, but you're a great, big, good lookin', some-account man!" Even after he has spent the whole evening with Bert and his girls and has become quite drunk, Mary says to him when he gets back, "They [her mother and brothers] don't understand you . . . but that doesn't matter." Since only her belief in him matters, he asks, "Do *you* understand me?" She nods and whispers (there is no title), "I love you."

Vidor uses the visit of Mary's family subtly to introduce a change of tone that accelerates into misfortune for John and Mary. "Whuzza idea . . . always doin' somethin' wrong?" John blurts in superstitious alarm when Mary sits up in bed and opens the umbrella he has given her. By April things are beginning to sour for the Simses, but bad luck is too strong a term for their bickering and bad temper, and what Vidor seems to suggest is that every marriage will exhaust an initial phase of romantic bliss and will degenerate unless a child is born— which is what happens. Ideology's (of course, hidden) point here is that it is unnatural not to have children, or that a couple will not find lasting happiness unless they form a family. "Take it from me," John shouts, "marriage isn't a word . . . it's a *sentence!*" He leaves the apartment, slamming the door behind him. Mary looks devastated, but gathers her wits sufficiently to rush to the window and beg him, with an affecting mixture of sweetness and urgency, to come back, and during their tender reconciliation she tells him that she is pregnant. He is transformed by the news. He is thrilled. "From now on I'm going to treat you different, dearest," he says. She becomes again "the most beautiful girl in all the world." John is still not particularly happy at his life-denying job, which partly explains the intensity of his pleasure at the prospect of fatherhood. When his son is born he becomes frantic looking for Mary and the infant at the hospital. The shots of all the other expectant fathers (including a black man) lined up in the hallway, and the sea of beds in the maternity ward, remind the viewer that John's experience is not unique but common to the crowd, and one is reminded of John's office where he is merely num-

9. Can "bad luck" explain why things start to go wrong for John and Mary Sims? (James Murray and Eleanor Boardman in *The Crowd*.)

ber 137. How different it all is from his own birth, which took place in a house, with one mother, one bed, and one very proud father.

The death of John's father coincided with the advent of mass society, which diminishes the individual. John does not, as his father did, predict greatness for his son, to the measure of Washington and Lincoln, those heroes for a former age, but falls to his knees and says to Mary, "This is all I've needed to make me try harder, dear. I'll be somebody now . . . I promise." The awful truth is that as a representative member of the crowd, John can never try too hard. He will never "be somebody." He will *never be enough.* Society's old superstructure (its ideologies of individualism and capitalist production, its values of industry and self-discipline, sobriety and thrift) are still in place, long after the base has changed. The great gap between ideology's demands and what is rewarded or even possible in mass consumer society registers painfully in John Sims' cry. If John were to "become somebody" he would no longer be our representative "Mr. Anyman," which it is his prime function in *The Crowd* to be.

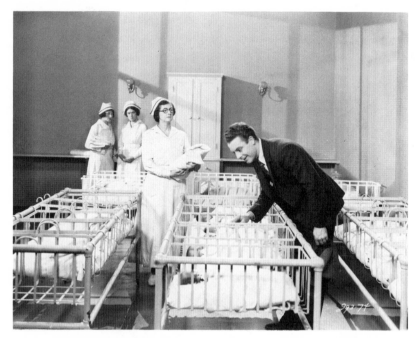

10. While the film describes the universal process of entering the symbolic order, the birth of John Sims' son is very different from John's own entry into the world.

The crowd (modern urban existence) provides no sense of community in the old sense of offering one a place within an order. Even within his own family, the last site for the inscription of a satisfactory identity, where he is a husband and a father, John feels alienated. The only scene of the whole family together indicates this. We see the Sims family on a picnic at the beach. A title tells us that only two eventful things have happened to the Simses in five years: "a baby sister was born . . . and John received an $8 raise." John is in an apparently good humor, strumming on his ukulele and singing, "All alone, I'm so all alone—" when the camera pulls back in the following shot to reveal that the beach is crowded, and like the man in the elevator in an earlier shot, who with a scowl ordered John to face the front (like all the others in the elevator), a grouchy old man now tells him to shut up. In this simple trope Vidor expresses the peculiar loneliness of the modern urban man. The pressures of the larger world to conform are too close, too ready to disrupt whatever peace or pleasure the family offers. The honeymoon love that buoyed John and Mary at Niagara Falls and throughout their first married months has been slowly giving way to grimmer imperatives. The strange fact is becoming more apparent: modern urban living is an intensified existence that can offer greater material comforts and more complex pleasures than the rural life of earlier times, but it can also be profoundly alienating, and the loss of one's job immediately threatens poverty and misery, with few support systems—the chief among which has always been the family and one's assured place within it.

Even this picnic is in danger of being disturbed by the paramount reality. How near and pressing that reality is. "Picnic my eye! I'm doing the same things I do every day!" Mary says, and suddenly the subject again has become John's adequacy, which more than ever is being measured by his difference from the crowd and his inability to "get ahead" financially. All happiness has been staked on an income. In a capitalist economy money speaks. It is money—more of it—that will bring John and Mary happiness, or so their socio-moral-economic world forces them to believe. "Don't crab, dear. Everything's goin' to be roses when my ship comes in," he pleads (or is it a confident assertion?). Just as melodrama streamlines the moral universe and is drawn instinctively to laws of familial desire, capitalism has invented money and is organized according to laws of exchange and profit. When all hope is pinned on John's "ship," happiness becomes a gamble. "Your ship? A worm must be towing it down from the North Pole!" Mary exclaims. While John believes in the system as the system advertises itself ("Don't blame me! It takes time to get any place in my firm!"), Mary understands that John must hustle in order to survive. This is the paradox: in order to *survive*, John must "get ahead." And getting ahead implies the opposite of harmony, order, or democracy—those values at the base of melodrama's vision of paradise.

In reproach, Mary alludes to Bert, who has apparently moved up the economic ladder by "hanging around the bosses." Buried in Bert's example, however, is a significant difference between the two men. In psychoanalytic terms Bert is a subject who does not embody or possess the phallus—as signified by his boyish appearance, obesity and, according to a stereotype, "compensatory" jollity. Bert, therefore, must position himself in favorable proximity to the phallus (the bosses, who have the power to promote employees and offer raises) although he will never, one suspects, embody it (become a boss) himself. John, on the other hand, is one of those who at birth inspire people to remark that one day he may become President of the United States. For the perpetuation of the phallocratic order there must be individuals who embody its significant principles, which in John Sims' world have more or less crystallized around an image of married, financially successful masculinity—the white American male "getting ahead."

John should not have to "hang around the bosses," for he was born to be a boss. One of the traits of the boss type, one might say, is his unshakable belief in the superiority, or at least validity, of his difference. "I've got big ideas!" John insists, "That slogan, *A Carload Full of Coughs* was mine! Only somebody sent it in first." Mary, as a woman and theoretically therefore more likely to understand the value and frequent necessity of compromise, tells him to stop tooting his own horn and get her some dry wood. In John's next action Vidor would seem to suggest a stereotype of heterosexual coupling: John breaks up the FOR SALE sign he has been sitting on and remarks, "This is the way I work! *I'm* the old go-getting kid! No matter what happens . . . you never hear *me* squawk!" He has not looked very far for some firewood, for there was no need to. Does he show pragmatic initiative only at Mary's inspiration? This may be the implicit understanding of what it is in which the married male-female partnership consists: masculine idealism and moral authority in partnership with feminine pragmatism and support. Mary must take a tempering, influential role, whether or not she is suited for independent action. John seems to be trying to convince himself of what he is (the "go-getting kid") in echoes of what, no doubt, he has been told all his life he is or should be.

One cannot help but read *The Crowd* as a critique of a system that undermines the masculinity of a good man like John Sims. John cannot even build a fire, and burns his finger in the effort, but we do not see any urban survival skills that have replaced lost ones like firelighting. The burned finger, like his broken-arm trick, is revealing of the core issue of impaired masculinity and its adjustments to a new age. Mary puts some butter on the burned digit and John recovers. The following scene in which John gamely scrambles around the beach on all fours giving his children "horsey-back" rides is, again, a clownish reference to his impotence.

John Sims, it is understood, will only succeed by personal initiative—which in his case we know amounts to no more than selling a talent for such slogans as, "Sleight O'Hand! The Magic Cleaner!" But an intertitle then undercuts that notion by returning the question of individually-determined destiny to a matter of luck: "Everybody wins a prize once in their lifetime . . . somehow. And $500 came to the Simses . . . all at one time!" It is bad luck, too, that their child is killed, which causes John so to lose his concentration that he must quit from the insurance company where he has toiled thanklessly for five years. The world becomes a malevolent place. With melodramatic logic, John must resist the whole world—the struggle is not within him—and Vidor expresses this poignantly in shots of John trying to persuade the world to make less noise while his daughter lies in a bed upstairs dying. He irrationally begs a newspaper seller to quiet down and tries frantically to stop the noise of fire engines and a curious mob running to the scene of a fire. One man against the crowd: John is the lone figure struggling to move in the opposite direction of the swarming mass of people. "Get inside!" a policeman advises him, "The world can't stop because your baby's sick!" An intertitle confirms this advice as a verity: "The crowd laughs with you always . . . but it will cry with you only for a day."

When John lands his fourth job in a week, a title explicitly states the danger of mass society: "We do not know how big the crowd is and what opposition it is . . . until we get out of step with it." The crowd, of course, is a broad metaphor. It does not only refer to mass society, but speaks in general terms for the Law, which in most melodramas is familial and is embodied in an idea of patriarchy. The father becomes the child's chief representative of the Law, as John's little boy indicates when he tells his suicidal father, "When I grow up I wanta be just like *you*." (Like most children, this child knows he will be better off if he becomes like his father, rather than if he opposes his father.) The father is the Law's most satisfactory representative, perhaps because—from the point of view of representation—he is more narratable than, for example, the crowd. And besides, one can *love* a father. "You still love me? You still believe in me, boy?" "Sure I do, Pop."

The best stories in film's history of melodramas are more familial than *The Crowd*, which buries the father somewhat, losing him to the crowd. If Vidor had given himself over completely to the melodra-

matic vision in this film he would have invented a more clearly defined Father, for as Deleuze and Guattari have observed,

American society—the industrial society with anonymous management and
vanishing personal power, etc.—is presented to us as a resurgence of the
"society without the father." Not surprisingly, the industrial society is bur-
dened with the search for original modes for the restoration of the equiva-
lent.[22]

The Crowd has an abstract, almost allegorical quality; nevertheless,
as a melodrama its represented object is that of the Oedipal drama.
The "dialectic of tenderness and hatred" Barthes wrote about, that
one enters into with the Father in telling stories, must reach from the
dominant metaphor of the film's title, rather than function within a
family or a context redolent with familial feeling. That Mary's brothers should come to take her away, because John cannot in their opin-
ion adequately provide for her, seems secondary; one does not hate
them for their action. John's trouble is with something larger and
more difficult to fight. John's Father, in a broad, metaphorical sense,
is History; it is the crowd. And so the movie ends, as it has mostly
played, in a metaphorical register. John and Mary reconcile, and with
their son go to a vaudeville theater. There, in the program, they spot
John's "Sleight O'Hand! The Magic Cleaner!" in an advertisement,
and John eagerly shows it to the responsive man sitting next to him,
indicating that it was he who came up with the slogan. The camera
pulls back a great distance, revealing the happy, laughing Sims family to be in a huge auditorium packed with people, and very quickly
their faces are, indistinguishable from the others in the crowd.

The Crowd is concerned explicitly with capitalist development: the
disappearance of bourgeois individualism (the production of goods
for the expansion of private wealth, motivated by self-interest and
tempered by Christian conscience) and the rise of industrial capitalism. Productive property as the economic basis of the family, as we
see it in *Way Down East* for example, has been replaced by wages. A
split between the home and the world (of production) has formed
and the discipline of the industrialized workplace for white- and
blue-collar workers alike has the effect of undermining the individual's sense of individuality, self-worth and belonging. As a family

[22] Gilles Deleuze and Félix Guattari, *Anti-Oedipus: Capitalism and Schizophrenia*, trans.
Robert Hurley, Mark Seem, and Helen R. Lane (Minneapolis: University of Minnesota
Press, 1983), 80.

melodrama, *The Crowd* shows some of the forces exerted on the family by the paramount reality within which it is located—the industrial-capitalist, urbanized State—and some of its effects: the soul-destroying monotony of John Sims' work at the insurance company, which makes him so irritable by the time he gets home, the need for money and the cruel pressure exerted by Mary's family on John to make more of it, the burden on Mary of making the home a refuge from the workplace, of household chores and raising children and being a loving wife, and so on. These forces put tremendous pressure on the family, threatening it with dissolution. *The Crowd* is animated by this threat and attempts, therefore, to understand this new kind of economy that had evolved in America. What this economy would eventually do to our psychology is described by John Berger in rather brutal Marxist terms: "The power to spend money is the power to live. . . . [and] those who lack the power to spend money become literally faceless."[23]

John Sims, obviously, stands on the threshold of a new class system based on economic power; indeed, he is one of its first victims. The era of bourgeois individualism that ended more or less in the late nineteenth century has given way to the development of large-scale industrial production, which no individual—certainly no John Sims—can affect. By the 1920s America has effectively become a mass society, and the relation between work and individual identity is broken or arbitrary, making work for the average man an alienating business, from which the traditional motive of self-interest harnessed to the activity of expanding private wealth has been removed. The new society offers only consumerism to satiate the hungers of the ordinary man, which of course is no substitute for the "personal life" he so desperately needs; and it is the cruelest answer to a man without a job.

During the 1930s in America almost everybody was out of a job, which partly explains the shift in the family melodrama that we see for example in *Stella Dallas* and *Ruby Gentry*, where economic factors in the determination of characters' identities and destinies are intertwined with class issues and psycho-sexual considerations. With villainy once again located and redefined, the struggle can continue.

---

[23] John Berger, *Ways of Seeing* (London: British Broadcasting Corporation and Penguin Books, 1972), 143.

For the time being, the site for melodramatic struggles will be the woman, for a story like John Sims' can only lead to revolution or the threatening subversiveness of Vidor's *Our Daily Bread*, which is a kind of proof of the impossibility for American ideology of the melodrama heading in this direction. Since American ideology will not permit communism, or a wholesale rejection of the city (which in *The Crowd* signifies our ideology), it must avoid the trouble that the common man's story will cause, leaving it to other genres.

"I DON'T WANT TO BE LIKE ME . . . BUT LIKE THE PEOPLE IN THE MOVIE!": *Stella Dallas*

In his *Histoire du cinéma*, Jean Mitry describes the melodrama as the bourgeois drama *par excellence*, "which is not to say that the bourgeoisie takes a special pleasure from melodrama, but that melodrama would appear to be an avatar of bourgeois morality and ideology. That is to say, melodrama ignores the class struggle, but not class *difference*, on which it is founded."[24] While *Stella Dallas* does not overtly critique the problems that are the film's subject matter, it exposes them with unusual clarity and candor. Better than the average American sentimental melodrama, *Stella Dallas* signifies—in an effective story and with remarkable economy—the dominant social values of its time. However, as Tania Modleski notes about mass art, *Stella Dallas* "not only contains contradictions, it also *functions* in a highly contradictory manner: while appearing to be merely escapist, [the film] simultaneously challenges and reaffirms traditional values, behavior, and attitudes."[25] Modleski goes on to observe that

while popular feminine texts provide outlets for women's dissatisfaction with male-female relationships, they never question the primacy of these relationships. Nor do they overtly question the myth of male superiority or the institutions of marriage and the family. Indeed patriarchal myths and institutions are, on the manifest level, whole-heartedly embraced, although the anxieties and tensions they give rise to may be said to provoke the need for the texts in the first place.[26]

Stella Dallas operates in just this way. In a stroke of self-reflexivity, a character within the text—Stella—is on the one hand shown to

---

[24] Jean Mitry, *Histoire du cinéma* (Paris: Universitaires, 1981), 593.
[25] Tania Modleski, *Loving With a Vengeance: Mass-Produced Fantasies for Women* (Hamden, Connecticut: Archon Books, 1982), 112.
[26] Ibid., 113.

have desires constituted by "popular feminine texts," which create her "dissatisfaction," while on the other hand she is shown resorting to these same texts to provide an outlet from the very dissatisfaction they produce. She is inscribed in an ideology that dooms her to perpetual dissatisfaction, unless she can find a way of desiring her own repression.[27]

As Mitry observes (and this is certainly true of *Stella Dallas*), the causes of the melodramatic situation are accepted rather than analyzed, and what is developed, "to absurdity if necessary," are the

real consequences for those who cannot acknowledge the causes, or who are incapable of dominating them without banishing themselves from society. The pathos of their situation derives from this, and the consequences are: impossible or forbidden loves, or wrongs committed against morality, customs, or social institutions. These wrongs are recognized as such in the name of the Law, or of a collective superego, and they produce a feeling more or less complicated by guilt, submission, or a fatality, from which the melodramatic character tries to escape—through dream—into an imaginary world which transfigures suffering or despair.[28]

The main problems in *Stella Dallas* that put the narrative elements into play and that threaten, at times, to tear the film apart, are twofold: there can be no social stasis under capitalism in America, nor *productive* desire under Oedipus. There are always people on their way up, and others on their way down, and desire, as understood by Gilles Deleuze and Félix Guattari, is inverted/perverted. Perhaps nowhere are these passages on the ladder more vividly represented than in a certain kind of American film melodrama—the domestic or family melodrama. Where Louis Althusser's concepts[29] imply a Marxian theory of ideology which is located in the superstructure, the "desiring approach" of Deleuze and Guattari rejects this division (infra/super-structures) entirely. For them, there is no "false representation of reality" any more than there is a division between causes and consequences (the Mitry quotation); desire is the driving force—it plays directly into social structures. They believe that Oedipus is

[27] Linda Williams begins her excellent article on *Stella Dallas* with a quotation from Marilyn French's 1977 novel, *The Women's Room*, in which the book's main character remarks to herself in wonder after recalling the last scene of *Stella Dallas*: "How they got us to consent to our own eradication!" (" 'Something Else Besides a Mother': *Stella Dallas* and the Maternal Melodrama," *Cinema Journal* 24, no. 1 [Fall 1984]: 2–27.)

[28] Mitry, *Histoire du cinéma*, 594.

[29] See Louis Althusser, *Lenin and Philosophy and Other Essays*, trans. Ben Brewster (New York: Monthly Review Press, 1971), 127–86.

responsible for the kind of malaise which the melodrama treats, and psychoanalysis (our way of understanding the family and "sexuality" itself) is perpetuated by Oedipus (these crippling structures) in a *mise en abyme*. In terms of the film, their approach represents, perhaps, a revolutionary hope for Stella's future, a way of rethinking desire and therefore of liberating Stella's desire, directing it away from repressive structures. However, in order to show how Stella is made to desire her own repression, she should be located first in the Freudian, bourgeois ideological field which, after all, is the terrain on which her destiny has been determined.

Although the first film version of *Stella Dallas* was made in 1925—before the stock market crash and Depression—it is no less true to say that America then, as it was in 1937 when the second version was made, was marked by a melodramatic imagination. The American Dream, in most of its versions dominated by hopes of riches and fears of poverty, is essentially a capitalist dream. Represented in *Stella Dallas* are some of the contradictions inherent in this dream and some of the acute tensions it can generate in the lives of those caught up in it. For the history of the melodrama, the hegemony in the twentieth century of the values and tastes of the middle classes represents an increase in the form's moral complexity. America's representations of itself in melodramas are, by 1937, a far cry from the more clearly-cut distinctions between villainy and virtue found in the cinema such a short time before—in the films of Griffith, for example. In *Stella Dallas*, particularly in the character of Stella herself (as she is defined by those around her—Stephen, Laurel, Helen), we see some of the problems of a society still not sure of itself, of its identity, of the class positions expressed by bourgeois-capitalist ideology.

The film equivocates in the character of Stella, and we wonder why Stella must, under ideological pressure, give up what she loves most (her daughter), or why, for example, nobody shows up for Laurel Dallas' birthday party. Most of the characters in *Stella Dallas* are basically the same people at the end of the film that they are when they first appear. This is melodrama's wish, its ideal: that characters be consistent. Their consistency aids in bourgeois ideology's attempts to mask its contradictions. But Stella herself is a site of contradiction, and through her character the film's ideological foundations, and the way in which subjects are formed within the repressive terms of dominant culture, are revealed. It is the final scene which exemplifies

11. Stella, an anonymous spectator at her own daughter's wedding,
pleads with a police officer for more time to watch. (Barbara Stanwyck in
Stella Dallas.)

most succinctly the kind of contradiction these pages on the film
hope to unknot.

Stella is standing anonymously in the rain watching the wedding
of her daughter Laurel to Richard Grosvenor III, scion of a rich, upper-class family. She has led Laurel to believe that she is in South
America with Ed Munn, never to return, for she feels that she is more
than an embarrassment to her daughter in this more elevated social
circle (to which Laurel can gain entry through her father), she is the
very obstacle to Laurel's social advancement and happiness. In psychoanalytic terms, Stella's gesture represents a radical assumption of
her castrated state. The heart-rending mises en scène of Oedipal
oppression and repression that we find so often in melodramas are
simply the concentrated representations of what we all suffer. As Deleuze and Guattari might put it, we are all oppressed in and by an
Oedipal drama that we have written, and here Stella is an exemplary
victim of desire as lack. William Rothman has it precisely right and

precisely wrong when he writes that Stella, in the film's final shot, smiling and walking towards the camera after witnessing Laurel's wedding, is some kind of "new woman" who has just demonstrated her "astonishing powers of metamorphosis or rebirth" and is "fulfilled."[30] Stella's smile, rather, is the sign of the absolute and thorough triumph of her own repression/oppression. Stella's sacrifice, read in terms of castration, suggests the overwhelming power of the Oedipal scenario, for it is only at the expense of a desperate loss to herself that Stella is able to take her place within the symbolic order.

As Deleuze and Guattari have written, Oedipus territorializes. Flows of desire are reduced to Oedipal codes and neuroticized territorialities. The result is a world in which everything is measured against neurosis and castration. The Oedipal-familial logic in which Stella Martin is inscribed can only end in castration, just as the Christian logic, for example, of Dreyer's *Ordet* (1954) can only end in a miracle. Wilhelm Reich's question with respect to the rise of fascism is the same one we ask about Stella: How could she be made to desire her own repression? Of course it is not her repression per se that Stella desires, but a place within an order. But there is, from our point of view, no satisfactory order within which she might inscribe herself—no "comprehensive feminism," no "adequately modernized religious sensibility," no "viable, sexually diversified culture."[31]

Stella's desire is colonized by the requirements of an ideology that operates through the transparent sign. Music, for example, at the beginning of the film, is fused with the image in a way that seizes *from* the Imaginary *for* the Symbolic. Music, which is at the origin of the term "melodrama," directly engages the emotions, and melodrama's use of music is symptomatic of the form's identity as an often irrational mode. Non-diegetic music in many Hollywood melodramas is constant, even excessive. As do the beautiful actresses so much on the screen in the "woman's film," music puts desire into the picture. Music seems to be an unsymbolized force, and it is on trajectories of sound waves that one is often carried to extremes of emotion in the film experience. Music is used in the melodrama to make us respond without thinking. As often as not we think we *know* because we can

---

[30] William Rothman, "In the Face of the Camera," *Raritan* 3, no. 3 (Winter 1984): 116–35.

[31] Ann Douglas, *The Feminization of American Culture* (New York: Avon Books, 1977), 13.

see something on the screen, when it is rather the music that has given the signification its overwhelming determination.[32]

The way in which music is used in the melodrama is not unlike the way in which Stella's desire is colonised. In the opening shots of the film there are three different types of music to match the three scenes that in true melo fashion establish the time and place and introduce the heroine: (1) nondescript romantic music for the titles framed in flower-decorated ovals (suggesting that the film will be, as Jean Mitry calls it, a romantic, sentimental melodrama), (2) jollier music for the shot of the town (a title tells us that this is Millhampton, Mass. and the year is 1919) and subsequent shot of the mill and bustling mill hands (this music conveys a lively sense of industry and, befitting a melodrama, seeks to present a picture of the world before the villain enters it),[33] (3) romantic and slightly expectant music for the introductory shot of Stella standing at the gate. This is melodrama in its simplest definition—melody and (silent) drama—the "appropriate" music for each shot, action or character. Since there is no voice-over narration—a device which borrows from the narrative voice always present in the novel—the image, with the help of this aural but not verbal underscoring, can make its significance more certain (in the tradition of silent film). Where the drama "shows," the novel "tells." This difference is at the heart of melodrama, its definition (if one is possible). It is in the *showing*, perhaps, that melodramatic "excess" is born. Of course a narrative voice is present in both the novel and the enacted drama, but the novel tends to realize that voice more concretely. The theater (the drama, the cinema, the actor or object or image present before our eyes) "pretends" that a narrative voice is not there, that the actors, the images, are conveying the story themselves. Different kinds of music establish different levels of narration that will be shown later to be at odds with one another in the film's attempt to make distinctions between Stella's "fantasy" and a world of the "real."

The image of Stella reading a copy of *India's Love Lyrics* is one that

[32] Incidentally, in the same breath Vidor once remarked that he did not think the music in *Stella Dallas* works very well (one of Sam Goldwyn's many contributions to the film) and that he had tried to inject the film with a little romanticism. (Cohn, "Entretien avec King Vidor," 19.)

[33] There is no character who is the villain in this piece; ironically this very industry— the mill and the system that divides the world into the haves and the have-nots—is indirectly the villain.

she herself has staged. She makes a picture and puts herself into a scene (for Stephen Dallas to see). But in melodrama's manner of concentrating information, the image tells us more than Stella would credit. The book, in conjunction with her clothing, her stance, and the house behind her, indicates a working-class girl's yearning for the exotic (represented by India) and for a more elevated level of experience (the lyrical), but, more important, this book tells us that she seeks her escape through *love*. Love, of course, is a word so full of meaning as to be nearly useless; the film repeatedly asks the question, "What is it that will make Stella give up Laurel?" The answer given so confidently in the reviews of the film in 1937—that it is mother love—is clearly inadequate. It is precisely a definition of "love" that the film seeks to offer, for Stella's book is linked to other forms of "love story" in the film—the newspaper article about Stephen Dallas and Helen Dane, the film within the film. Love is a fiction pursued throughout *Stella Dallas*; it can only exist in its absence (as it does to an extreme extent in Ophuls' *Letter from an Unknown Woman*), in a staged scene, a representation. Stephen Dallas, for whom the scene (Stella at the gate, reading) was staged, walks by, totally unaware of Stella's yearning presence.

After the shot of Stella standing at her garden gate hoping to see— and to be seen by—Stephen Dallas, we are given a shot of Stella reading about Stephen Dallas in a newspaper. This is typical of the phenomenal narrative economy that is one of the Hollywood melodrama's specialties, turning on compressions and improbabilities, chance and coincidence. She is fascinated with his story, which draws her into the vortex of the situation that will eventually force her to suppress her own desires in favor of a sacrifice to the paternal Law. He is a millionaire's son and a Harvard graduate. The slightly prolonged fade-out on Stella's face as she contemplates what she has read functions like the tableau of traditional stage melodrama—a moment held for the special significance it contains or for an amplification of emotional effect,[34] stressing the moment's status as some kind

---

[34] What can we read there on Barbara Stanwyck's face? It has been observed by Jean Marsh, who was one of the creators of (and who plays the character of Rose in) the British television drama series *Upstairs, Downstairs*, that "most scenes in all soap operas end in a close-up of a character thinking—thinking worried, thinking puzzled, thinking sneering, thinking triumphant, but thinking." (Jean Marsh, "Soaps: The View From England," *The New York Times*, March 22, 1987: 31.)

of turning point or crisis, be it internal/psychological or external/(f)actual.

When Stella's brother, returning from the mill, teases her ("Stella's got a fellah! Except he don't know it!") she becomes furious—furious because her own motives have been exposed to her, and because his demand that she give him a kiss strikes precisely the chord (of repressed incestuous desire) that she is making an effort to transfer and transform. The brother's primary function, however, is to recall Stella to her class. He invokes the difference between Stephen and the mill hands, and her rejection of his embrace because he has dirty hands begins a motif which recurs throughout the film in which cleanliness is linked to class.

The causes that propel Stella towards her destiny are identified early in the film. In a single shot the entire Martin family is represented, with the mother confined to the house, yelling, "Supper's ready!" This family is something to escape, and yet it is posited as a source of stability. Later, when Laurel and Stella are living in an apartment, Laurel will yearn for just such a house, with a little garden. This is the paradox, and it applies generally to the role of the family in melodrama: the family frees and imprisons at the same time. It provides a stable order at the cost of repression. In *Stella Dallas* the *idea* of family itself is not rejected; rather, two types of family are presented, one negative (the Martin family) and one positive (the Morrison family), with Stella caught in between. Often melodramas suggest that material poverty is the villain of the piece, not Oedipus; melodramatic villainy, as we have noted, changes historically. But the tendency is to give economic factors a human origin or Oedipal cast, since any chance of improving one's lot, or at least of understanding one's unhappy situation, usually seems impossible in the impersonal face of the larger economic situation.

Following the sequence in Stella's bedroom, we are given a shot of Stephen Dallas in his office at the mill, reading the same newspaper (which announces the engagement of his former fiancée, Helen Dane, to a banker by the name of Morrison). The connections are all made (Stella Martin, Stephen Dallas, Helen Dane, the past, the present) and soon, according to the logic of melodramatic montage, their paths intersect, in a moment typical of the melodrama's narrative economy.

While costume has perhaps always been the most reliable index of class and character in the movies—and it is Vidor's use of costume that has made *Stella Dallas* almost notorious—there are dozens of other ways to indicate a character's class and personal peculiarities. When Stella meets Stephen, it is lunchtime at the mill, and she sees him cleaning an already-clean glass for some milk he is about to pour himself. This gesture, and the fact that Stephen is played by the always perfectly groomed John Boles—a supremely dull, smooth matinee idol—links repression and the upper classes. It is a popular notion, with some basis in Freudian theory, that the upper classes (the most successfully civilized) are the most successfully repressed.[35] Stella notes the gesture, and when she and Stephen start to eat the lunch she brought her brother (in the hope of a chance meeting with Stephen) she picks up a glass, reaches for the cloth, and remarks casually, "I hate glasses that don't shine." This masquerade to seduce Stephen is achieved with the effortlessness of habit.[36]

But Stella surely does not fully appreciate the complexities of what she is getting into. Stephen's glass-cleaning is class-determined behavior, and it is class difference, more than sexual difference, that the film will finally identify as the insuperable obstacle between Stella and Stephen. To the extent that Stella *does* know what she is doing, we cannot help but admire her for refusing later to submit to (or for being unable to recognize, to understand) the repressive codes of behavior that the Dallas-Morrisons live by. Her violation of upper-bourgeois codes is confusedly conceived, however, and it results in the pathetic self-parody and eventual self-sacrifice which ends the film. Regardless of whether Stella's smile in the last shot suggests that it was all worth it, both the self-parody and the self-sacrifice are distressing for the viewer, and call into question Stella's challenge to bourgeois codes from the start.

Her remarkably sure sense of what to wear on the occasion of her visit to the mill seems, later in the movie, to be a contradiction, for an utterly disastrous taste in clothes becomes one of Stella's distin-

---

[35] The connection is made explicit in the Bette Davis character in *Now, Voyager*—another film based on a novel by Olive Higgins Prouty, the author of *Stella Dallas*. Also, a line of John Kenneth Galbraith's in the February 22, 1985, issue of *The New York Times Magazine* comes to mind, describing the 750 students which the Harvard Business School graduates every year as "an extremely bright and diverse convocation with, as students go, exceptionally high standards of dress and personal hygiene."

[36] Cf. Laura Mulvey, "Afterthoughts on 'Visual Pleasure and Narrative Cinema' Inspired by *Duel in the Sun*," *Framework* 15/16/17 (1981): 12–15.

12. A lower-class Stella, unable to fit in, makes a spectacle of herself at the exclusive resort where she has taken Laurel.

guishing features. Stephen's sartorial sense is subdued, safe. Only his pencil-thin mustache gives a clue to the fastidiousness and degree of self-possession that make him in the final analysis not particularly likeable. He looks after his body. It is an upper-class body; he is sleek and slightly plump, unlike Stella's scrawny, haggard mother or wiry brother. When Stephen steps out of his office for a moment, Stella feels his expensive jacket which is hanging behind the door. While the gesture might indicate that Stella appreciates fine clothing, it simultaneously equates good clothes with human superiority and suggests that Stella understands these fine clothes to be "proof" that Stephen is a fine being. It thereby hints subversively that Stephen could be merely the sum of such external, acquirable parts. It is a question that is raised and dropped throughout the film.

The question of the respective degrees to which genetic inheritance and social environment determine destiny is played out in the character of the daughter Laurel, who is the product of Stella and Stephen, two people from radically different social backgrounds. The film finally endorses a dubious genetics according to which Laurel inherits only the best from both parents, while each parent remains in the class into which he or she was born. Once it becomes clear that neither money nor marriage to Stephen Dallas will upgrade Stella to a higher class, the differences between classes are presented in a rich variety of ways.

In the main, social class in this film is a matter of taste written in phallic terms. The differences between Stella and her upper-class counterpart, Helen Morrison, are particularly revealing. Helen was Stephen's fiancée, before the shame of his father's suicide drove him to seek the anonymity of Millhampton. Clearly, power and privilege are phallic, and Helen Morrison unconsciously effaces her "femininity" in order to ally herself with the phallic. Femininity as a patriarchal construct varies with social class. This upper-class femininity of Helen's is paradoxical in its subtle incorporation of masculine aspects. One cannot say that Stella is either more or less feminine than Helen, only that her kind of femininity is different from Helen's, and that it is to some extent a function of her lower social class. Whether it is by close association with what is phallic in the world, having it, or becoming it, Helen will always, in a sense, be "inside," where it is warm and dry, while Stella will find herself "outside," in the rain.

To Laurel, Helen is like a goddess in one of her mythology books. What we see is a tall, flat-chested, square-shouldered, handsome woman with short, dark hair, wearing a blazer. When Laurel first meets her in Helen's New York townhouse (New York, the phallic city) a Great Dane follows Helen down the impressive stairway to meet her. Helen's children are all boys, all of whom are dressed like little men and are wearing hats when Stephen first meets them in the city. These little boys, the eldest of whom is called Cornelius (an American would think immediately of Vanderbilt), are well-groomed, and are already learning the ways of capitalism. The youngest has been saving his pocket-money and is taking his family out to lunch the day Stephen meets them. He knows exactly how much a lunch should cost, and has also saved a little extra in case another person should join them unexpectedly.

For all the signifiers of masculinity that surround Helen, however, she is presented also as a mother—which is what Stella is. There is an appeal by the film to all mothers (in patriarchy, by extension, to all women), and there are moments in the film of recognition for the female viewer—moments of comfort, inspiration, or self-pity. When the two women meet, one senses that Helen's heart goes out to Stella, that she understands the peculiar position Stella has put herself in. And on Laurel's wedding night Helen instructs the butler to leave the curtains open, knowing, without being told, that Stella will be out there. Earlier, when Laurel is born, Stella complains that everybody else seems to think that they know more about childbirth than she does. The maternity experience was not one that Stella "got from books." Scenes like these suggest why films like *Stella Dallas* are sometimes called "women's films." They contain such moments of recognition, given to the female viewer before she must face again the fact that she lives in a man's world, and this is the way things are, have to be, or even should be.

Such are the ways in which the melodrama—simultaneously a progressive and a non-progressive form—works. Helen Morrison's motherhood is dealt with only briefly, almost parenthetically; this preserves her masculinized identity and avoids favoring Stella's brand of femininity too strongly, which would make the film's conclusion in support of the patriarchy too difficult. There are no scenes of Helen feeding her sons, sewing clothes for them, or directly engaging in the details of throwing a party for them—all of which we see Stella do for Laurel. While motherhood can certainly be presented as a phallic principle, as it is with Helen, who has produced sons rather than daughters, this is obviously not how the film chooses to present Stella. By film's end we must understand somehow that Stella is standing in the rain not because she is a woman or a mother, but because of a lack in *her* (as a person, a character).

It cannot be recognized without surprise that the film betrays an underlying fear of motherhood. On the one hand, motherhood is fetishized, in order to circumvent the threat it poses the male-female married relation. On the other hand, limits are set for it and it is sacrificed (in its own name!) to a conventional heterosexual coupling and the imperatives of upward social mobility. The fear that *Stella Dallas* reworks for ideological gain (for the patriarchy) is not simply the masculine fear of motherhood's unique relation, but specifically of the female child's desire for her mother. This desire is a problem which patriarchy refuses to address. As Edna O'Brien explains:

If you want to know what I regard as the principle crux of female despair, it is this: in the Greek myth of Oedipus and in Freud's exploration of it, the son's desire for his mother is admitted; the infant daughter also desires its mother but it is unthinkable, either in myth, in fantasy or in fact, that that desire can be consummated.[37]

Stella Dallas' main point, it could be said, is to show how Laurel must transfer her desire for her mother to a young man, and how Stella must give up her daughter (both lessons of the patriarchy).

The film appeals consciously not just to women, but to moviegoers *as* moviegoers, and describes a problem that movies, the movies that made America, can cause. When Stella and Stephen go to the movies shortly after they first meet, Stella is enraptured by what she sees on the screen. We see the closing shots of it, a romantic melodrama, intercut with shots of Stella and Stephen. Stella is looking at the screen, Stephen is looking at Stella, we are looking at *Stella Dallas*, the movie within it, and at ourselves. When they leave the theater Stephen and Stella have a particularly revealing conversation, the gist of which, from Stella, is "I don't want to be like me . . . but like the people in the movie!" In Deleuzian terms, Stella suffers from an "incurable insufficiency of being." Her sense of lack is the counter-effect of desire—desire repressed and blocked. (In Freudian terms, of course, desire springs from a lack.) Hers is every moviegoer's prob-lem, only worse. What registers vividly is the gap between Stella and the idealized world she sees on the screen, like the gap between Emma Bovary's actual life and her fantasy life. Stella does not appre-ciate the fact that nobody can really be like the people she sees on the screen, and the propaganda of the screen-kiss on which the film-within-the-film ends (the kiss that is, and justifies, closure) is in its implications the most dangerous form of romanticism. As we have noted, the melodrama is the bourgeois drama for the bourgeoisie, and in this scene Stella is explicitly identified as one among the masses who, like us—the bourgeois audience—goes to the movies.

Although Stella enjoys life and is not embarrassed by her lower-class (and in clothes, "feminine")[38] tastes, she is aware that the upper classes generally do not have the same tastes that she has. When Mrs. Phillibrown (of the anglicized accent and austerely elegant and

---

[37] "A Conversation With Edna O'Brien: 'The Body Contains the Life Story,' " by Philip Roth, *The New York Times Book Review*, November 18, 1984: 40.

[38] Feminine here in the sense of fetishistic masquerade. See n. 9 above.

somewhat masculine attire) asks if Laurel could spend a weekend with her in Boston, Stella says she would love Laurel to have the opportunity to see some "real shows—I don't just mean movies." Again, as she did not with Stephen, Stella does not appreciate the extent of the difference between Mrs. Phillibrown's moral universe and her own, for Mrs. Phillibrown replies with excessive dignity: "I had more in mind museums and galleries." During the after-movie conversation Stephen is quite explicit on this pattern of self-denial in our culture, the repression of desire with desire founded on a cult of lack: "It isn't really well-bred to act the way you feel." This is Stephen's problem in a nutshell, and Stella's too.

We, of course, understand Stephen's role, but it should alarm us that we do. We, too, have been "oedipalized," "territorialized." Consider an early scene in the movie, which corresponds to early scenes in Stella's life, set in the family, where it all begins. Stella is not at home for breakfast because she is out with Stephen, and her father becomes unreasonably angry. But his anger is understandable if one sees it as a countereffect of desire. Deleuze and Guattari see the family as

the delegated agent of psychic repression, or rather the agent delegated to psychic repression; the incestuous drives are the disfigured image of the repressed. The Oedipus complex, the process of oedipalization, is therefore the result of this double operation. *It is in one and the same movement that the repressive social production is replaced by the repressing family, and that the latter offers a displaced image of desiring production that represents the repressed as incestuous familial drives.*[39]

The family alienates the entire network of desiring-geneaology by "confiscat[ing] the Numen (but see here, God is daddy)."[40] Stella's father "stages" the repression that is the result of this Oedipal confiscation. In the same instant, Stella's brother threatens to leave home. This response to the father's unwieldy exercise of patriarchal "right" is for Stella. The situation is neurotic, to be sure, but reorganized within the patriarchal system a moment later when Stella arrives home with a wedding ring on her finger and Stephen in tow.

We see here, as in all melodrama, the obvious and vivid functioning of what Louis Althusser calls Ideological State Apparatuses. There might clearly be scenes of the Repressive State Apparatus in

[39] Deleuze and Guattari, *Anti-Oedipus*, 119.
[40] Ibid., 120.

action (such as the scene in Griffith's *The Mother and the Law* in which troops fire on strikers at the Jenkins factory), but the deeper criticism of this action is offered in an ideological, private domain.[41] In the family melodrama the favorite Ideological State Apparatus is obviously the family, and what we see in *Stella Dallas* is a story that takes a particular course because of Stella's role in a family. She must leave her parents, but only so she can take her place in the formation of another family unit. After she marries Stephen it follows "naturally" that she will have a child: the couple in bourgeois society is not so stable as the "mommy-daddy-me"[42] unit of the family because the couple itself is formed by chance, by desire, which, undesirably, is (potentially) unstable. Sexual desire must be transformed into, or redirected towards, desire for a child as soon as possible, to put the unit under Law: the Law of the Father, the Law of the Family, the Law of Oedipus. (Many melodramas do of course deal with the couple's desire,[43] but in a sense these dramas are part one in unrealized two- and three-part series.)

A turning point, perhaps, in the story of how Stella comes to desire her own repression, is the birth of Laurel. Barely concealed is the fact that *Stella does not really want this child*. Stella wants to have fun, to dance and "have some good times." There is no doubt that she grows to love the child, but in a telling phrase of Stella's, Laurel is "a regular pal" to her.[44] The film has a little difficulty in representing the

[41] In the example of *The Mother and the Law* we are given to understand that the strike is the result of a complex of factors, not the least of which is Jenkins' personal selfishness, and the "unresolved" bond (unconsciously suggested) between Jenkins and his unmarried sister for whom he established the Jenkins Foundation for Moral Uplift, which has cost so much money as to necessitate a cut in workers' wages, and so on.

[42] An eccentric but apt term Deleuze and Guattari use frequently in *Anti-Oedipus* to refer to the Freudian family.

[43] Frank Borzage's *Seventh Heaven* (1927) is just one, splendid, example among thousands.

[44] In *Mildred Pierce* (1945), we see a more grotesque version of this mother love which, being so intense, betrays a truth about love in general—that it is in no way neutral or "innocent." Tania Modleski points out that while the preoccupation with children in nineteenth-century fiction can be attributed to the high infant mortality rate, "in the woman's film, on the other hand, it is the mothers or the mother-surrogates who are the martyrs, sacrificing everything for their (often ungrateful) children. This shift in attitude may be explained by the fact that women in the twentieth century, much more than their nineteenth-century counterparts, have had to depend on their children for fulfillment, since the 'support networks' of women have virtually disappeared. This increased dependency generates increased resentment, a dilemma

conflict, for it avoids showing how Stella makes her transition from "person" to "mother." It occurs off-screen, in the fade-out that covers Laurel's progress from crib to highchair. At least, and one should say, significantly (how melodrama vacillates in its relation to the patriarchy!), the film makes it obvious that the "mystique" of motherhood is not instantly conferred with the birth of a child. As Ann Douglas observes,

The cult of motherhood [in the nineteenth century], like the Mother's Day it eventually established in the American calendar, was an essential precondition to the flattery American women were trained to demand in place of justice and equality. It offered them, of course, a very genuine basis for self-respect. It gave them, moreover, an innate, unassailable, untestable claim to charismatic authority and prestige, a sanction for subjectivity and self-love.[45]

Whether or not Stella will opt for the mystique of motherhood becomes the next question, for it does, as we know, have its rewards. In her article "The Case of the Missing Mother," E. Ann Kaplan observes that after her initial resistance to mothering, Stella enthusiastically embraces Motherhood, but

In getting so much pleasure for herself out of Laurel, Stella violates the patriarchal myth of the self-abnegating Mother, who is supposed to be completely devoted and nurturing but not satisfy any of her needs through the relationship with her child. She is somehow supposed to keep herself apart while giving everything to the child; she is certainly not supposed to prefer the child to the husband, since this kind of bonding threatens patriarchy.[46]

A day or two after Laurel is brought home from the hospital where she was born, Stella persuades Stephen that they should go dancing. The dilemma is suggested squarely: convention requires that Stella stay in bed, whether she feels like it or not, because she has just given birth to a child. Likewise, convention requires us to condemn Stella for indulging herself, when maternal duty dictates that she spend this evening at home with the baby. If we recognized the fraud sometimes concealed in words like duty, there would be no dilemma. Under patriarchal Law, marriage and motherhood is meant to con-

reflected in the child obsession of the woman's film as well as in soap operas." (Modleski, *Loving With a Vengeance*, 24.)

[45] Douglas, *The Feminization of American Culture*, 88.

[46] E. Ann Kaplan, "The Case of the Missing Mother: Maternal Issues in Vidor's *Stella Dallas*," *Heresies* 16 (1983): 84.

tain (Stella's) sexuality, which in Stella's case is still dangerous,[47] as signified, for example, by the metallic, glittering dress she wears to the dance. We are conditioned to see something fraudulent and deceitful in the shining surface; it derives, perhaps, from the trouble we have with that original shiny surface, the mirror. At any rate, our cultural conditioning produces shock waves of melodramatic conflict at the sight of this mother in a slinky, sexy dress.

Motherhood has failed to phallicize Stella, and she is presented as still desiring. Since the part of Stephen is played by John Boles, whose screen persona is on the dull, stuffy side, the viewer might be inclined to explain Stephen's failure (or the failure of marriage) to contain Stella's sexuality in these terms: Stella is too sexy for him, and her erotic energy is understood somehow to be a function of her social class, which ties in with the antiseptic hygeine of the upper classes discussed earlier. If it is our passion that makes us legible to others, Stephen becomes more hazy, less sympathetic, as his desire for Stella falters and diminishes. As he withdraws from Stella, his own masculine appeal begins to derive exclusively from his money and social origins, which are not enough for Stella, since her passion is not produced by that nexus. Stella does not find money and social position sexy enough. In effect, the movies and magazines have betrayed her. She expected more than what she gets—but she had no clear idea of what she wanted in the first place (unlike, for example, Craig's wife, in the movie of that name,[48] who marries a rich, bland man, also played by John Boles, and gets exactly what she wanted: money, social position, a house).

When Stephen desperately begs her, "Stella, can't you . . . won't you understand?" we are not sure, as he is not sure, whether she can't or won't. "Why did you marry me?" he asks in a grave voice. When she answers, 'Because I'm crazy about you," she unties his

[47] As Deleuze and Guattari have written, "If desire is repressed, it is because every position of desire, no matter how small, is capable of calling into question the established order of society: not that desire is asocial; on the contrary. But it is explosive; there is no desiring machine capable of being assembled without demolishing entire sectors." (Deleuze and Guattari, *Anti-Oedipus*, 116.)

[48] *Craig's Wife* (Dorothy Arzner, 1936). In the 1925 version of *Stella Dallas*, whose advertising campaign gave Ronald Coleman top billing, Stella's desire for Stephen is defined more in terms of social advancement. She gives a "swell tea" at the country club because, as she says to Stephen, "Honey, you're such a big, important man. I can't be a little wife poking along behind."

bow tie, and his face softens as the question recedes. This silent gesture reveals again the psychoanalytic subtext. We know at least why he married her: the way to this man's heart was through his eye. Stephen's desire is produced in vision. Stella is a fantasy for his scopic drive, in which the eye functions as phallus. He is blinded (to the incompatibilities of their class differences) by his desire for her.

The unlikely union of Stella and Stephen produces Laurel who, from the beginning, is represented as a successful combination of her parents' attractive character traits. In early scenes we see the baby Laurel in her highchair wiping up the mess she has made eating a bowl of porridge. "Get that!" shrieks Stella. "The spit of her old man!" The implication, of course, is that Laurel has inherited this "good" behavior from Stephen—a point emphasized by the contrast of Stella's "lower-class" language. It is doubtful that Stella's interpretation of the child's gesture can be valid. Stephen has lived in New York since the birth of the child, and cleanliness, we know, is not a question of chromosomes; but the child's gesture and Stella's remark establishes the link again between cleanliness and the upper classes, which, we saw, is one of the means by which the film attempts to grapple with the slippery terms of the issue of social class. This same bowl of porridge becomes the ashtray for Ed Munn's cigar when he lifts Laurel from her highchair for a bounce on his knee. The image, which includes a glass of whiskey near the bowl, is confined in close-up. It is the image of how others see Stella and her household, for Stephen unexpectedly walks through the door, sizes up the situation in an instant, and in a fury of dismay stutters, "I can't have our child living . . . like this."

The problem of Ed Munn in Stella's story, presented as he is in images like this one, as a gross masculine presence, is that Ed, for all his crude boisterousness, is an immensely likeable character and in no sense a villain. In an extraordinary performance, Alan Hale makes Ed Munn a sympathetic character, as Stanwyck makes Stella fundamentally good and endearing. One cannot fault Stephen for his indignation, and one can only put it down to melodramatic fate that he sees the worst of Ed. One Christmas night Stephen turns up in time to see Ed maudlin drunk,[49] and it must be remembered that Laurel's

---

[49] Again, Ed is associated with a gross sexuality: he brings Stella a plucked turkey, which he attempts to shove directly into the oven. Incidentally—from the outer limits of the intertext—Sylvia Plath, whose benefactress at one time was Olive Higgins

birthday party is a fiasco all because Mrs. Phillibrown saw Stella and Ed giggling with unseemly mirth on the train to town. One's fate, the movie asserts, is directly or indirectly always determined by *others*, and how they see things.

From his geographically remote position, Stephen tries occasionally to exert a "good" influence on Laurel, although she would hardly seem to need it. For example, Stephen sends her *Rebecca of Sunnybrook Farm* for her birthday, while Stella complains, "Books can be got free in the library, but there's no place you can get a fur coat for nothin'." Laurel refuses any frills Stella tries to put on her birthday dress and tells Stella that she (Laurel) is too young to wear a fur coat. The child is congenitally kind and sweet, as if such a thing were possible, and sometimes shows a fineness of feeling that we suspect not even her father, whose excellent genes Laurel supposedly has inherited, would possess. For example, when Laurel, on her return from her visit to the Morrisons in New York, is rhapsodizing about Helen to Stella, she says, among other unintentionally cruel things, "She hardly ever puts anything on her face" as Stella is slathering cream on her own face and fretting in front of the mirror about the appearance of dark roots on her peroxide-blonde head. She screams with dismay when she thinks Stella is smudging a photograph of Helen with her cream-covered fingers, but she then sees the cruelty and selfishness of her unintentional comparison, and in a silent gesture of love and apology takes up the hair-dyeing business Stella was in the middle of. The scene is truly extraordinary. It displays with vivid overdetermination the vital materiality of the codes of feminine beauty.

On the train to Millhampton after Laurel's spectacular humiliation at the resort hotel, Laurel again shows her integrity as a truly loving daughter when, with tears in her eyes, she slips into the sleeping berth with Stella. While it is implied that Laurel is, like her father, a genetically finer being than Stella, she is still, in relation to the phallic principle that organizes the world, found wanting; she is, after all, female. For example, at the resort she orders a chocolate ice cream

---

Prouty, the author of *Stella Dallas*, has her heroine say in *The Bell Jar* when that "fine, clean boy Buddy Willard" drops his pants and she contemplates the naked male body for the first time: "The only thing I could think of was turkey neck and turkey gizzards and I felt very depressed."

sundae with fudge and whipped cream, whereas Richard Grosvenor III[50] orders vanilla ice cream "without the frills."

Stella is the supreme avatar of this theme of "feminine" frivolousness. The image of Stella in her room at the resort hotel functions like a tableau of nineteenth-century stage melodrama or an engraving illustrating a character in a Dickens novel. She is shown, with her blonde hair fantastically curled, propped up in bed (all bedclothes and lingerie wildly florally patterned) eating chocolates and reading *True Confessions*. Stella believes, as Emma Bovary does, that life (if not her own, then life *somewhere*) is like life as represented in *True Confessions*. It is this belief that is her tragedy and that produces the smile on her face when, standing in the rain outside the Dallas-Morrison residence, she sees her daughter marrying Richard Grosvenor III in a scene that could be taken from *True Confessions*. The extremity of Stella's outfit at the resort, and her effort later to disgust Laurel into running back to the Dallas-Morrisons in New York by playing loud music, puffing on a cigarette and reading a magazine while she is supposedly waiting for Ed Munn, is the film's extraordinary, and one should say, successful, effort to induce a crisis by the sheer hysteria of a delirious mise en scène. The two moments differ, however, in that Stella in the first scene is in some sense being "herself," and in the later scene is staging a conscious suicide/sacrifice.

The upper-bourgeois sons and daughters at the resort are seen in tennis outfits—clothing at its most understated, and clothing associated with upper-bourgeois leisure—to push to the most extreme degree possible a contrast with Stella. The film's primary effort, hysterical because it is not sure that it will succeed, is to reestablish an older, reassuring order, of villains and figures of virtue, upper classes and lower classes, good taste and bad taste.

The problem is that Stephen is not a clear-cut villain in Stella's story. Society—bourgeois ideology itself—is the villain, even though its ideal as represented by Stephen and the Morrisons is not unattractive. Stella, the film's heroine and chief figure for audience identification, is likeable, warm, earthy, generous—but an extravagant attempt must be made to make her seem not quite to fit the mold that would, to use Helen's phrase regarding Laurel, make her "one of us

---

[50] Grosvenor, one might recall, is the family name of the richest man in the United Kingdom, the Duke of Westminster.

really.'' On the one hand, the film encourages us to identify with Stella, and to recognize how she is constituted by the fictions of popular culture. On the other, the film suggests that Stella is the universal mother, from whom we must all establish our independence—for our Oedipal resolutions—or drown in the "chaotic carnal atmosphere of infancy"[51] and be swallowed up in maternal identification and dependence.

In recognizing ourselves in Stella we recognize the degree to which in America, to use Baudrillard's terms, the simulacrum has become the real. That Stella *knows* the stories in *True Confessions* are just stories, but is then revealed by film's end to be a character herself in one of them, proves Baudrillard's point that "it is no longer a question of a false representation of reality (ideology) but of concealing the fact that the real is no longer real, and thus of saving the reality principle.''[52] She has lived a sentimental romantic melodrama, has been inscribed in its language. Our own image is thrown back to us by the fact that Stella is a character in a *True Confessions* story or in a movie she has seen. *Stella Dallas* is only a movie, we say; but to talk about how Stella believes in the simulacrum (the film-within-the-film, the stories in *True Confessions*) we imply that she herself is a sign, a vestige of the real. She is not. While she is indeed a character in a movie, there is essentially no difference between her position and ours. Her fantasies, fed by popular culture, become her reality, and it is a reality that demands a profound repression.

In Stella's case it is first her class origins that she must overcome, and then it is the pleasures of motherhood that she must repress, in the name of an ideology that defines "motherhood" in terms meant

---

[51] Dorothy Dinnerstein, *The Mermaid and the Minotaur: Sexual Arrangements and Human Malaise* (New York: Harper and Row, 1977), 133. Dinnerstein explores several implications of the fact that we all have (had) mothers—that the main presence in infancy and early childhood is female. She articulates eloquently much that is relevant to an understanding of melodrama and how Stella Dallas is made to desire her own repression: "the way in which adult feeling resonates with the emotional atmosphere of infancy; the overwhelming power, attractiveness, and hatefulness of the person or persons who tend the body, and support the emerging personality, of the pre-verbal child; and the ways in which men and women differ emotionally, and evoke different emotions from others, as a consequence of the fact that the persons who provided this crucial early care for all of us were female" (xiii).

[52] Jean Baudrillard, "The Precession of Simulacra," *Simulations*, trans. Paul Foss, Paul Patton, and Philip Beitchman (New York: Semiotext[e], Inc. Foreign Agents Series, 1983), 25.

to contain female sexuality and limit female subjectivity. When Stella has performed the functions of motherhood as it is conceived by patriarchal ideology, she must, with grace, step back into the shadows to expedite the patriarchal imperative that will put Laurel into circulation—to be exchanged between families in the name of the Father—according to the fictions of popular culture. Bourgeois ideology (the social discourse) and Oedipus (the psychoanalytic discourse) produce a "reality" which exacts a toll from the likes of Stella. For, when she succeeds in her desire "to escape—through dream—into an imaginary world which transfigures [her] suffering or despair," she succeeds only in desiring her own repression.

From the Wrong Side of the Tracks: *Ruby Gentry*

The first figural image in *Ruby Gentry* is on the title card. It is of Ruby herself in half-silhouette, framed in a doorway, wearing a tight pair of jeans and a blouse that accentuates the feminine curves of her body. Athletic and voluptuous, boyish and womanly, she appears to be posing in a way that shows off her physical charms to best effect, and trying at the same time to break out of the narrow frame that imprisons her in a tiny rhombus of light. The narrative, however, begins with a voice-over and with shots of Ruby now (that is, as she appears also in the film's last shots)—"strange, gaunt," asexual. There is undoubtedly a story to tell here. Why does this woman apparently live on a boat? What happened, that will be so worth telling?

The French title of the film, *La Furie du désir*, would suggest that the film is about just that: the fury of desire. The American title, on the other hand, and the voice-over that begins and ends the film, suggest that it is about class and social prejudice (gems and gentry). The film of course is about both—about a dialectic between class and sex.

The voice-over directly offers an interpretation. It suggests that Ruby is still "suffering in atonement for all the tragic consequences of her willful acts." This voice of official condemnation, however, belongs to a man who has been in love with Ruby from the moment he first met her. He is Dr. Saul Manfred who, as the one telling the story, represents the film's declared point of view. What Saul says in the opening shots makes explicit the story of struggle that her present image conceals:

There was a time when Ruby was beautiful and alive, and I believe that it was this spirit of life and love that caused so much envy and resentment to be foist against her by the narrow, class-conscious citizens of our town. For Ruby was born on the wrong side of the tracks, and although she struggled valiantly to overcome this stigma, the townspeople never let her forget it.

Ruby's being "beautiful and alive" is where the trouble starts. The first image of her—the silhouette framed in a doorway—represents how society (and men in particular) see her and would like to keep her. Ruby's spirit of life and love that everyone finds so dazzling is also what they are afraid of. If she were not so in possession of herself, if she would only submit to the frame and take a passive, "feminine" role, her having been "born on the wrong side of the tracks" would, one is made to understand, be overlooked by the citizens of Braddock. Ruby's sexuality comes in some way to be identified with her social class, as her will to self-determination produces the vitality that is found to be so attractive and dangerous. While the film bears out Freud's remark that "anatomy is destiny," it tries to give equal weight to the notion that environment (social class) determines individual destiny. The voice-over at the beginning cannot articulate just *how* social class and sexuality are linked in Ruby's case—but that is what the film is for.

Saul, a Yankee (i.e., from the less European, more industrialized, capitalistic North), does seem to think the citizens of the Southern town of Braddock are exceptionally narrow-minded, which would suggest that he believes social class—or rather, class difference—is the obstacle to Ruby's happiness, not sexual difference, about which nothing can be done anyway. Saul wants to believe that it is only class prejudice that ruins Ruby's life, when in fact we observe that gender has as much to do with it. Ruby was born not just on the wrong side of the tracks that divide people socially, but also on the wrong side of the tracks that divide sexually. The way in which the film handles the issue of social class reveals that sexual difference as a problem is, wherever possible, pressed into class terms.

When, for example, Jim Gentry married Letitia, he married above his social class and did all right by it. But it was his wealth, one presumes, that made it possible for him to marry her. It should be observed, also, that she is an invalid, which suggests that a marriage across class lines is an aberration that will, at the very least, result in sterility. When he later marries Ruby, however, Jim Gentry is mar-

13. The death of the aristocratic invalid, Letitia, paves the way for Ruby's marriage to Jim and entry into a different world. (Josephine Hutchingson, Jennifer Jones, Karl Malden, in *Ruby Gentry*.)

rying within the social class of his origins, although he has adopted the manners of a gentleman—as Letitia had hoped Ruby might adopt the manners of a lady. As in *Stella Dallas*, social class in *Ruby Gentry* is an issue computed in particular combinations of money and manners. Both commodities can be acquired, but the films are ambivalent on the matter, for if a subject does not take on the characteristics of the upper class after being presented with opportunities to do so, social class is then understood to be an immutable law. The real point is that the melodrama posits a sexual and social ideal, and sex and social class are never insuperable obstacles if the subject will only conform to the ideal. But Ruby will no more put down her guns than adopt the code of femininity that is traditional for Southern ladies. The implicit question, as with Stella Dallas, is whether Ruby cannot, or will not. She is offered the chance to "overcome" her social origins, and a chance to efface the very kind of femininity that makes her attractive in the first place.

When Saul first sees Ruby, standing in the doorway of her father's hunting lodge, he is struck dumb. "Don't let it shake you, Doc," Jim quips. "It's just anatomy!" Ruby's tight clothes reveal her womanly figure, but also suggest that her body is straining to burst free. She has a deep, throaty voice, and we see immediately that she shares a gun-fetish with all the men. She is, in short, a tomboy. The film celebrates a phallic sexuality, of which Ruby is the only female example, and as a tomboy with an ostentatiously female body Ruby signifies perfectly the desires of the men—desires which, in the end, prove too contradictory to be supported (Ruby will not play the "backstreet" lover for Boake Tackman after he marries Tracy McAuliffe).

There are basically three kinds of woman in *Ruby Gentry*: a lower-class virago (Ruby), a middle-class wimp (Tracy), and an aristocratic invalid (Letitia). Tracy, in Boake's words, "is gentle, and she's as bright as a dollar." His description says even a little more than Ruby's immediate response to it tells ("I know! She's got 'brains and breeding'!"); Tracy's father is lending Boake the money he needs to drain the plantation that for years has been a swamp. If Boake's masculine presumptuousness is in almost every case unforgivable, his lucid understanding, at least, of what his priorities are in the tricky area where love and work meet and sex and social class interact, is to be admired—whether or not it is fair to Ruby.

Charlton Heston is one of Hollywood's "straightest" actors, while Jennifer Jones has, before and since *Ruby Gentry*, played "unstable" or contradictory characters in the movies.[53] He represents "what has to be done," something admirably American. As Boake Tackman he stands not for love, or desire, but family, property, personal energy, and progress. When he says of his marriage to Tracy, "Our families have more or less planned it since we were kids," the film means more by his words than he does. *Ruby Gentry* may be Ruby's story (the fury of desire . . .), but it is also a family melodrama, and as such believes in what Boake represents. The family is a microcosm for society; it is held to be the model for other forms of social organization. The family is the human organization that this kind of film knows best, and what Ruby offers, or represents, is the antithesis of this sort

[53] A few examples of "unstable" or contradictory characters Jennifer Jones has played in the movies: the amnesiac in *Love Letters* (1945), the half-breed Pearl Chavez in *Duel in the Sun* (1946), Emma in *Madame Bovary* (1949), the compulsive liar in *Beat the Devil* (1954), the distraught, indecisive woman in *Indiscretion of an American Wife* (1954), and the mentally unstable psychiatrist's wife in *Tender Is the Night* (1962).

of order. She embodies, rather, (in Boake's words) something "sweet and wild and crazy."

As a melodrama, a form that emphasizes conflict, *Ruby Gentry* is not inclined to offer a happy medium between terms. The alternative to Ruby is a ninny like Tracy, or an invalid like Letitia. These women are the price a man must pay for his patriarchal order. Boake knows that the most thrilling times of his life have been spent with Ruby. "But when it comes to settling down for the rest of my life, you see, I like the little corner of the world I was born in. I like everything about it." A corner is something one knows. It can also mean property. Whatever it is, it is always there. When Boake says he likes everything about it, Ruby says, "The money!" and to his clear-headed credit, Boake replies, "The money's part of it, so I can do the work I want to do. For a hundred years the Tackmans have been sliding downhill—ever since the tide swallowed our plantation. Not one of them lifted a finger to do anything about it!" He does not want to end up like his father, who just sat on the veranda drinking bourbon. The film in this way makes clear the driving logic of the symbolic order, and the kind of threat to it represented by the Imaginary—on the one hand, something "sweet and wild and crazy," and on the other, an alcoholic image of slothful inactivity.

Resonating throughout Saul's story are associations which produce an equation in which a Northern kind of vigor, represented by Boake, must struggle with the Southern forces of lethargy and langor (the heat, the men who sit around talking, the swamp) and desire (Ruby). Boake is considered by the other men to have "too much energy for a Carolina boy." He will not give in to the swamp, that grand metaphor of the film. It represents disorder, the formless, nearly-uncontrollable forces of nature, and later, by association, Ruby's sexuality. The swamp is useless, unproductive, but beautiful (as Ruby agrees with Saul it is), and dangerous. The hard, dry sexuality of Boake must protect itself from Ruby's amorphous, mysterious, voluptuous, drowning sexuality. "There are all kinds of love," Boake tells Ruby; never was a truer observation made, but it is the film's endeavor to sort them out.

What is clear on a specific level, and implicit on a general level, is that men and women love differently. A man loves differently from a woman because love is tied up with identity. Boake's sense of who he is derives from the corner of the world he was brought up in; it derives from his work, his personal achievement in a materially productive sphere. Ruby's identity is a more complex matter. She is a "swamp girl" from "the wrong side of the tracks," but like Emma Bovary she has passion, will, determination. And there is the significant matter of Ruby's extended stay with Jim and Letitia Gentry.

In a flashback Jim explains to Saul how Ruby came to live with them after an incident in which Boake Tackman (then a local football hero) had "tried to get fresh with" Ruby and she stabbed him with an oyster knife. Letitia insisted that Ruby stay with them "so that she could have the protection and care a young girl needs." So Ruby stayed, and Letitia "taught her how to dress, how to act towards the servants, how to manage a big house," and so on. But Ruby eventually went back to her father's house, and Jim says to Saul, "So maybe we weren't as kind as we meant to be—training her for a life she can't have. You see, Ruby doesn't belong." Saul is incredulous. "You mean socially?" he asks. Jim explains matter-of-factly that she is from the wrong side of the tracks. When Saul asks, "Do you mean to say, in this day and age . . . ?" Jim exclaims, "You're forgetting where you are, Doctor!" He goes on, "Those fools are so full of pride about who they are . . . their fine old family names . . . they can't even see what she is . . . how wonderful . . . !"

Families. Names. These Southerners cling to old signifiers of order, without, as Boake sees it, doing anything about fighting to keep "the swamp" of disorder and desire from drowning them. They need to abandon inherited, invalid indexes of identity and to start over, to find out "who they are." Jim realizes that this Southern class system and he and Letitia have played significant parts in Ruby's destiny. Jim and his aristocratic wife helped to complicate Ruby's sense of who she is, and she now carries two worlds within her; she has been permitted to see that the life of a "swamp girl" need not be the only life. Her desire for Boake Tackman can only have been increased by her stay with the Gentrys, since the hope of its satisfaction was surely planted at this time when Ruby learned about the corner of the world Boake inhabited, and when she understood that she could be "worthy" of his love.

"He's mine!" she tells her brother. He has belonged to her at least from that night when she marked him—stabbed him with her oyster knife (truly a wound of desire!). As only an oyster knife can pry open an oyster, Ruby, sometimes as hard and brilliant as her name, has a power over Boake that no one else has. Their relationship will be a struggle to the death, because Ruby is as strong as he. Her strength and her will are what attract Boake; he sees himself in those traits. He does not, as he will with Tracy, always have the upper hand. Married to Tracy, Boake's struggle with the other is displaced into the land and his ambitions for a wealth-producing plantation. Tracy becomes only a medium, a commodity of exchange between Boake and other powerful men from whom he will derive his identity in terms of social class.

From the moment of their first encounter after his return from South America, Boake and Ruby's attraction-repulsion magnetism is obvious. The desire Ruby signifies is more vivid than the mediated, repressed terms of the desire in which Boake eventually chooses to inscribe himself with Tracy. When Ruby hears Boake's car pull up outside the lodge, she grabs a flashlight and darts into the shadows of the veranda. When he strides up the stairs, she whistles their code call. He calls her name softly into the dark. She laughs throatily and turns on the flashlight and points it at his face. "You have me at a disadvantage! I can't see what you look like," he says. "But I can imagine! Gimme that light! Let's see what I been missing!" As Laura Mulvey puts it, the one who controls the look controls language, and the one who controls language controls the world. Ruby will let herself be looked at, but she will also turn the tables and bear the gaze herself. It puts Boake "at a disadvantage," which he cannot tolerate for long. There is no question that the one who is looked at also exercises a certain kind of power over the one who looks,[54] but not like this, in a scene analogous with voyeurism where Ruby has complete power over Boake trapped in her beam of light.

Throughout the movie, however, Boake exercises his "to-be-looked-at-ness"[55] to powerful effect, filling the screen with his tremendous shoulders, and at one point by taking off his shirt. The men in the locker room banter about how he must have fairly sizzled the night before when he and Ruby careened into the ocean after driving along the beach, and suddenly, when he pulls off his shirt and stands there in his underpants, we remember what Ruby has to sizzle about, too.

---

[54] Cf. Miriam Hansen, "Pleasure, Ambivalence, Identification: Valentino and Female Spectatorship," *Cinema Journal* 25, no. 4 (Summer 1986): 6–32.

[55] "To-be-looked-at-ness" is a neologism of Laura Mulvey's.

Ruby's vacillation between bearing the look and being looked at is what makes her thrilling.[56] As Jim says to Saul, shaking his head at the wonder of it, "No woman like her! One minute fighting, scratching. Next minute she's as sweet and soft as any woman alive. Guess I like that wild side best. Can't help bein' glad that Lettie didn't really tame her." Ruby has not achieved what one could call a stable identity. She has been brought up among men and guns, in the woods, and also at the Gentrys, under Letitia's old-world, Southern guidance (just as the Jennifer Jones character, Pearl, is brought under the taming influence of the Lillian Gish character in *Duel in the Sun*). She starts out as a "swamp girl" and becomes the richest woman (the richest person) in Braddock. She tries many roles, and all of them are unsatisfactory to her.

The night before the hunt, Ruby decides to wait on the men at table. It is the first time, as one of them remarks, that they have seen her do this, and Ruby replies, "It may be the last time, so take a good look." She is waiting on table in order to be seen by Boake. Ruby and Boake exchange looks during this scene (he mostly pretends not to look) while the men talk about Ruby, and Boake keeps returning the conversation to his plans for the future. "I says it's time she was learnin' to do a woman's work," Ruby's father says, which prompts one of the others to ask if she will sell her gun ("You got no use for it!"). "Don't you just wish!" says Ruby. Ruby has become too independent, too masculine for the men. Or rather, she has become too femininely beautiful for them to continue treating her as one of the boys. She now signifies their desire. "I raised Ruby like she was a boy!" her father says proudly. "Somethin' sure musta got outta hand. Look at it! 'Cept for those pants she wears . . . !" The way those pants fit Ruby's body prove she is not a boy. Pants are for men, on whom they do not create noteworthy contours. The thrilling synthesis of masculine and feminine traits in Ruby is not the kind of sexuality these Southern men know how to deal with. It is Tracy, rather, in her great, flouncing dresses, her white gloves, and with her

[56] It is what makes the Queen of Sheba thrilling, too (in Vidor's last feature film, *Solomon and Sheba*). When Prince Adonijah asks in wonder, "Has the screaming eagle been transformed into a cooing dove?" she replies, "How dull the world would be if people never changed! I am wiser, Prince Adonijah. I no longer do battle with a sword." As the Prince leaves, he remarks, "I think I understood you better as the screaming eagle!"

14. Tracy McAuliffe, the "nice girl" with "brains and breeding," pays an unaccustomed visit to Ruby's father's hunting lodge. (Bernard Phillips, Jennifer Jones, Phyllis Avery.)

conventional "spontaneous" Southern charm, who is the norm for women in this corner of the world.

Ruby as an androgyne is emphasized again in the scene where she dances with the dress Letitia hopes to wear to Boake's wedding. She swirls around the room, flirting with and complimenting it as if Letitia were in her arms and she were a male suitor. Letitia's dressmaker is "a spinster lady, poor thing. Got no idea what catches a man's eye!" although she makes a dress "that bowls men over and makes all the women green with envy." This small phrase of Ruby's about the dress inciting feminine envy says a great deal. All "feminine" masquerade (dresses, etc.) are for men, to catch their eye, while women can only be envious, wishing that they had whatever some woman has (a dress, for example) to catch that man's eye. A woman is made to desire what a man desires, since she has no existence outside of his gaze. It is never suggested that Tracy, for example, desires Boake, for his shoulders or for anything else; her destiny is to marry him.

Ruby's fighting and scratching one minute and the next being "as sweet and soft as any woman alive" is really not such a paradox or contradiction as the men who know her seem to find it. The men in her life, Boake Tackman particularly, will not permit her any self-determination, and she fights and scratches whenever they "take her for granted," or, as she says later, "tramp back and forth over my life treatin' me like I was trash." The first example of her "scratching" makes her reasons for it clear. During the dinner the night before the hunt, as we have seen, Ruby takes it upon herself to serve the men. She pours coffee for them, one at a time, leaning forward to reach their mugs on the table. When she gets to Boake's mug, he discreetly puts his hand on Ruby's tight-jeaned thigh and presses her towards him, in a possessive gesture, as he continues to talk to the men about his plans. Quick as a flash she scratches his face and pulls away. Boake is shocked, and one of the men remarks, "Tryin' to brand him, Ruby?" Boake then smiles privately, as the shot dissolves.

Clearly, Ruby is blamed here for being attractive and provocative, and for scratching Boake in a gesture that they can only interpret as wild, "feminine" contradictoriness. No one, of course, sees Boake's gesture that provokes Ruby's response. Her Old Testament-spouting brother takes the hardest line, with the reproach that Ruby is "invitin' damnation to [her] soul."

Boake does take Ruby for granted; he will not recognize that she is as much a sovereign individual as any man. When they go hunting they fire at a deer simultaneously, and when they reach the dead animal Boake says proudly, "It's the best shot I ever made!" His egocentricity is staggering. Ruby's flat response is, "Naturally, I missed." She had sent the doctor off on his own hunt trail as quickly as possible in order to be with Boake now, and yet he complains that she took too long about it and he "won't be kept waiting." We hear her yearning, pained reply, although Boake does not even seem to notice that she is speaking: "I've done some waiting! Bo, you don't know!" The film is very direct about Boake's chauvinism. When he says, "You can have South America. You can have the whole world. But *this* is for me!" Ruby asks the very question to which we are afraid to hear the answer. What, specifically, does he mean by "this"? It is almost certain that "this" is not the same thing for Ruby as it is for him. Without a trace of irony or tongue-in-cheek, he replies, "Real country liquor, tidewater cooking, and North Carolina women. I've always said, there's nothing like a dame!" Ruby of course is not "North Carolina women" nor, as she points out, a "dame," but his reply is only, "Why don't you *give up*, Ruby!"

There are several scenes like this in the film. It does not occur to Boake, for example, to open the car door for Ruby ("I hope you noticed, you got a gal who can open a door all by herself," she says to him), and when they listen, late one night, to the sound of the pump that is draining the flooded field, Ruby remarks that it sounds like a big heart beating, Boake says, "It is. It's *my* heart!" Ruby has every right to ask the question which it seems Boake will never consider—"*What about me?*"

Leo Bersani has observed that, "from the man's point of view, the only way in which the woman can be reduced is not by a change in her identity, but rather by her *enslavement to the male version of her difference.*"[57] Boake decides to stake Ruby's difference from him on the notion of "a man's work." "Do you really think you can compete with a man's work?" he says derisively. Women (Tracy, Letitia) are essentially passive; they live *through* men, who work. Boake is suggesting that a man's work is more important to him than anything else in the world, that a man's identity derives from his work. Certainly, when Ruby resolves to take her revenge on Boake, Saul believes her mistake to be that she never understood that "a man and his dreams, a man and his work are one and the same." Ruby does finally understand, which is precisely why she floods Boake's field. She wants revenge, and knows how best to exact it, even though she still loves Boake—her love now being indistinguishable from hatred.

On some level Boake and Ruby are not distinguishable enough, one from the other—not the way Boake and Tracy are. Difference is clearly marked there. The universe of the melodrama depends on clearly legible differences on all levels. It is a world of binary structures: men and women, masculine and feminine, the "right" side and the "wrong" side of the tracks, North and South, dry land and water, brother and sister, work and love (action and passion), material wealth and poverty. After showing how these structures can be crippling and frustrating, however, *Ruby Gentry* shows some frightful consequences of any merging of opposites. Ruby's androgyny, her moving across class lines, Boake's implicitly "Northern" ideas about

---

[57] Leo Bersani, *A Future for Astyanax: Character and Desire in Literature* (Boston: Little, Brown & Co., 1976), 296.

agricultural redevelopment, Jewel Cory's incestuous obsession with his sister, Ruby's sudden access to great material wealth, her attempt to make Boake love her as much as he loves his "work," all contribute to the breakdown of the moral order which the film criticizes and— finding no alternative—must reinstate.

The swamp is the logical place for the final unraveling of codes. After Jim drowns in a boating accident and Ruby, now the richest person in Braddock, is accused of murder (even by Boake), Ruby takes magnificent revenge. Dressed with severe elegance, wearing black sunglasses, gloves, stylish hats, and puffing on a cigarette, she sets about destroying every man in Braddock who has ever humiliated her. When she floods the field Boake has struggled for so long to reclaim, she throws herself finally into a dizzy orbit.

Ruby and Boake go for an inexplicable "hunt" in the swamp at night (all logic reversed). They embrace with weird passion; it is not clear whether Boake is strangling Ruby or not. When Boake asks Ruby if she is afraid, and she asks, "Of what?" he says, "Of me—the kind of man I am now." He has, quite possibly, lost all reason. If she has destroyed his bid for identity, what "kind of man" is he now? That Ruby's brother Jewel should fire the shot that kills Boake (and that Ruby kills Jewel) has its own logic. Ruby and Boake are an equal match; she has already destroyed him, and she must live to suffer in the knowledge of what she has done. What she has done, though, is not the evil in the story. The real source of evil in this story, as the "moral occult" locates it, is a wrong identification of evil, given voice to by Jewel moments before Ruby shoots him and kicks his dead body into the swampy water: "Woman is the very root of wickedness . . . in her beauty, a snare!"

Ruby's last words to Boake are the most urgently spoken words of her life: "Say you love me! Boake, say you love me!" If he would only say those words, and mean them, Ruby could at last see herself, and if Boake could say the words, he would not be trying to kill her now. The concluding voice-over narration ("Yes, Ruby Gentry was born on the wrong side of the tracks, and the people of Braddock never let her forget it!") is, we appreciate, inadequate, but it does not matter. Ruby's story, as we have seen and heard it, tells the more complex truth, which is still not settled, as signified by the fact that Ruby, piloting her own boat, does not live on dry land (in Braddock), nor has she joined Jim and Boake beneath the water or in the swamp.

Vidor and the Social Discourse:
Provisional Conclusions

The social discourse in the American melodrama as we see it in the Vidor films does not dominate for long. The prime reasons, no doubt, are the entertainment values of the American film industry, and the optimistic nature of the American Dream.

While audiences may have been impressed by the dignity and vigor of such films as *The Crowd* and *Our Daily Bread*, on the whole they would not put their faith in a spirit of community. And if Americans, as we see them in the movies, were at first a little baffled by the nature of mass society, it did not take them long to find ways to combat some of its alienating effects. In true melodramatic fashion, the melodrama reduced the problem to smaller, more manageable terms: nineteenth-century ideologies of individualism were refashioned to fit the new conditions, and the terms once again became decidedly familial.

In *The Crowd* Vidor finds that he (or the form—melodrama) is not equipped to make American capitalism visible for what it is. The forces that oppress John Sims cannot be satisfactorily figured in the narrative terms of the Hollywood melodrama. The film is ambivalent about the class positions it expresses, because it inadequately comprehends mass society. (This mass society, we are learning, is not a classless society.)[58] The film attempts to find answers for contradictions but experiences some difficulty in this because the narrator will not erect straw villains. It vacillates between modes. Melodrama is the one mode, and the other is Vidor's own: a peculiar combination of the "political," an expressionistic-documentary style, and an aspiration toward some sort of transgeneric purity (which the MGM production values perhaps serve).

Stella Dallas is a story that attempts to grapple with issues of social class, but it translates them into personal terms. There is some confusion in the translation as an effort is made, on the one hand, to make it appear that Stella's problems are her own fault (her taste in clothes seems wilfully outrageous; she will not modify some of her vulgar mannerisms in order to keep Stephen), and on the other

[58] Cf. Fredric Jameson, "Class and Allegory in Contemporary Mass Culture: *Dog Day Afternoon* as a Political Film" 1977; reprinted in *Movies and Methods II*, ed. Bill Nichols (Berkeley and Los Angeles: University of California Press, 1985), 715–33.

hand, to suggest that she is representative of a class (the great majority of the American movie-going public), and, moreover, suffers difficulties because she is a woman in a man's world.

The class system that is produced by capitalism, which divides the world inevitably into the haves and the have-nots, seems in Vidor's later films to be implicated in the sources of our eroticism. Ruby Gentry may be from the wrong side of the tracks, but she is the sexiest figure in the movie, and she is probably so (like Stella Martin/Dallas) *because* she is from the wrong side of the tracks: her social origins have determined her aggressive-passive volatility, and her ambition is contrasted with the paralysis of an exhausted Southern aristocracy (which represses female sexuality).

The Hollywood cinema is a cinema of vivid storytelling, and a film's narrative flow is helped immensely if the story's moral outlines are clear. The social discourse, in short, is (for the "moral occult") too complicated ever to be very popular in the commercial cinema; the American film melodrama rarely finds imaginative alternatives to the bourgeois-capitalist system which—in spite of all the miseries it has produced—is so obviously bound up with America's economic success and great vitality as a culture. Americans like to think that theirs is a classless society, or that American society aspires to classlessness. However, there is evidence everywhere that America is deeply class-ridden, and one of the problems is that rich people tend to be more fascinating subjects for films, and villains are always more exciting than figures of virtue. Consequently, Hollywood has always been ambivalent in its attitude towards class issues. The critique of upper-class behavior and upper-class milieux is invariably confused with their celebration. Usually, poor people are no fun, unless they are funny (which explains why the social content of comedies can be so high, as almost any Chaplin film shows), and class issues are hard to handle in a country that does not like to admit that there is a class system.

The melodrama discovered a long time ago, however (long before the cinema), what the contradictions inherent in the social discourse are. In *The Factory Lad*, for example, an English stage melodrama written in 1832 by John Walker, a factory owner is forced by the realities of industrial progress to make an unpopular decision. He embraces the law of supply and demand by resolving to propel his looms by steam, which will render half of his work force unnecessary to him.

He is not inherently an evil man, and yet we know that if he does not make the switch to steam-driven looms he will lose in the competition for profits, and then all his workers will be out of a job. Capitalism produces impossibilities of this sort, with which ordinary men—and the melodramatic form—cannot usually cope. The response is not reasoned, but emotional: the only aesthetic, textual solution in melodrama's terms is to make the factory owner a villain.

In the sexual discourse the terms are more immediate and visceral than they are in the social discourse, but we cannot say that the social discourse is just left behind, or abandoned for this reason. It is, rather, incorporated into a psycho-sexual discourse. In America, as far as Hollywood is concerned, entertainment and utopia are the terms, not analysis, plausibility, facts, and history—which explains why the social discourse as we see it in *The Crowd* must give way to something else. It gives way to a more sentimental vein in *Stella Dallas*, and to an erotic one in *Ruby Gentry*. Class conflict must be *figurable*, but the figuration must not seem facile or outdated; this is melodrama's challenge, and it is why the form's syntactic dimension changes constantly.[59]

Unlike the musical or the comedy, the melodrama (to the extent that it is constrained by its own generic tradition) generally does not find release for the contradictions inherent in social material in dance numbers, dream sequences, songs, or comic business. The mise en scène, we have said, and a certain use of music, have been the main formal areas in which we see the marks of excess in the melodrama. As for the represented object, it was not to be explicitly the complications of capitalism and class for very long. Even in its heyday as the studio most identified in the 1930s with themes of social consciousness, Warner Brothers, we know, produced films that demonstrated both "a gritty feel for social realism and a *total inability to give any coherent reasons for social difficulties.*"[60] Where it might have given coherent reasons for social difficulties, the Hollywood cinema did not, for it has always been dominated by the entertainment values of an industry that depends on mass public approval—approval that is

---

[59] Television soap operas, prime-time serials, and special mini-series are fascinating for this reason. They are watched avidly for their topicality. They offer an absolutely up-to-the-minute report on the "moral occult" according to the texts of popular culture.

[60] Bergman, *We're in the Money*, 92. (Emphasis added.)

given, usually, to movies that affirm the optimism of the American Dream. As a medium that would seem to be very much attracted to the *body*, to surfaces and to things, the cinema could not help but tap an erotics of vision, that led the family melodrama away from what I have been calling the social discourse, towards a psychoanalytic (which is to say, sexual) discourse.

8. Vincente Minnelli

15. Minnelli (right) with Van Heflin on the set of
Madame Bovary.

VINCENTE Minnelli's melodramas, more than Griffith's or Vidor's, resonate with the logic of Eric Bentley's dictum that "melodrama is the Naturalism of the dream life."[1] The film melodrama, whatever its excesses, is rooted in realism, but of course it is Hollywood realism, and within that tradition there is a discernible hyperreal "look" to the MGM film, which Minnelli's style typifies. It is a heightened realism that explicitly approaches artificiality in its lavish production values. The stylizations achieved through CinemaScope and Technicolor,[2] for example, and expensive attention to costumes and set decoration, elaborate lighting schemes and camera movements, give the MGM/Minnelli movie a brilliant sheen which in the melodrama somehow contradicts the often "everyday reality" of the represented milieu.

It has become a commonplace observation that Minnelli's most persistent theme is the relationship between dreams and reality.[3] Art and life, imaginary and real worlds meet, parallel each other, substitute for each other. There is something postmodern, even, in the implicit epistemology of Minnelli's approach to the cinema: for him, the cinema is not "about" or "reflective of" life; rather it is about and reflective of cinema. Life exists in the image; there lie its truths, in the "dream life," which is a realm organized largely in images. Although the dialogue is often very good in Minnelli's melodramas, it is the mise en scène, the decor, that usually tells us what we need to know.

Minnelli's remark about *An American in Paris* (1951)—"I was determined that this would have to be a story of emotions rather than an actual story, you know"[4]—speaks for almost all of his films, and most especially the melodramas. What he means by "an actual story" is a story that must conform to the requirements of realism—plausibility and the *vraisemblable*. The musicals, obviously, are the most free to depart from realism's anchors, but the conventions of the melodrama develop to such a sophisticated degree by the late 1940s and 1950s

[1] Eric Bentley, *The Life of the Drama* (New York: Atheneum, 1967), 205.

[2] From his third film onwards (*Meet Me in St. Louis*, 1944), most of Minnelli's films were shot in Technicolor or Metrocolor. All of his films from *Brigadoon* (1954) through *A Matter of Time* (1976) were filmed in CinemaScope or Panavision, and all of his films, except for the last two and *Goodbye, Charlie* (1964), were made for MGM.

[3] François Guérif, *Vincente Minnelli* (Paris: Edilig, 1984), 16.

[4] Vincente Minnelli, with Hector Arce, *I Remember It Well* (Garden City, N.Y.: Doubleday, 1974), 255.

that a hyperreality, a stylized "Naturalism of the dream life," makes the genre look more than ever like its cousin, the musical.

Where the musical is inherently an "up" and "happy" form, the Eisenhower-era melodrama, as D. N. Rodowick observes, is "plagued by fears of the internal subversion of its ideologies," seen in "the inability of the melodramatic text to evolve as either a fully affirmative or fully subversive form. Split between madness and authority."[5] These terms, madness and authority, are the sinister counterpart of other terms that are used throughout this study: the Imaginary and the Symbolic. In the more benign terms that Minnelli himself would probably use—dream and reality—we see the correspondence as well. And to push the link still further, into ideological terms, we see that sometimes in Minnelli's movies it is felt instinctively that hope for a better world will come out of madness,[6] dreams, the Imaginary—those realms traditionally signified in our culture by woman, or the "feminine" position. The so-called "feminine" streak in Minnelli as an auteur finds its most consistent expression in a love of objects, of beauty (in decor, clothes, color, etc.). The number of dream sequences, ballets, camera movements, characters who are artists or in pursuit of a dream, are a testament to the attraction Minnelli feels towards the "dream life."

Minnelli evidently admires the figure of the artist, who can, or at least attempts to, combine his or her life and dreams in a continuum (Jonathan Shields in *The Bad and the Beautiful* (1952), Van Gogh in *Lust for Life* (1956), Laura Reynolds in *The Sandpiper* (1965), or less successfully, Emma in *Madame Bovary*, and Dave Hirsh in *Some Came Running*). To find that space, somewhere between madness and authority, between the Imaginary and the Symbolic, between (in the narrator's words in *Madame Bovary*) "one kind of dream, and another kind of life," is the central passion of several Minnelli protagonists.

There is between the home and the world (or desire and discipline,

---

[5] D. N. Rodowick, "Madness, Authority, and Ideology in the Domestic Melodrama of the 1950's," *The Velvet Light Trap* 19 (1982): 45.

[6] As Minnelli says in his autobiography on the subject of *An American in Paris* and cinematographer John Alton: "I knew he'd approach the light changes in the ballet with the boldness—and the madness—that was needed." (*I Remember It Well*, 241.) And Joel Siegel makes a mysterious remark in praise of *The Pirate*: it is the closest Minnelli has ever come to realizing "the abstract, deeply personal world of whirling forms and colors which seem to haunt the best and the worst of his films." (Quoted by Minnelli, *I Remember It Well*, 192.)

or play and work) a split that Minnelli is concerned to narrow. As a Hollywood filmmaker, himself in the business of "working" to create fantasy worlds, Minnelli is peculiarly in a position to believe that this is possible, which accounts for the returning element of self-reflexivity in his movies—movies about filmmaking, about the theater world on Broadway, about artists, about characters whose imaginations are fed by media-fabricated images, and so on. Whether or not this fusion of one's work with one's "life" is possible only for men, or sometimes for men and never for women, is the question that cannot be left alone. In *The Bad and the Beautiful* the wife of Jim, the screenwriter on Jonathan's picture, says to Jonathan after the couple have spent two weeks in Hollywood, "Thank you, Mr. Shields, it was wonderful fun. I like being a successful author's wife. It took me a long time to learn the secret: his work comes first!" This is the same ideology we hear in Vidor's *Ruby Gentry* (Boake Tackman's "work" comes before anything Ruby represents), and from Gwen French in *Some Came Running*. Gwen advocates work first: Dave is to write books, not make love to her. And in *The Bad and the Beautiful* when the screenwriter's wife is killed in an airplane crash, work is the only means through which Jonathan believes his grieving screenwriter will recover: "Let's get to work, you and I," he tells him.

Dream/fantasy spaces appear easily in the musical; they require little justification owing to the peculiar conventions of the form. Sometimes the dream-reality tension-affinity is kept well within a realist framework, but more often in the musical fantastic scenes become the diegetic "reality," as when Judy Garland imagines her hero in *The Pirate* (1948), or Gene Kelly's fantasy of himself and Leslie Caron in *An American in Paris* ends the movie on seventeen delirious, balletic minutes. These scenes, to repeat Metz's observation about the cinema generally, have an imaginary, that is, perfectly *real* power.

In Minnelli's first melodrama, *Undercurrent* (1946), the textual presence of the unconscious, the very source of any melodrama's peculiar power, is couched in Gothic terms. A man appears everywhere to be alive, but he is not *seen*—in fantasy or in the "fact" of the diegetically "real"—because he is supposedly dead. Alan (Robert Taylor) accuses Ann (Katharine Hepburn) of being in love with his "dead" brother Michael, to which she protests, "No! How could I be in love with someone I've never seen?" He answers with a logic that all melodramas depend on: "Why not? You've seen a lot of Mike: a book, a poem, his house, a girl who once loved him." Minnelli's style, primarily a visual one, observes this way of producing information—in the things around and of a character. Of course all filmmakers must do this, but Minnelli seems particularly to relish giving proof in the visual. In *The Bad and the Beautiful*, when Jim complains that Jonathan has cut some dialogue in a scene, Jonathan says "she doesn't speak. We move in the camera close . . . she opens her mouth to talk . . . but she can't. She's too emotional to be able to speak. And what she's feeling, we'll leave for the audience to imagine. Believe me, Jim, they'll imagine it better than any words you and I could ever write."

This assertion of Jonathan's, while no doubt true as Jonathan means it to be understood, just for a moment returns us to Luce Irigaray's questions in response to Lacan's assertion that all you have to do is "go look at Bernini's statue in Rome, you'll see right away that St. Theresa is coming, there's no doubt about it." *What*, indeed, will this character that Jonathan and Jim have created be feeling? She is silenced, but all the signifiers around her will tell the audience—will make the audience imagine—what she is feeling. As a character within a fictional world of characters, her existence underscores a truth about the speech of woman: that it is given to her by men. Even her silences are legible in a specific register, determined by men. Or is there hope in such a space, such a silence, for the indescribable—that which escapes (masculine) language? The desire, the aspiration, is beyond language, whether or not we can say it is not-masculine. "The truth," as Flaubert writes in *Madame Bovary*, is that

fullness of soul can sometimes overflow in utter vapidity of language, for none of us can ever express the exact measure of his needs or his thoughts or his sorrows; and human speech is like a cracked kettle on which we tap crude rhythms for bears to dance to, while we long to make music that will melt the stars.[7]

In the cathartic climax that Minnelli excels in producing, perhaps a truth is released, for whenever some logic is brought to breaking point, the terms of that logic can suddenly become starkly clear. As the Kirk Douglas character says in *Two Weeks in Another Town* (1962) after that film's most climactic scene: "Well, *now* we know!" Unlike the musical, which can explode in scenes of singing and dancing, the

[7] Gustave Flaubert, *Madame Bovary*, trans. Francis Steegmuller (New York: Random House, 1957), 216.

melodrama, with its roots in realism, must find other ways to release the energies produced by the terms of the form. In Minnelli's hands, returning repressions produced by the familial terms of the melodrama appear primarily in decor, but in a climax such as the one in *The Bad and the Beautiful*, the release comes in vivid cutting and music, with Lana Turner driving in an hysterical frenzy in the pouring rain after she learns that her mentor has taken up with another woman. The outrageous commandeering of the natural world to speak human states is typical of the melodrama, but the metaphoricization of the natural world—its inscription in emotional terms for human purposes—is rarely so spectacular and outrageous in realist cinema as in Minnelli's melodramas. In *Some Came Running* the climax occurs in the carnival scene where Raymond drunkenly pushes his way through the crowd, past flashing lights and brilliantly colored surfaces, with a pounding, discordant music on the soundtrack, before shooting at Dave Hirsh and killing Ginny Moorehead. The hunt in *Home from the Hill* and the waltz at Vaubyessard in *Madame Bovary* are kept more or less within Hollywood's rather flexible standards of realism for the melodrama, but Minnelli supercharges them.

The crisis expressed in the climactic scene is one of personal identity, always. Across the three Minnelli films under examination we see an increasing emphasis on stark Oedipal struggles between characters, with social factors subsumed under Oedipal logic. While social and economic factors still inflect the destinies of the main female characters (Emma Bovary in *Madame Bovary*, Ginny Moorehead and Gwen French in *Some Came Running*, Hannah Hunnicutt in *Home from the Hill*), a sexual logic charges the conflicts in their lives, as is the case of the male characters also (Dave Hirsh and Bama Dillert in *Some Came Running*, Wade Hunnicutt, Rafe and Theron in *Home from the Hill*).

In *Madame Bovary* Minnelli's treatment of Flaubert's novel is not unlike the psychoanalytic session in its re-inscription of a story in discourses not available to those characters involved. Living through men, seeking an identity through them, is the choice Emma Bovary makes; it is shown to fail. The film suggests on the one hand that if only Emma had found the right man, the man worthy of her love, she would have been happy. On the other hand, it is suggested that Emma's struggle for control over her life, her efforts to gain an identity that does not erase her, will never be achieved through a man. Female subjectivity under the patriarchy in which Emma lives cannot be realized, and in Emma's case no conventional compromise is achieved, for she kills herself. Before her death, in a final, desperate attempt to enter the economy of desire, of exchange—in a curious literalization, that of circulating money—Emma is denied the money she so desperately needs by all the men whom she approaches for it. The "hom(m)o-sexual" principle of the socio-cultural order in which Emma Bovary is inscribed determines that she can as a woman never be anything other than a commodity in its exchanges.

Some Came Running presents a microcosm of American bourgeois society at its most oppressive. The social determinants of earlier melodramas have become too difficult for the form to handle, and *Some Came Running*, though highly critical of bourgeois society in general, largely puts the blame on women. The film divides its characters between those who are of and in respectable bourgeois society, and those who are outside it. The struggle for a compromise or synthesis of the different social and sexual positions which the two women (Gwen French and Ginny Moorehead) represent takes place within the character of Dave Hirsh, who is attracted to both. On the masculine side, Dave's friend Bama Dillert is one extreme reflection/projection of Dave's character, and his brother Frank is the other. The impossible struggle of opposing forces and interests is resolved in the end, and can only be resolved, by the death of one of the women, Ginny Moorehead, returning Dave to his bourgeois inheritance.

In *Home from the Hill* the question of legitimacy and paternal legacy underlies Rafe's and Theron's search for a satisfactory identity within the family and bourgeois society. The film is concerned with what it means to be a man in bourgeois patriarchal society, and is concerned therefore with the moral authority of the patriarch, Wade Hunnicutt, who does not recognize his illegitimate son Rafe, and who has "given up" his legitimate son Theron to his wife Hannah. Rafe, the masculine son, seeks a legitimization of his identity which his father's recognition will confer, and Theron, the "mama's boy," seeks a masculine identity which his father can teach him. The film thrashes out one of melodrama's big concerns: the putting right of the moral order, signified in family relations, for the perpetuation of the patriarchy.

What a Woman Really Wants, or What She Really Means:
Madame Bovary

By 1949, the year *Madame Bovary* was released, a more acutely psychoanalytic understanding of the world is being reflected in the fictions of Hollywood cinema, as much in movies from directors who started in the silent era as from younger directors, like Vincente Minnelli, who is really a generation removed from the likes of King Vidor and two generations away from Griffith. The dozens of psychological thrillers that we now call *films noirs* that were made in the 1940s represent the psychoanalytic vision in its most paranoid, sexualized manifestation, but in almost every film genre individual psychology and a keener awareness of sexuality and of how human subjects are shaped by class, gender, childhood, the familial context, the media—in short, ideology—is better understood. The melodrama of moral simplicity disappears as the many factors that shape human destiny emerge more distinctly from the shadowy regions of a fate that once knew only right from wrong, God's hand, luck, and not much else.

Minnelli's *Madame Bovary* is really about the insidious dangers of the melodrama—about a woman who "waits for experience to duplicate literature, unaware of the fact that literature didn't duplicate life in the first place."[8] As in *Stella Dallas*, the heroine struggles against the pressures of social prejudice and class, but the biggest obstacle to her happiness is her blindness to the fact that life and romantic fictions about life differ significantly. Emma's not unreasonable desire for vivid experience, for a keenly lived life, is made by those around her to seem frenzied and extreme in proportion as her desire is thwarted. But her desire is doomed to be thwarted because it is not tempered by imaginative compromise. She is, as Leo Bersani observes, "finally crushed by the weight of an insubstantial imagination which has been unable to discharge itself of its fables, which has never found a world."[9]

Even as a young girl, she harbors "ridiculous dreams of high romance and impossible love."[10] But like Flaubert, Minnelli does not

[8] Leo Bersani on the Emma Bovary of the novel, in *A Future for Astyanax: Character and Desire in Literature* (Boston: Little, Brown & Co., 1976), 96.

[9] Ibid., 98–99.

[10] These are Flaubert's words, during the courtroom defense of his book. References to Flaubert, unless otherwise indicated, are to the character played by James Mason in

blame Emma for her actions. The whole point of *Madame Bovary* is a melodramatic one: to show Emma's struggle against the world, to try to come to grips with why she suffers, to gauge the validity of her desire, to learn the lesson her story offers, and, in Flaubert's words, to discover what her dreams are made of, where they come from, and how this "kitchen drudge who had dreamed of love and beauty," this "flower beyond the dunghill," had grown here, in a place not worthy of her. Near the end, unhappy and defeated, Emma asks helplessly, quietly, as if to the universe and in no expectation of an answer, "There's not something wrong with things being beautiful, is there?" The melodrama of *Madame Bovary* seeks to understand how Emma comes to ask such a question, and tries to answer it.

Minnelli collapses Emma's aspirations into a quest for beauty, a physical beauty of fine clothes and richly furnished houses, but this attains a metaphorical dimension, since we see how she loves to laugh, to love, to dance—in effect, to heighten her experience of life through all her senses, which in sad irony the priest at her deathbed asks God to pardon. "May the Lord pardon all the sins that you have committed through the sense of hearing. . . . May the Lord pardon all the sins that you have committed through the sense of sight," and so on. The priest lists the five senses in this manner, driving home for the viewer the tragedy of Emma's fate, since any sins she may have committed through her senses have been made to seem inevitable, forced by the pressure of her destiny, which has been articulated in terms of melodrama.

Emma's destiny is established as a destiny by the film's first image, of the book *Madame Bovary* by Gustave Flaubert. The book (Emma, her story) is on trial literally and figuratively in this trope made possible by filmic adaptation and putting a fiction within a fiction. The effect is to seal Emma Bovary's destiny before it begins, which quintessentially speaks the melodramatic understanding of existence, in which the world is a theater and we are all characters who play out our parts in it. As Charles says in the novel, when Emma's story is finished and she is dead: "Fate willed it this way."

The Public Prosecutor in the case against Flaubert and *Madame Bovary* (the book which the James Mason Flaubert will defend) holds

---

the film, just as quoted dialogue is from the film, not the original Flaubert and his book on which the film is based.

the book aloft and shakes it in a gesture of outrage, demanding that its author be found guilty of "committing the misdemeanor of an outrage against public morals and established custom." Emma Bovary, this character created by Flaubert, "is at once a disgrace to France and an insult to womanhood." As the representative of "public morals and established custom," the prosecutor cannot understand "this woman of insatiable passions, this monstrous creation of a degenerate imagination." She is an enigma; there is no way to explain why she is the way she is. As a modern melodrama about a past time, however, the film can inscribe Emma in a different language and can present her in a light by which poor Charles Bovary, for one, will never see her. Flaubert will go back to the time when Emma Rouault was in school, and piece by piece describe her development, her construction as a human subject and how and why her story turns out the way it does—from Emma Rouault to "Madame Bovary"—in much the same way that Vidor describes how Stella Martin becomes "Stella Dallas."

Like the intertitles of so many silent films, Flaubert's intermittent narration tells us what to think, or at least to consider the moral complexity of the story we are about to hear, and not be too quick to cast blame. Minnelli has Flaubert tell the courtroom (us, the audience watching the film) that while he has shown them "the vicious," he did so "for the sake of understanding it so that we may preserve the virtuous." And while Emma may be monstrous, "it was not I who created her. Our world—your world and mine—created her, as I shall attempt to demonstrate." The book is rather more complex and oblique in its laying of blame for Emma's fate, and ends with the striking report on the pharmacist Homais' progress towards his much-coveted award of the Legion of Honor. Implicitly, it is this kind of man—the ambitious, self-satisfied bourgeois, with some education and the power of printed language at his command, the man of pseudo-science and vanity, the pursuer of fraudulent values—who is really to blame. The film, however, is more explicit in identifying the origins of Emma's misfortunes, and it makes clear its melodramatic purpose beyond that of entertaining us.

Minnelli's *Madame Bovary* identifies itself as a melodrama in its differences from classical tragedy. As Jacques Goimard notes,[11] classical

[11] Jacques Goimard, "Le Mélodrame: le mot et la chose," *Les Cahiers de la cinémathèque* 28 (1979): 17–65.

(French) tragedy is an art for the elite and one that for all its majestic distancing is easy to read and stage anywhere, being dependent less on mise en scène (on decor, music, dance, or photogeny and gesture) than on action generally reduced to its simplest expression. The text of classical tragedy is sacralized and given a life of its own by virtue of its stylized diction, and the interest tends to be focused on states of the soul, to the near exclusion of *"jeux de scène."* The classical tragedy, unlike the melodrama, keeps a consistent tone and has its principal characters hesitate among the several roles or choices that their situation presents to them.

Already we can see, from this incomplete list of the traits of classical tragedy, how modern, or melodramatic, the treatment of Emma Bovary's tragedy is. The film depends heavily on mise en scène and *jeux de scène* for its meanings, and harsh truths are represented not in the stylized diction of moral distillations but in realism's detailed and episodic profusion. Emma does not hesitate before an array of choices; her only choice is whether to die of ennui, or fight it, whether to live or not to live with a consuming sense of unappeased desire—which is no choice at all. She has no flaw in her character which causes her downfall after a great many torments of (in)decision and choice, as it is observed the tragic hero does. Hers is not a question of internal moral dilemmas, but of survival: Emma versus the world, not Emma versus Emma. While tragedy has a predilection for subjects taken from historical and literary traditions and retains the unifying control and tone of a single author, melodrama does not, as Minnelli's *Madame Bovary* shows in true Hollywood fashion. Flaubert points out and describes the function of his melodrama when he says to the court,

There are thousands of Emma Bovarys. I had only to draw from life. And there are hundreds and thousands of women who wish they were Emma Bovary, and who have been saved from her fate not by virtue, but simply by lack of determination!

Her story is meant to apply like a lesson to our lives. The audience is encouraged to see itself in her.

While Emma is like many women, however, she is exceptional. She has determination, but she is also driven by forces over which mortal control is scarcely possible. Emma will not accept the impossible gap ideology posits between the idea (the ideal) and the reality. As Flaubert says more than once in his voice-over narration, there is "one kind of dream, and another kind of life." With Emma, "the dream did not end. She had learned to be a woman for whom experience would always be a prison and freedom would lie always beyond the horizon." This belief in the dream is at the heart of the melodramatic impulse, at the heart, indeed, of most cinema.[12] When Flaubert says that "in Emma there was a terrifying capacity for pursuing the impossible," he is describing that will to *realize* the dream, which Emma—surrounded by poverty, ugliness and mediocrity—*must* attempt.

How did "our world" create her? The camera pans right, from Emma in her room in the rude farmhouse where she lives with her father, to a wall she has covered with pictures and illustrations from magazines and books, which Flaubert's voice-over tells us "had taught her that the strange was beautiful, and the familiar contemptible."

Unlike so many melodramas of an earlier type, *Madame Bovary* presents a victim who is not merely passive and virtuous but seen, rather, to be implicated in her own undoing even as she is clearly still a victim. The villain is no longer a man who twirls his mustaches, but is in "our world," which includes the lying promises of our fantasies. More fully and explicitly than *The Crowd* or *Stella Dallas*, *Madame Bovary* develops this awareness of ideological effects in the construction of the human subject—of the influence of narratives and images (the media) in making people what they are. Flaubert's trial and his voice-over commentary directly address the melodrama's increased sense of responsibility to locate and define causes more precisely.

Her dreams animate Emma and make her charming, vivacious, seductive, selfish and capricious. When after their wedding Charles brings her to Yonville where they are to live, Emma exclaims, "It's like a picture in a story book!" which of course very quickly it will cease to be for her. She wants theirs to be a storybook existence in Yonville. Of course Charles had told Emma about the town—in terms she chose to interpret as glowing—in his effort to persuade her to marry him. "Yonville!" she says in her breathy, romantically in-

---

[12] It is, fittingly, the main theme of Minnelli's last film, *A Matter of Time* (1976). In that film the dream sustains the contessa in her solitary old age, and it launches the young girl on a magnificent life of adventure and beauty. In a sense, *A Matter of Time* is Minnelli's dream wish-fulfillment for films like *Madame Bovary*; it is the story of how one might wish things to have turned out for poor Emma.

flected voice, "It sounds like Heaven! Tell me all about it again!" What we had in fact heard Charles say on the subject of Yonville was banal in the extreme, and it is no surprise that he feels compelled, at her intense responses, to remark that he is easy to get along with and will make a good husband, but "I'm . . . I'm . . . not very exciting."

During the early hours of the morning following their wedding night Emma weeps while Charles sleeps, but she rallies when Charles awakens, and she promises with fervor and wishful intensity to make him "the most beautiful home in Yonville—this side of Rouen! This side of Paris! . . . I will, I will. I'll give you a home you can be proud of. We'll be gay. We'll entertain."

To judge by Flaubert's defense of Emma in court, Emma's tears the morning after her marriage to Charles Bovary could not have been "otherwise." Even if Emma were a "normal" woman and had not so much "determination," she would have felt a keen disappointment at the reality of married life, no doubt of her first experience of sex itself, of the shabby room in the cold light of early morning. Emma is deluded by what she has read and the pictures she has seen, just as Stella Dallas is.

And yet the cinema by the 1940s sympathizes with her and appreciates her predicament. After all, the cinema is in the business—one of the most expensive and extravagant in the history of representation—of creating fantasy worlds, of providing the very sort of escape to which Emma is so susceptible. The cinema is quite aware by this time of its ideological power, even though its commitments are first to profits and entertainment. This growing awareness of how ideology functions finds its best expression in the influence of psychoanalysis on the cinema—both implicitly, in how stories are told, and sometimes explicitly, as in Hitchcock's *Spellbound* (1945). As psychoanalyst Dr. Constance Petersen (played by Ingrid Bergman) in that movie says to John Ballantine (played by Gregory Peck), "I think the greatest harm done to the human race has been done by the poets. . . . Why, they keep filling people's heads with delusions about love—writing about it as if it were a symphony orchestra, a flight of angels. . . ." Half humoring the cerebral but beautiful woman, Ballantine eggs her on: "Which it isn't, eh?" "Of course not!" she asserts, "People 'fall in love,' as they put it, because they respond to certain hair colors, or vocal tones, or mannerisms that remind them of their parents." ("Or sometimes for no reason at all,"

Ballantine interjects.) "Oh, that's not the point. The point is that people read about love as one thing and experience it as another."

While Hitchcock wanted fantasy in *Spellbound* to be kept to a minimum and to "use a logical approach to the man's adventure,"[13] the film does treat love "as if it were a symphony orchestra," in Miklos Rozsa's score especially. Narrative cinema almost cannot help itself from melodramatizing and romanticizing, which is how love itself works (willingly misrecognizing the other) and is what Emma Bovary does with life. The question of who has the more valid approach to life and "love"—Dr. Petersen in *Spellbound*, or Emma in *Madame Bovary*—becomes valid because, after all, Dr. Petersen does fall in love with John Ballantine (responses to certain vocal tones? mannerisms?), and Emma falls in love with a fantasy Prince Charming. Gregory Peck can fit the bill for Dr. Petersen, and for us, but Van Heflin is "only a man," which is to say he falls short of Emma's ideal, although Emma is unwilling at first to recognize this. Emma marries Charles Bovary to escape the farm and in the vague but urgent hope for a better life through him.

Curiously, Emma is "motherless," although nothing beyond its mention is made of the fact.[14] We are meant to understand, perhaps, that without a mother's presence, as a model, Emma as a child gains an imperfect sense of just how constrained the feminine position under patriarchy must be. Any child, of course, will believe that his or her powerlessness is a function of being a child in an adult world, but while Emma probably interprets childhood (its aspects of dependency and thwarted desire) as a *female* condition (with her father representing the masculine, *adult* condition), she no doubt believes on some level that adulthood will release her from the (maternal) authority of the convent and the gender-determined chores she must perform on the farm. As Dorothy Dinnerstein has observed, "Male authority carries the breath of the rationally controllable world, the world that the child—even, in a qualified way, the girl child—looks

---

[13] François Truffaut, *Hitchcock* (New York: Simon and Schuster, 1967), 119.

[14] Cf. the chapter on *East Lynne* (novel, stage, and film versions) in E. Ann Kaplan's forthcoming *Motherhood and Representation* (New York: Methuen). Kaplan identifies the reason for Lady Isabel's unfortunate attraction to the villain Levison in terms of a loss of the "maternal function." In losing her mother, Isabel loses and is driven to experience again a "passionate, merged feeling" that Kaplan identifies in the maternal relation. Perhaps Emma is driven by this same desire.

forward to being part of when it becomes an adult."[15] Emma's father may be only a peasant farmer, but, to borrow Dinnerstein's words, "even if his work in the world is menial, he has the status of a participant in history, because he is above female authority: he has identity outside the immediate family circle. *So the essential fact about paternal authority, the fact that makes both sexes accept it as a model for the ruling of the world, is that it is under prevailing conditions a sanctuary from maternal authority."*[16]

Emma may have grown up "motherless" in the conventional sense, but she had several surrogate mothers (the old women we see in the film's opening shots, the sisters at the convent). Nicely enough, Charles Bovary appears on the scene at a critical moment in Emma's life: the night is stormy, attributing a cosmic intention to the occasion, and her father has broken his leg. Structurally (psychoanalytically) Charles must appear in order to replace the father, and from the old hags' apprehensive remarks about his beardlessness and youth we sense that Charles will probably not be able to fulfill the masculine principle for Emma, which Mr. Rouault (as long as Emma was a child) managed to embody by virtue merely of being her father.

From her first meeting with Charles, which she brings about with a great degree of calculation,[17] it becomes clear that Emma's destiny will be shaped by the men in her life. Later, her conviction that only men enjoy unlimited freedom becomes so strong that she wishes, with a crazy passion, to give birth to a male child through whom she might live out her own dreams:[18] "A man can be free. If he doesn't

---

[15] Dorothy Dinnerstein, *The Mermaid and the Minotaur: Sexual Arrangements and Human Malaise* (New York: Harper and Row, 1977), 190.

[16] Ibid., 176.

[17] So does Stella Martin take some trouble to "catch" her man in Vidor's *Stella Dallas*, and the Dear One in Griffith's *The Mother and the Law* must make a calculated effort to attract the attentions of a young suitor.

[18] "Thus, with regard to 'the development of a normal woman,' we learn, through Freud, that there is and can be only one single motivating factor behind it: 'penis envy,' that is, the desire to appropriate for oneself the genital organ that has a cultural monopoly on value. Since women don't have it, they can only covet the men who have, and, since they cannot possess it, they can only seek to find equivalents for it. Furthermore, they can find fulfillment only in motherhood, by bringing a child, a 'penis substitute,' into the world; and for the woman's happiness to be complete, the child must have a penis himself. The perfect achievement of the feminine destiny, according to Freud, lies in reproducing the male sex, at the expense of the woman's

like his life, he can change it." The camera, as if to associate this desire with Emma's other "impossible dreams," pans right from her
beseeching face to the picture-covered wall of her fantasies that it
seems she has brought with her from her childhood home and re-
created in the attic of her house in Yonville. Her distress has been
provoked by the chance visit of the Marquis d'Andervilliers whom
Emma saw chuckling to himself in the hallway at the sight of her
provincial soirée. It is a classic moment of melodramatic excruciation:
in our identification with Emma, it is that unhappy glimpse of how
others see (us). Emma knows instantly that her soirée of babbling
voices looks like a parody of the real thing, and that the Marquis
would know the difference.

Charles does not know the difference, which is why he suffers
none of the torments Emma does. The embarrassment of class difference is traditionally felt by Americans to be more of a European problem than an American one, and yet it is often a crucial experience in
America where it is not uncommon for huge class differences to exist
within the same family between only one generation and the next.
The Frenchness of *Madame Bovary* (the film) is almost irrelevant—the
pretext for some "period" charm and spectacle, a matter of costumes
and names; it does not posit a social milieu that is peculiar to the
French, or suggest that the narrated events are the sort of thing that
could only have happened "long ago." The film is as American as
any movie Douglas Sirk ever made, or Minnelli's own *Some Came
Running* and *Home from the Hill*.

Rodolphe, whom Emma meets at the Marquis' ball, asks a friend
who she is. "Some doctor's wife," the man says; at which Rodolphe
remarks, "Oh, yes, the peasant." As American movies repeatedly
show, class mobility is generally limited to one leap per generation,
and Charles Bovary seems to feel that his progress from peasant to
professional (doctor) is as much as any sane man should dare: "I
have a right to be a doctor, just as long as I know my limitations."
Emma, as a beautiful woman, reveals clearly the way in which under
patriarchy women are commodities—objects of exchange—between
men, having no fixed identity of their own voluntary inscription. Until she marries Charles, Emma is a daughter, whose charm and

own." (Luce Irigaray, *This Sex Which Is Not One*, trans. Catherine Porter [Ithaca, N.Y.:
Cornell University Press, 1985], 86–87.)

16. Though escorted by her husband, Emma realizes a dream: she is received by the Marquis at his chateau, where she will meet and dance with her Prince Charming. (Paul Cavanagh, Jennifer Jones, Van Heflin, in *Madame Bovary*.)

beauty could take her almost anywhere, but once married to Charles she will derive her identity from him. She becomes "some doctor's wife." It is her beauty and grace that obtained Charles and Emma their invitation to the ball, but the evening is like one of the fantasies pinned to Emma's wall at home: it is not the real thing, as it is for the aristocrats, but a brief chance for Emma to forget her middle-class reality. Smooth-faced, wide-eyed Charles is pathetically out of place among these laughingly confident aristocrats—suave, bearded men who appear not even to see him in their midst. But for Emma it is a dream come true.

The Marquis leads her in the first dance of the evening, and men clamor to be her partner in the dances that follow. During a moment of rest she sees herself in an ornately framed mirror on a wall—an image of loveliness in a magnificent ball gown, surrounded by handsome young men. In this moment time seems to stand still, like a tableau of stage melodrama or a picture on Emma's wall at home. But in being marked as an image—framed, static—the moment speaks its own doom and underscores its own unreality. Of course it is "real," but as an image it will evaporate in the effort to realize it.[19]

She meets Rodolphe, who almost literally sweeps her off her feet, and they waltz in a swirling delirium that achieves an oneiric giddiness that matches Emma's emotional state. When the Marquis hears that she "is going to faint" unless she gets some air, he orders the great French windows of the ballroom smashed. The scene is magnificent, fantastic. As melodrama does so well, it pushes at the very limits of realism, making Charles' maudlin intrusion on Emma's waltz with Rodolphe the most embarrassing, shattering moment of Emma's life. She will never be the same after this: she knows better, now, what she wants. She has glimpsed something that will help articulate her desire,[20] and she begins to hate Charles, whom she will blame as the obstacle to her freedom.

Before the ball—before Emma knew of their invitation to it—she had remarked, "Do you know, Charles, why that clock strikes? To announce the death of another hour." Excluded from desire's exchanges, denied active participation in Symbolic operations, Emma as a non-subject experiences life as a living death, as time without pulse. Charles can only wish he were clever. "If I were clever," he says to her, "I could understand you. If I could understand you then perhaps I could help you. I love you so much, Emma. . . . What is it

---

[19] It takes imagination to realize the image: this is Minnelli's point in so many of his films. *A Matter of Time* offers as its moral lesson the dictum: *You should never wish to be like anyone else in this world, unless you want to be a copy. If you are not an original, you are nothing! Be yourself! That's the important thing. The world worships the original!*—which Minnelli represents not just in the narrative (story, dialogue, etc.) but, paradoxically, in the privileged trope of the mirror, a particular, elaborately framed mirror that inaugurates and concludes the narrative.

[20] The question remains, nevertheless, *whose desire?* For a fascinating "parable of [patriarchal] femininity attempting its own representation," see Abigail Solomon-Godeau, "The Legs of the Countess," *October* 39 (Winter 1986): 65–108. Solomon-Godeau examines how throughout the second half of the nineteenth century the Countess de Castiglione had hundreds of photographs taken of herself in what may be seen as "an extreme and immensely stylized recapitulation of fetishistic mechanisms dispersed throughout the culture that produced her." What is Emma Bovary but (like the Countess de Castiglione) "a tabula rasa on whom is reflected a predetermined and delimited range of representations? And of what does her subjectivity consist if not her total absorption of them, her obedience to a scopic regime which inevitably undercuts her pretended authority as orchestrator of the look"?

17. "Do you know, Charles, why that clock strikes?
To announce the death of another hour."

you want, Emma?" Poor Charles is not very clever, but even if he
were, there would not be much more he could do for his wife. Emma
answers, "How do I know what I want?" and after Charles leaves
the room asks her child rhetorically, "Berthe, are you filled with
madness too? Are all women?" Melodrama deals in this sort of painful irony. We know that Emma is not mad, but we are powerless to
prevent her, our chief figure for identification, from beginning to believe it of herself.

On the other hand, Emma *is* driving herself mad. She finds the gap
between men as she would like them to be (that is, life as she would
like it to be—since she believes that her only access to "life" is

through men) and men as they are (life as it is) impossibly frustrating. In the absence of much experience of actual men, Emma has come to understand men in terms of images of men, and her desire has been formed through the desires of men. Charles, too, is arrested by an image—of a woman—and finds women's difference from men (the difference between "image" and "self") insurmountable. "Oh, I don't suppose a man could ever know what a woman really wants, or what she really means," he sighs. Emma knows that if she cannot *be* a man, or have a son through whom she might realize her desires vicariously, or that if she will never have enough money to make her house as beautiful as she would like it to be, or that if her chances for a life among the aristocracy were dashed the day she married Charles, then she might as well try to be "in love"—with Léon Dupuis, or with Rodolphe—since to be "in love" is to be in a fantasy world (the realm of the image) that can keep unhappy realities at bay.

There is no doubt in Emma's mind that Charles loves her,[21] but she does not really love him. All her roiling desires have coalesced into an idea of love that is passionate, romantic, unrealistic. "I know you [Charles] love me. I know you're good to me. Oh, I'd rather you were worthless and dashing and brutal and that you'd strike any man who looked at me!" It is the kind of contradictory declaration Charles will never understand. "Emma, this is story-book," he says helplessly. She urges him, on an idea from the apothecary, to become a famous doctor by performing an operation on the clubfoot of Hippolyte, a local peasant; she senses it as her last opportunity to gain a satisfactory identity through Charles. "If only you could be famous," she says, "If you could be the kind of man who wears the Legion of Honor! Charles, you could push me aside and ignore me. But how I could love you!" Charles' identity derives from his profession as a

---

[21] But what is it, after all, that he loves? Irigaray remarks on "the *fabricated* character of the [woman as] commodity, its trans-formation by man's (social, symbolic) 'labor.' " Charles loves an image of Emma that he and his sex have created, but as Irigaray notes, "Man endows the commodities he produces with a narcissism that blurs the seriousness of utility, of use," which is why Emma holds Charles' love in such indifferent regard. "The mirror that envelops and paralyzes the commodity specularizes, speculates (on) man's 'labor.' Commodities, women, are a mirror of value of and for man. In order to serve as such, they give up their bodies to men as the supporting material of specularization, of speculation. They yield to him their natural and social value as a locus of imprints, marks, and mirage of his activity." (Irigaray, *This Sex Which Is Not One*, 176–77.)

country doctor, and every other man in Emma's life is at least more or less satisfied with his identity, except perhaps Léon Dupuis, the lawyer's clerk. His example, curiously enough, is the exception that proves the rule.

Léon throughout the film is some kind of proof of the constructedness of identity. He is the first man with whom Emma will distract herself from the boredom and mediocrity of life with Charles, but Léon is not exactly the kind of man who wears the Legion of Honor. He is young, handsome and charming, but, in the words of the lawyer, "Léon's value to Yonville is largely cultural . . . er, shall we say, ornamental. He has no mind for details." Like Emma, he is a bit of a dreamer—dreams are his response to limitation, to the unattractive details about his situation which he prefers not to see. He enthusiastically helps Emma decorate her house when the Bovarys first move to Yonville, and like Emma dreams of Paris, the great city which it is enough to live in, a city like Rouen with the power to confer an identity on every one of its inhabitants. On the same day that Emma is informed by Léon's mother of Léon's impending permanent move to Paris, Rodolphe reenters her life.

Rodolphe, ironically, is pretty much the "worthless and dashing and brutal" lover of Emma's dreams. He courts her ardently and at first is unafraid of her passion, but he will only play the lover, on his own cavalier terms, and Emma is only one lover among several Rodolphe has had. (He sentimentally keeps Emma's letters among others from former lovers.) A man like Rodolphe can no more understand a woman than Charles can. "I adore my bachelor privacy," he tells Emma; it is obvious he is glad she is married: it safeguards the constraints without which he would be afraid to pursue their love affair. Rodolphe thinks of his infatuation as possession by a witch (as Stefan—also played by Louis Jourdan—in *Letter from an Unknown Woman* sees Lisa as a "sorceress"). This lovers' conceit comes out of a profound inability to come to terms with otherness. Rodolphe loves Emma's difference, but, quite understandably, fears the loss of his own identity, which as a movie *Madame Bovary* represents largely in the mise en scène of environment:

> Emma: I could take my revenge on you, Rodolphe. You know I could. I could straighten up this room. The way you live! With everything piled every which way . . . guns and boots and pipes and magazines and books . . .

Rodolphe: I like it.
Emma: What a woman could do to this house!
Rodolphe: Oh, I know what a woman could do to this house. She could
           destroy it. And you, you witch. If the woman were you . . .
           [They kiss.]

Their love, we must infer, is a vital, virile affair, for it is represented mostly in a few brief shots of Emma galloping on her horse to and from Rodolphe's great house, in embraces, and a fire in the hearth.[22] In one early scene the banality of married life with Charles is juxtaposed with what Rodolphe offers: at the Yonville agricultural fair Emma and Rodolphe seclude themselves in a room within earshot of Charles and the other local men who are droning on in speeches about agricultural matters.[23] Rodolphe attempts to convince Emma of what we know she has always felt: that she deserves a better fate. His extravagant praise of her beauty—of her face that is wasted on the shopkeepers of Yonville, her hands that were designed for a thousand pleasures, her lips that were meant to speak only of love . . . not grocery lists—clearly plays into the long-harbored fantasies that she has tried so hard to realize. *This* is love(making). For, as Leo Bersani has observed, "Like all abstract concepts, love is a phenomenon created by its own definition. It is a synthetic product (the result of a synthesis, and existing nowhere in nature), and its only reality is on the level of the sign."[24] The consequences of Emma's inadequate grasp of this truth are disastrous, tragic. She allows herself to be destroyed by the impossibility of desire. She will not accept the fact that all desires are essentially unfulfillable, and she chooses, rather, to believe in the melodramatic signifier, which we know makes "large but unsubstantiable claims on meaning."[25]

On her return from her first afternoon alone with Rodolphe at his

[22] As always, the Breen office (the most overt of Ideological State Apparatuses operative in Hollywood) had something to do with how the passion between Emma and Rodolphe would be represented. Minnelli quotes from a letter sent by the Breen office to L. B. Mayer: "The kissing in these scenes is obviously completely unacceptable, by reason of its quantity and its passionate quality. We urge upon you the advisability of playing all scenes between Emma and Rodolphe without any kissing or lustful embraces." (Minnelli, *I Remember It Well*, 204.)

[23] Robin Wood has alerted me to the curious fact that the speech is about manure, with a reference to "our se(a)men."

[24] Bersani, *A Future for Astyanax*, 97.

[25] Peter Brooks, *The Melodramatic Imagination: Balzac, Henry James, Melodrama, and the Mode of Excess* (New Haven: Yale University Press, 1976), 199.

house, flushed with excitement at her triumph, this dream becoming real in spite of everything, Emma looks at herself in a mirror, as she had done at the ball, and she smiles. It is a curious gesture that is in some ways emblematic of Jennifer Jones' unique acting style which here, as in *Duel in the Sun* and *Ruby Gentry*, seems exquisitely controlled, hard-working, self-regarding and phony, and yet utterly sincere. The actress, perhaps like no other, achieves conviction through a kind of absolute intensity, in highly mannered displays of Hollywood acting conventions. Jennifer Jones' elaborately wrought performance suits *Madame Bovary* (as a melodrama, a festival of clichés) and it suits Emma's passionate, contradictory nature. This gesture of looking at herself in a mirror, to "see" herself and to register her own responses, has poignancy because it reenacts the original drama of the mirror, in which one's sense of self, alone and separated from life's continuum, is underscored in the very moment that a better self is offered in the (unattainable) image. The dream of one's ideal self is born in the same moment that its realization is denied as an impossibility. The returned gaze that Emma looks for cannot be found in a literal mirror, except in as much as she succeeds in seeing herself as she imagines Rodolphe sees her.

Emma's ideal self is ineluctably tied to the male gaze. Her identity is conceived in it, bound up in the "mirror games" Irigaray mentions in her observation that the use of and traffic in women maintain the reign of masculine hom(m)o-sexuality, "in speculations, mirror games, identifications, and more or less rivalrous appropriations, which defer its real practice."[26] As Emma in effect indicates to Charles, she would not mind effacing herself totally if he were worthy of her love; an identity derived from a man, the film perhaps implies, is not in itself what destroys Emma, but the fact that she never finds the right man.

When she looks in the mirror almost for the last time, Emma does not see her better self. The cracked mirror throws back the truth of her flawed ("castrated") state. "Is this where I end up?" she asks Léon, "In a dirty little hotel bedroom. Broken mirrors, no curtains on the windows. You know me, Léon, this wasn't what I ever wanted. Did I ever want anything cheap or ugly? Is it a crime to want things to be beautiful?" Near the end, Emma's bad luck (for want of a better

[26] Irigaray, *This Sex Which Is Not One*, 172.

term) is so relentless that the film seems to suggest, after all, that her fate is not a question of luck—of marrying the right man—but rather, a question of feminine destiny.

At the end, as Emma is dying from arsenic poisoning, she asks, "What did I do?" What transgression, in other words, did she commit, that she must now be so punished? There is no answer, of course, except that she was born female, born into a world that told her and then proved to her that, in the psychoanalytic metaphor, she is castrated. The phallocratic organization of this world in which subjectivity depends on *having* or *being* the phallus—this world in which Emma must forever be marked as lacking—is emblematized in a conversation between her and Léon in the hotel room of their last meeting. Emma had hoped to salvage her situation by drawing from the estate of Charles' recently-dead father, but Léon tells her that the estate is worthless. To mask his frustration, he says, "Oh, Emma! Let's forget it. What's money!" to which Emma retorts, "You can afford to say that! You've got money!" So roughly reminded that indeed he does not have money (that he is not phallic, significant—as gloriously masculine as he knows Emma wants to believe all men are), he becomes conscious suddenly of his surroundings, as Emma herself has always been. The image of himself thrown back by the hotel room is a poor one. "Why is it that I should suddenly be overwhelmed by the vulgarity of this room?" he asks. The truth is that everyone, women *and* men, are subject to the castrating power of the Law, and when Léon is forced to recognize this truth, he turns to fantasy with as much longing and fervor as Emma ever did: "Oh, Emma! Someday you and I, we'll go to Paris!" But for Emma the support of fantasy is crumbling: "Someday, Léon, I'll probably stop hoping for anything."

Overwhelmed with debts, rejected by Rodolphe, and disappointed by Léon, Emma finds herself no longer able to believe in the image. Since the old Swiss seamstress whose songs promised Emma the world, there have been no women in Emma's life, only men. Every man has offered her something, but at an exorbitant price (the price of her subjectivity), including L'Heureux the shopkeeper (literally, a price) and the apothecary at whose laboratory Emma gulps down handfuls of arsenic. The "hurt inside" that she has felt all her life becomes hideously literal.

In the novel Flaubert perhaps identifies the stark elements of Emma's fate when he writes, "In her desire, she would confuse the sensuous pleasures of wealth with the raptures of the heart, the refinement of manners with the delicacy of sentiments."[27] She is a victim of her confusion about how love and money go together in the bourgeois world. As Albert Thibaudet has suggested, Emma's life follows a parallel course on the financial and sentimental planes, in which "the disappointments of the one coincide with the troubles of the other. Rodolphe and L'Heureux . . . exploit and destroy her, not through malicious intent, but because they act in accordance with the law of nature and society,"[28] which respects the rights of seducers and usurers.

Emma does not adequately comprehend this law (the "right" of the seducer and the "right" of the usurer) because she received a skewed version of how it functions. After her junky diet of popular fictions, and according to its principles, she recklessly abandons herself to "the system," and thereafter can never quite credit the terms of femininity under patriarchy. As an excessive (i.e., melodramatic) character, she does not temper her desire, which is what "normal" women do when they mask, efface, ignore, do whatever must be done to overcome, the injustice of the "feminine" position under patriarchy. That all Emma's hopes must always be pinned on a man points to the underlying problem of her destiny (and that of "the thousands of Emma Bovarys" Flaubert refers to in his courtroom defense), and when she sobs, "I can't help it! It's how I am. Save me, Charles!" we must believe that Emma is trapped. It is too late for her to conceive of her place in life differently, to change her desire, and all she can do is helplessly throw her impossible situation back at Charles, who picks up a copy of *The Therapeutic Review* in dumb anguish and stares at it sightlessly. The last refuge, the only way out of the problem (the impasse to which Emma's "problem" brings the masculine point of view), is a *medical discourse*. The medical discourse, as Mary Ann Doane has written,

makes it possible once again to confine female discourse to the body, to disperse her access to language across a body which now no longer finds its major function in spectacle. Yet, de-specularized in its illness, that body is

[27] Quoted by Albert Thibaudet in Chapter 5 of *Gustave Flaubert* (Paris: Gallimard, 1935). The chapter has been translated by Paul de Man and reprinted in the Norton Critical Edition of *Madame Bovary* (New York: Norton, 1965), 371–83.

[28] Thibaudet, in *Madame Bovary* (Norton Critical Edition), 382.

nevertheless interpretable, knowable, subject to a control which is no longer entirely subsumed by the erotic gaze. What the body no longer supports, without the doctor's active reading, is an identity.[29]

Charles can only think that his wife must be sick, but perhaps we have seen or heard something else, something different, which it has been one of *Madame Bovary*'s main functions as a melodrama to hold out as a possibility. Quite clearly, it is not a question of "what a woman really wants, or what she really means," but a question of how we define "woman." And what it means to be a man or a woman is *our* responsibility. As Flaubert says of Emma near the beginning of the film, "Our world—your world and mine—created her. . . ."

COMING HOME: *Some Came Running*

"The audience had to be knocked out by their vulgarity," Vincente Minnelli wrote of the characters in *Some Came Running*; "I decided to use the inside of a juke box as my inspiration for the settings . . . garishly lit in primary colors."[30] There is no doubt that audiences *are* knocked out—by many things that the best film melodramas are famous for, and by Minnelli's exuberant mise en scène and his success in conveying the throttled passions produced in these middle-class characters by the profoundly ambivalent feelings they have about themselves. Class difference and the eroticism that can be produced by it, and conflicted familial feeling, form the chief sources of energy in the film, driving it relentlessly forward, like a flood.[31] Minnelli exploits every stereotype about the American middle classes, and the truths he represents (those that stereotype and cliché express) are frequently ugly—harshly satirical without satire's saving edge of humor or irony.

The disgust that Dave Hirsh (Frank Sinatra) feels, and that extends from his character to dominate the tone of the entire film, is explained by the fact that the "moral occult" of the bourgeois society

---

[29] Mary Ann Doane, "The 'Woman's Film,' " *Re-Vision: Essays in Feminist Criticism*, ed. Mary Ann Doane, Patricia Mellencamp and Linda Williams (Los Angeles: The American Film Institute, 1984), 77.

[30] Minnelli, *I Remember It Well*, 325.

[31] The French title of the film, more appropriately, or definitively, than the American title, is *Comme un torrent*.

represented in the film (the American middle class in the 1950s) is severely disordered. Dave's search for "home"—his desire for an identity in familial terms that, for better or for worse, cannot be taken away from him, an identity that is as firm as the fact of familial origin—reveals that "home," as in *Home from the Hill*, is a special kind of fiction.

The film's central theme of individual identity, carried primarily in the character of Dave Hirsh, neatly organizes most of the film's conflicts. These various conflicts are overdetermined in the narrator's hatred of bourgeois mores, represented in the film's critique of misogyny, to create in the narrative a complex network of essentially masculine imperatives that result in the sacrifice of a woman.

Dave is of two worlds, and that is the problem. Everything in the film—all spaces, all characters—belong ostensibly to the one world or the other, but as the narrative progresses we see many similarities between the two worlds, just as there are obvious differences. However, according to melodrama's insistence on moral clarity founded on principles of *difference*, the two worlds cannot, must not, become one. Smitty's Bar, and the country club at which the Hirshes and the Frenches dine, cannot become the same place; Gwen French and Ginny Moorehead are not the same person; Dave cannot, it is asserted, be an artist and a non-artist at the same time. The World, and the Subject, then, are forever divided, and a unity between them, or within the subject ("coming home"), can only be achieved at some expense, some repression, or ultimately, by death. The question of which choices Dave will make from the array of unattractive ones before him provides the film's hermeneutic code.

If every melodrama must provide somewhere an image of perfection, or good, which will either be destroyed, or destroyed and reconstituted, *Some Came Running* does it briefly—almost not at all—at the end of the film, and only indirectly at the beginning. The utopian image, as it might be called, is in this film a natural one that excludes human figures. In the final shot, at Ginny's burial on the hillside, the camera moves gracefully over the tombstones of the cemetery, past Bama who at last takes off his hat, to an unobstructed view of the river beyond. In its compositional perfection a cosmic harmony is suggested: Order at last. But in the foreground we can see the tombstones, just as we see Wade Hunnicutt's tombstone in the final shot of *Home from the Hill*—silent reminders of how we pay for that utopian image.

The opening shots of the film show natural landscapes also, but they are framed by a bus window, with Dave asleep in a seat in the foreground. The Great American Outdoors, flitting past like images on a strip of celluloid running through a projector, is, bit by bit, compromised. Mountains and rivers give way to houses, bridges, and finally, to Parkman, Indiana, which "used to be" Dave's home town. Dave Hirsh's journey in search of himself begins with this literal journey. He may not have realized that, while he was drunk, his friends put him on this bus bound for Parkman, but the logic is there: he is returning to his origins, to uncover, as Frank McConnell suggests, "his own heritage, his own relationship to that central law that is the sanction of all other laws which surround him and define his world."[32]

Dave's army uniform introduces the film's central theme of individual identity. The uniform has the effect not only of effacing his individual identity, but of making him look out of place in Parkman, where people wear civilian clothes and look like ordinary mothers and fathers, or children. Dave is like an unhappy orphan let out of the institution at last, but with nowhere to go, no *family* to return home to. Even all the bars in Parkman are closed at this hour. If Parkman does not represent Dave's heritage, what, then, is that "central law that is the sanction of all other laws"? And what relationship to that law will he uncover?

Some Came Running, we find, describes a loss of faith in the Father. The Father, the Family, Home, are bankrupt, although every law derives from that symbolic nexus. Ginny, whom Dave cannot believe took this bus ride with him from Chicago, assumes he will ask her "to meet his folks and everything," and she adds that she is not unaware that it is "just about the highest compliment that a fellow can pay his girl." Her assumption is that Dave has a family. All social interaction, after all, depends on assumptions of this sort; most people do have families. But another code is invoked in Dave's reply— the extrafamilial code of casual relationships. He gives her $50 to get herself back to Chicago and explains to her, "Look, I'm really sorry,

[32] Frank McConnell, *Storytelling and Mythmaking: Images from Film and Literature* (New York: Oxford University Press, 1979), 161.

but you know a guy gets loaded, and meets a girl, and . . . you know. . . ." The scene echoes down from Griffith's belief in man's polygamous instincts. In effect, this relatively small misunderstanding between Ginny and Dave begins a sustained articulation by the film of an ideological imperative: to organize all relationships in familial (or extra-familial) terms. The film as a melodrama will represent the confusion, trouble and hurt that occurs when the familial pattern is not followed. Moreover, the film suggests that we are all both members of a family, and orphans.

Dave does have some actual family, as it turns out. His brother Frank is a successful Parkman citizen of good standing, although he represents everything that Dave despises and that *Some Came Running* has contempt for. At the very least, he is smug, hypocritical, and boring. While Frank is becoming frantic over the rumor that Dave has deposited $5,000 in the other bank (not Parkman Savings, of which Frank is a director), Dave is in his hotel room unpacking his books: Faulkner, Steinbeck, Thomas Wolfe, F. Scott Fitzgerald, Hemingway . . . and a manuscript entitled, "Unfinished Story," by Dave Hirsh. These books and his manuscript serve as shorthand for Dave's values. Dave cares about art, and meaning, while Frank, a jewelry store owner, cares only about money and social standing—the media of exchange, rather than the point of it all.

Frank's speech is as bankrupt as his bank account is not. He speaks (or rather, bellows) in clichés. For example, when he happens to be standing in front of a mirror in Dave's hotel room and Dave glances in his direction, he says, "Oh, I know. I know, it's getting a little thin on top [he looks at himself anxiously and strokes his hair], but like they say, not much grass on a busy street!" Dave's dry response is, "You may be losin' your hair, but you haven't lost your razor-sharp wit."

Stereotype, sterility, bankruptcy. These are the terms of existence in Parkman. But what of desire, in Parkman? Frank has an affair with Edith Barclay, his secretary, which his daughter learns of. His wife, Agnes, is coolly unsexual. Gwen French, whom Dave meets and becomes attracted to, puts all her energies into marking school papers. And at Smitty's Bar, where the women wear too much makeup and the men drink too much liquor, desire's economies seem perverted as well.

When Dave asks after his father, he is told that the old man died a

18. The "Unfinished Story" is both a manuscript and a man. (Frank Sinatra and Martha Hyer in *Some Came Running*.)

long time ago, of alcoholism, and that towards the end "he was just Hell on wheels." ("Phew! What a family!" Frank complains.) However, there is, there must always be, hope invested in the next generation: "Oh, wait 'til you see the new generation, Dave. Why, that niece of yours is a *real* lady!" As it turns out, Dawn (the name says it all) will eventually escape Parkman, as Edith the secretary does, which does not, we observe, say much for the town's future. All the other women in the film belong to one of two types: respectable, inflexibly cool, domineering women, such as Agnes and Gwen, and "pigs," as Bama Dillert calls the kind of women (Ginny, Rosalie) who work in Parkman's brassiere factory by day and can be found at Smitty's Bar in the evenings. "I don't know what it is about them pigs, but they always look better at night," says Bama.

Shockingly misogynistic as Bama's dictum is, it is the most unambiguous sign of the breakdown in the dialectic of give-and-take between men and women in *Some Came Running* into all (power and control), or nothing. The film, as James Jones said of his book on which the film is based, is about "the separation between human beings—the fact that no two people ever totally get together; that everyone wants to be loved *more* than they want to love."[33] The women are either castrating or not worth it, because—psychoanalytically speaking—the space normally occupied by the Father is empty. The hierarchy, or sex-power economy, in other words, is out of kilter. Frank Hirsh puts on a show of being the patriarch, but Dave knows, Agnes knows, we know, and so eventually does Dawn, that it is all merely a hollow show. Agnes has been reminding her husband for eighteen years that it was *her father's store.* Money, in other words, is all that is left of the Father, which explains Frank's hysterical references to money and financial success. If nothing else, Frank at least knows how to make money; he has staked his very masculinity and paternal authority on it, and is dismayed by Dave's relative indifference to it.

By depositing $5,000 in the "other" bank Dave is aiming where he knows it will hurt his philistine brother most—at the heart of his money-based values. When Frank first shows up at Dave's hotel room to complain about this and other things, he says, "You might have called, Dave. You owe me that much"—a remark which Dave turns around to critique his brother's consignment of him to an orphanage when he was a little boy: he offers Frank a check to cover the cost of his years there.

The origins of the corruption of values that Dave's return to Parkman will uncover are thus located. Not everything, the film makes clear, can be valued in financial terms. Money—only a medium of exchange—cannot be substituted for the thing itself, which in Dave's case is love—an identity secured through love. But Frank's notions of family and masculinity are fraudulent, or at the very least, inadequate. He has not been able to establish a convincing identity in terms of either, perhaps because, as we know, his own father was an alcoholic. If Dave has looked to Hemingway and other American writers for models of how to "be a man," Frank looked only as far as a jewelry store and how to make profits. For Frank, family is an image: a beautiful wife, a house as grand as Tara in *Gone With the Wind*,

---

[33] Quoted in Minnelli, *I Remember It Well*, 324–25.

a pretty daughter dressed in white. The logic of his morality has a stark simplicity: everything has a price and can be bought.

To Frank and Agnes, all that matters are money and a notion of "family" that we can see is empty. When Dave is at their grandiose house, their strained chatter reveals the poor limits of their imagination. Frank assures Dave that the Frenches, who will arrive shortly, are *"well worth* meeting. They're, er, *really, really* an old family." Agnes' remark is even more telling: "Bob French owns all that land between the river and the reservoir. They're *really* wonderful people." Dave will have to wait and see whatever it is in which their wonderfulness consists, since his own values put no premium on the moral superiority of owning all the land between the river and the reservoir.

The image of "family" that the Hirshes present is completely at odds with the reality of it. For example, while Dave and Dawn chat in the Hirshes' luxurious living room, Agnes and Frank (ostensibly fixing drinks) conduct a vicious, whispered exchange in the kitchen. Agnes is furious that Frank has brought Dave home, and the effort Frank expends to maintain an appearance of gracious hospitality makes him hysterical. "Well, well, well!" he brays, as he marches back into the living room. "The old hearth and fireside! Family all together! Nothing like it, eh Davie boy?" (Dave grunts in ironic response, and draws on his cigarette.)

All traffic in this scene circulates around the huge, pale blue, satin-covered couch on which Dawn is perched in her pretty, blonde perfection, as she and it are being depended upon to anchor the scene and stand as "proof" of the Hirshes' enduring integrity as a "good family." Frank is shouting, "Now, what we've got to do is get you settled down, Davie—put your money to work! I wanna see you save some *real* dough!" Dave's presence there is a reminder that the real thing, which Frank's money is meant to signify the presence of, is missing from Frank Hirsh's life. If only Dave would make more money, and stay in one spot, and take a wife (again, a signifier to make good the lack), everything would be just fine.

Earlier, Frank had asked Dave if he were married. When he said no, Frank chortled, "Oh, oh. Ha ha. Guess we'll have to find you a girl!" The "girl," of course, is Gwen French, who has always expressed a great interest in Dave's writing. The inferences we draw from her cool blonde appearance and excessively dignified manner are soon confirmed. As she says to Dave later, when he tries with all the charm he can muster to romantically ingratiate himself with her, "I know my eyes are not fascinating. I wear my hair this way to please the school board. If you want to flatter me, I have only one good feature—that's my mind."

A shift in the power relations within the family accelerated in America in the 1950s, making the truth-telling arena of sex itself an impossible embarrassment for men as much as for women. If, as Leo Bersani puts it (to quote him out of context), "sex is the power to make someone else powerless, and the joy of sex is given by reflected images of that power,"[34] then Agnes and Gwen will not submit to it (nor, on the masculine side, will Bama)—for, if the Father is seen to be a hollow show, where is the power and pleasure in making him powerless? Women still stand to lose more than men in such an exchange. So, Agnes and Gwen withhold their bodies, leaving "sex" to women like Ginny and Rosalie, who indeed belong to another class. As Foucault argued, sex has played the role for the bourgeoisie that blood played for the aristocracy—that is, as a means of defining the body. If Agnes and Gwen are to distinguish themselves from women like Ginny and Rosalie, their most powerful way to do it is with their bodies.

Gwen wears her hair in a "French Roll," like a phallus pinned closely to her. She teaches "Creative Writing and Criticism," and has "read every word" that Dave has written. She does not herself write (the phallic activity of commanding the Word), she only teaches it and is a critic—which suggests a different order of appropriation. Dave, whatever he is, or now thinks he is not, was once a writer, and that is what Gwen wants. She wants the writer, the Phallus. The whole subject, however, gives Dave "a pain" (we know where), for it signifies his lack; he is "feminized" by it. The issue is absolutely central to *Some Came Running*. It is a question of identity; it is the very reason for the film:

Gwen: I'm an admirer of yours, Mr. Hirsh.
Dave: Well, until people get to know me they usually are.
Gwen: Oh, I meant as a writer. That's why I wanted to meet you.
Dave: But I'm not a writer. Haven't been for years.
Gwen: I'm not sure I agree with you. The fact that an author is inactive—
         that doesn't necessarily mean that he isn't an author.
Dave: Exactly what does it mean?

[34] Bersani, *A Future for Astyanax*, 296.

Everyone treats her answer ("I suppose it could mean he should get back to work") as a witticism. The tension of the moment is amplified by the composition of the scene. Gwen is seated on the couch in the middle of the shot; her father is standing to the right; Dave is standing on the left; and Frank and Agnes are standing behind the couch, with their arms around each other, posed in the image of the united, still-deeply-in-love couple. In a self-conscious gesture Gwen adjusts her skirt. She will not be discomposed by this man with a silky voice and huge blue eyes.

The fact that ours is a logocentric, phallocratic culture overdetermines the relationship between Dave and Gwen, making it clear that the film wants Gwen, as teacher-critic, to give up her control of the Word (since it does not "suit" her, makes her "un-feminine"), and wants Dave to take up his control of it (i.e., become a writer again, restore his "masculinity").[35] There is pressure on Gwen—from her father, from Dave—to be more "sexual," so that Dave, as it were, can become less so. If the film seeks to distinguish between "lived" and vicarious experience, it is for men to live, and for women to live (vicariously) through men. Dave likes Gwen because she is "respectable"—she has the respect of the middle-class community in which Dave wishes to feel "at home"; she is hard to get—value being determined inversely by availability; she is offering to give him back his identity. He likes her for liking his writing. He has found a woman worthy of his love—which is to say, to the measure of his regard for his best self.[36]

From Dave's point of view, however, these upper-bourgeois characters have lost something vital as they have allowed a materialistic ethos to dominate their lives. They are not interested in ideas, or—

[35] The patriarchy, most especially for *Some Came Running*, should probably be defined as Heidi Hartman defines it: as "relations between men, which have a material base, and which, though hierarchical, establish or create interdependence and solidarity among men that enable them to dominate women." (Quoted in Eve Kosofsky Sedgwick, *Between Men: English Literature and Male Homosocial Desire* [New York: Columbia University Press, 1985], 3.)

[36] Later, when Gwen reads Dave's "unfinished story," and pronounces it already finished in her view, the logic of Dave's desire becomes more apparent. Dave himself is his unfinished story. He is looking to Gwen to represent his lack. He is looking for the Phallus (Mother/Father), but is doing it in the conventional heterosexual manner—identifying himself with a woman, alienating his desire in a signifier. As signifier of lack, Gwen (the woman) can—paradoxically—complete the story. She represents the irretrievably lost object (the maternal body).

since *Some Came Running* is a melodrama—in emotion, identity, or feeling, but only in appearances. To put it more simply, Ginny is all feeling and all emotion; and Gwen is all mind. Dave represents the hope for a healthy synthesis of emotion and intellect, but the film makes him choose between Ginny and Gwen. And when he has made his choice, he must try to make her conform to his desire. By intellect, of course, the film means something high and dry. We see it in Gwen—it is understood to be a form of discipline, something involving inhibition. It is not too much to say that the film critiques the belief that intellect is natural, or proper, in a man (Dave as a writer), but unnatural and inappropriate in a woman (Gwen is "frigid," and not a "real" writer anyway). In the spirit of the familial universe of the melodrama Dave must also find a satisfactory identity as a brother, a brother-in-law, an uncle, a son, and perhaps as a lover and a husband.

So far, Dave has had some success only as an uncle, and his past identity as a writer, we infer, was "not enough." Dawn has expressed an admiration for her Uncle Dave. She sees him as some sort of independent, free-spirited adventurer ("A girl couldn't do that!" she exclaims), although he wants her to know—since honest advice helps to make him a real uncle worthy of the name—that "bumming around only helps to make you a bum." At one point, after offering a particularly avuncular piece of advice, Dave tells his niece, "You make me feel like one of the family. It's a new feeling to me, and I like it."

It is, as we have said, only because of his writing, however, that Gwen takes any interest in Dave. Her valuation of writing, we infer, derives from a partial displacement of her love for her father, who was or is a professor. Dave can only become a lover and a husband (and then become an acceptable brother and brother-in-law) by becoming a writer. The price that he is being asked to pay, though, is to give up everything that can make him a writer in the first place: he must give up attempting to experience life more vividly, attempting to gain more direct accesses to the flows of desire. Writing, as we know, is an effect of desire, which the film admires but as a melodrama does not find immediate enough. The film must turn the desire of the "writer" into more suitably filmic significations of desire: camera movements, embraces, a beautiful woman's face, a man's voice—the film's own writing. Gwen's "theory that writers create to compensate for some lack in their personal lives" is consistent with the film's understanding of the psychology of writing, but when she says she is not offering herself "as compensation," we know that the film, like Dave, thinks it is "a peachy idea." Dave's suggestion that they "go park somewhere and talk it over" is not such a bad one, after all, for love is always a written text; it is not a feeling. In fact, that is what the film does: it talks it over. What kind of film would *Some Came Running* be if, as Dave facetiously suggests, they became pen pals?

Where Gwen represents overdisciplined, throttled desire, Ginny represents undisciplined desire, and the film roots this in class difference. Gwen's desire is associated with intellect and the upper-middle classes, and Ginny's desire is both "female" and associated with the lower classes. While Dave begs Gwen to recognize that his "passions are pretty conventional," Gwen is afraid of those conventional passions and urges Dave to regard her "one good feature"—her mind—where they "will be on safer ground." But the film, of course, is rooting for Dave when he asks, "Who wants to be on safer ground?"

Dave might succeed in sexualizing Gwen's desire, thus combining sex and sensibility, but he will never be able to discipline Ginny's desire or make her understand the short story that, with Gwen's help, he gets published in *The Atlantic Monthly*. The publication of his story does not permit Dave to break through Gwen's reserve, nor does it enable Ginny to understand Dave any better.

On the day of its publication, Ginny waits for Dave at Bama's house, where he has been staying. With a copy of the magazine in her hand, she tells him eagerly that everybody at the brassiere factory has been congratulating her. "Really? What for?" he asks. "Because I'm sort of a friend of yours, like," she says. She has been signing autographs all day. Dave is horrified, and screams at her, "Why don't you get it through your thick head that nobody signs their name to a story that somebody else wrote!" He also rather crudely insists that she is not his girlfriend, regardless of whether, as she says, "everybody" thinks she is.

Ginny is truly devastated. She sits by herself on the porch, trying to make sense of what has happened. Eventually, softened by just a little remorse, Dave asks her to come inside. When she says, "You got no right to talk to me the way you did, Dave. I'm a human being and I've got as many rights and feelings as anybody else," Dave says,

"Okay. So you're a human being." Ginny tells him that she knows he is still in love with Gwen French, but when he says he is not in love with anybody, she runs over to him and pleads desperately, "Dave! Dave! Be in love with me! . . . Oh, I love you so awful, awful much! . . . You know I'll do anything for you. I'll do anything if you ask me!" Dave considers this for a moment, and says, "Would you . . . would you clean up the place for me?" Ginny is ecstatic: "Oh, could I? . . . Oh, I'd love to! I'd love to!"

Later, Dave asks her to listen to his story in *The Atlantic Monthly*. When he has finished reading it to her, she asks, "Is that the end?" The scene gets more ugly, and more pathetic. She says that the story makes her "feel like a terrible failure" because Dave "can put those words down on paper like that, and all [she] can do is hem brassieres." Dave is persistent, cruel. He demands to know what she liked about the story, and when she is unable to say what, he shouts that she didn't understand a word of what he said. (She doesn't, in other words, understand *him*. She does not provide the reflection of himself that he wants to see.) "No, I don't," she pleads, "But that don't mean I don't like it. I don't understand you neither, but that don't mean I don't like you! I love you! But I don't understand you."

In this moment Dave seems to have learned something truly significant from Ginny, and he asks her to marry him.[37] To Bama, who is outraged and indignant that he has "lost" a friend to a "pig," Dave says, "I'm just tired of being lonely, that's all. The way she feels about me . . . well, nobody ever felt that way about me before. And besides, maybe I can help her. I sure can't help myself."

When Bama says, "the fact remains, she's still a pig," he thinks he means only that she is inappropriate for Dave—that she is a certain kind of woman—but the problem is really ("the fact remains") that Ginny is female. Sexual difference is the insuperable obstacle to satisfactory relations between people. The film, in fact, is ambivalent about whether class difference is the main problem (in Dave's search for an identity), or whether the problem, intractably, is heterosexuality itself. Dave frequently calls Gwen "teacher" in embarrassed ref-

[37] It is one of the great flaws in the epistemology of the melodrama: that love answers to nothing; you do not have to understand love. The buck stops there, at love, which is its own justification—mysterious, transcendent, conquering. Perhaps this is true, and fine, if both parties are in love with each other. Perhaps explanations then are indeed irrelevant.

19. Dave's other world of liquor, gambling, and women. (Frank Sinatra, Shirley MacLaine, Dean Martin, Carmen Philips.)

erence to the humiliating role he feels she subjects him to, and once, when she pulls away from him, saying, "I'm not one of your bar room tarts!" he puns, "You're right teacher! You're a hundred per cent right. I've been a bad boy. I've been naughty. Matter of fact, I don't even belong in your *class*!" As both teacher and upper-middle-class intellectual, Gwen would rather read about love than experience the phenomenon that writers write about in the name of love. Not only is it safer, it provides a kind of guaranteed satisfaction. Gwen may suffer, but her suffering will never be on the order of Ginny's suffering. The film as a melodrama drives itself to distinguish between one kind of desire and another—between the desire of "writing," and the conventional desire of heterosexual love and marriage. The film, as with all melodramas, knows, but does not know, how to break free of the shackles on (or *of*) our desire; the least it can do, however, is establish some categories, define some terms.

If there is some split, as the film posits there is, between writing and living, the question becomes, how to write *and* live, how to make desire a positively animating force rather than a force requiring repression and painful re-channeling. Perhaps there is no answer. The film, certainly, gives no grand, radical answer. It urges, rather, a synthesis between the positions represented by Gwen and Ginny, and suggests that such a synthesis is possible in Dave, if not in either of these women.

Desire—to state it as unambiguously as the film does—is a dangerous thing in *Some Came Running*, and the final scene in which Raymond stalks Dave at the fairground is the culminating explosion of repressed desires that can no longer be contained. Fittingly, Minnelli handles the scene like a dark, dramatic musical number. It is wildly unreal, in the sense that it takes off from the diegetic reality that the film has maintained to that point. The music pounds in great, crashing chords, and Raymond's shadow lurches drunkenly across a red wall. He lumbers past swirling lights, blinking neon, and through the crowds of noisy, excited people. The screen suffuses with orange light, then blue, cutting from time to time to Bama, who is trying to save his friend from the deranged lover, and to Dave and Ginny who are walking together among the crowds. When Raymond starts shooting, one cannot be sure in the confusion whether Dave has been shot, or whether Ginny has flung herself onto his body to protect him. The moment is frenzied and disturbing.

In *Some Came Running* the repression of desire, as I have suggested, is clearly implicated in class issues, and it produces violent impossibilities. The film, however, can only "resolve" its problems by repressing them. Ginny's death perhaps frees Dave to marry Gwen, who may well accept him. Ginny represents all the obstacles to a union between Dave and Gwen, but when she is finally removed, we know that nothing essential has changed. Bama, to whom "somethin' bad happens" every time he takes off his hat,[38] takes off his hat for Ginny at her burial, but one doubts that he can have changed very much, even though his gesture suggests that there is always room for hope, for change.

The melodrama must believe in the possibility of change, no matter how small and slow advances are. When Dave shows up at the Frenches' house to propose marriage to Gwen, he says to her, "Look,

[38] Is there any need to explain the sexual symbolism of Bama's hat?

I've quit drinking, I've changed. I know I haven't changed a hundred per cent, but I *have* [changed]." The melodrama posits that we are all, in Gwen's words, emotionally "rather commonplace" people. A premise of the melodrama is that no matter how baroque or particular the circumstances and plot details of a story (our lives) might be, the emotional core is constant and common. There lies the truth to guide us: in the unchanging and universal nature of emotions produced by the familial matrix. One may not be a writer, as Dave is, or a frigid schoolteacher, or a factory worker, but one is always a son or a daughter, a brother, a wife, and so on. The bourgeois patriarchal system in *Some Came Running* may be out of kilter—as evidenced by the fact that all the men and women are in some way mismatched and desiring in the wrong directions (Raymond wants Ginny, and Ginny wants Dave, Edith Barclay wants Frank, Dawn goes to Terre Haute with a man old enough to be her father, Rosalie wants Bama, who wants Dave, who wants Gwen, who wants her father, and so on)—but the film does not advocate its overthrow. It asks for a restoration of order, of a particular moral universe, and suggests that if Dave can achieve a satisfactory identity, all other identities will fall satisfactorily into place.

Both Bama and Gwen believe that it is only through writing that Dave will gain the sense of self-worth that he so obviously needs, and they urge him with different advice on how to regain the identity of "writer." Bama's world, however (a world of bars and drinkers), poses as much of a threat to Dave's ability to write as Gwen's excessively ordered world of bourgeois repressions. When one morning, hung-over and bleary-eyed, Dave remarks to Bama, "You know, I figured you drink three drinks to my one, and you look like a milk-fed quarterback," Bama replies wisely, "Well now, that all depends on what a man's cut out for. I can drink, and you can write. Oh, I know about them two books!" This is the same advice that is offered implicitly in Vidor's *The Crowd*: do whatever it is that you are "cut out for." Bama's proposal to Dave of a gambling partnership is not such a bad one, after all. As Bama reckons, it would give Dave "time to write." We are thus returned to the film's two discourses of desire: "writing" and "drinking"—or, to put it less metaphorically, desire in symbolic mastery, and desire in the Imaginary, of the body.

The real origin of Dave's unhappiness, the problem that precedes the issue of his becoming a writer again, is familial. Although Dave despises his hypocritical brother, he advises Dawn not to judge him (her father) too harshly. He does not want to destroy the Father; he wants to restore the (good) Father's power and authority. Dave comes home in order to "uncover his own heritage, his own relationship to [and seek affirmation of the solidity of] that central law that is the sanction of all other laws which surround him and define his world."[39] The film does not condemn outright the system that is indirectly the cause of Ginny's death; it only asks that it function better—that the Father resume his proper place, so that Dave can "come home."

To Be a Man: *Home from the Hill*

By definition, the bastard is a victim of society, for which reason the theme of bastardy proliferates in melodrama. The issue, of course, is legitimacy: as Captain Wade Hunnicutt tells his son Theron in *Home from the Hill*, "you're my next of kin—legal, legitimate, born in marriage, with my name and everything that goes with it. And that's the way of the world. There are the ins and the outs, the haves and the have-nots. You're lucky, you've got yours." But although Theron is legally Wade's son, he feels far from lucky, since he is a "mama's boy." For a masculine counterpoint we must look to Rafe, Wade's illegitimate son, who has inherited his father's manly characteristics and is loved by him. *Home from the Hill* is as much about Rafe's search for a legitimate identity—as the theme of the bastard son traditionally dictates in melodrama—as it is about Theron's search for a masculine identity. Theron's (failed) effort to find a satisfactory place within the family, under the law of the Father, will hinge, finally, on his discovery of his half-brother Rafe's bastardy. The two searches are inversely related. Theron, as seducer (then killer), takes Rafe's place as social outcast—and vice versa.

The wrong, then, that must be put right in this familial universe, concerns Rafe's legitimacy, his *recognition* by his father. The most active agent of this re-constitution of the divided family—this expiation of sin, this purging of corruption and effort to see justice prevail—is Theron, whose identity, it becomes apparent, has been indirectly determined by it. His mother Hannah has refused to sleep with Wade

---

[39] McConnell, *Storytelling and Mythmaking*, 161.

ever since she learned of Rafe's birth, although she has agreed to stay
with Wade on the condition that Theron be hers exclusively. In *Home
from the Hill* the old melodramatic question of an obstacle to happiness is posed in terms of familial legitimacy. On the side of happiness
there is the survival of the family, the transmission of the right values, proper inheritance, and the finding of suitable identities for family members within that symbolic order and in bourgeois society.
That obstacle begins with Wade Hunnicutt and is identified in the
film's opening scene.

The hunter implied in the film's title (he who returns from the hill)
is first Wade himself, and the hunt is the film's chosen metaphor for
masculinity. It dramatizes a law according to which there is the *masculine* and the *not-masculine*, an axis that divides the world into hunt-
ers and the hunted, the strong and the weak, protectors and the pro-
tected. The hunter survives, prevails, and rules by earned "right,"
gained usually by force of strength and endurance, cunning and violence. Implicitly, from a title that precedes the narrative, the hunt is
"out there," in the world, from which the hunter must always return, to home, where he may find rest, nourishment, tenderness,
beauty, and love.

The world of men—and the part women play in it—is set in place
immediately with the hunt. In the film's opening shot we see Wade
with his dogs and his men crouched in a swamp, aiming at a formation of ducks flying overhead. Seconds before we hear the shot that
hits Wade in the shoulder, we see Rafe note that the attention of one
of their dogs has been distracted by something, and Rafe flings himself forward to knock Wade out of the line of fire. (The man who had
tried to kill Wade is the unhappy husband of one of the many women
Wade sleeps with.) Back in town Wade has his wound dressed by the
doctor. Even wounded, he looks powerful, sitting on the table in the
foreground, erect, bare-chested, wearing his Texan ten-gallon hat
and knocking back a shot of whiskey. He submits to the doctor's
ministrations and reproach:

Wade, I'm goin to tell you how we small-town Texans get our name for violence. It's grown men like you still playin' guns and cars. You never will
grow up will you? It's gettin' to where a man ain't a man around here anymore unless he uses up a car . . . You hear? . . . goes down a road at a
hundred miles an hour, owns six or seven fancy shotguns, knows six or
seven fancy ladies!

Manliness is posited in the discourse of authority from the very start—it frames and defines the actions of the characters in such a way that each narrative "event" becomes an illustration of the code of masculinity. A definition of masculinity is also articulated in Robert Mitchum's body and dress, and in the remarks of the doctor who, in contradistinction to Wade, is short, plump, balding, bespectacled, and perhaps Jewish. The doctor is no hunter, and he objects to what he thinks is an adolescent conception of masculinity, based on speed, the power to kill, conquest and ownership.

These opening scenes tell us a great deal. In terms even of the metaphor, Wade *has* been wounded in a hunting accident, and the doctor will prove to be right: Wade eventually is made to pay for his sporting life, "poaching on the preserves of love"—fatally shot by a man who believes his daughter's child was fathered by Wade. The "right" that Wade claims, the right to cross any man's fence when he is hunting, is that of the usurper, and it signals Wade's original corruption. Wade breaks the rules; he believes rules are for other people—for lesser men, for women, children. In his role as the very embodiment of the Law of the Father Wade should be, as it were, beyond desire. But we see that he is not, and his desire is subversive of the paternal metaphor.

Female sexuality in this universe is determined by these masculine imperatives. Hannah, we learn, will not entirely let Wade get away with breaking the rules. After the shooting "accident" Wade tells Rafe to drive more slowly, for he is in no hurry to get home. By violating the rules of symbolic exchanges between men, by betraying the "hom(m)o-sexual" system according to which women are exchanged between men and according to which marriage is meant to remove a woman from the market, Wade has forfeited his right to a happy home life.

As Robin Wood has written, "in a society built on monogamy and family there will be an enormous surplus of sexual energy that will have to be repressed; and . . . what is repressed must always strive to return."[40] We see that return of the repressed everywhere in *Home from the Hill*, in the story, in the mise en scène, and in the music. Rafe is the single most obvious sign of Wade's excessive sexual en-

[40] Robin Wood, "The American Family Comedy: From *Meet Me in St. Louis* to *The Texas Chainsaw Massacre*," *Wide Angle* 3, no. 2 (1979): 5–6.

ergy, which marriage has done nothing to contain, and all the problems this has created turn up in the body of the text, like symptoms in the body of an hysterical patient.[41] The energy attached to the idea of Wade's virility and the patriarchal principle he embodies is invested in his clothes (leather jacket, white suits, Stetson hat), his swaggering walk, his obedient hounds, his study cluttered with his hunting trophies, and so on. And in the same way that repression always seeks a return, punishment for transgression in melodrama is sooner or later exacted. In fact, Wade will only come home from the hill, finally, when he is dead.

Rafe's desire (for legitimation based on the recognition that he is Wade's son) structures much of the film. This repressed desire—so central to a satisfactory identity for Rafe—returns in several ways, as in Rafe's asking Wade for "that double-barreled, twelve-gauge bird gun you keep locked up." A man like Wade, however, should not have to pay for anything: "I'm not payin' you for my life, Rafe, I'm just thankin' you for it!" The gun, of course, is here the symbol of phallic continuity between father and son, which Wade will withhold until the end of his life. (This masculine inheritance, appropriately enough, will be mediated through women—Hannah and Libby—in a deft reordering of power lines that keeps patriarchal principles intact.)

The film begins with a dilemma for Wade: he has two sons, but in effect he has no sons. Theron belongs to Hannah, and Rafe is a bastard—an orphan so far as the world is concerned. The film proceeds to show Wade's last, perhaps only, effort to reclaim Theron, for Wade's own identity is to some extent inflected by questions of dynastic bequest and paternal legacy. Wade's dilemma is precisely a function of his paternal status. As supreme embodiment of the patriarchal function, Wade owns everybody and everything around him. Unlike John Sims in *The Crowd*, a man like Wade Hunnicutt does not work for wages. He takes and he owns. The phallic power that he possesses in the familial sphere is conflated with property ownership. Wade even seems to think that he owns Rafe, in the way that aristocrats in Old Russia owned serfs. Theron, however, as his legal heir, presents Wade with a different problem. As Wade sees it, if

---

[41] Geoffrey Nowell-Smith, "Minnelli and Melodrama," *Screen* 18, no. 2 (1977): 117.

Theron is to be his worthy successor, Theron must learn "to be a man."

The whole hunting metaphor of *Home from the Hill* aptly expresses the masculine sexuality that the film as a melodrama simultaneously critiques and celebrates. It is above all a *phallic* sexuality, which charges everything. When Wade before the hunt teaches Theron how to fire a gun, the camera cuts to a close-up of Mitchum's face—one of the very few in the film—and his voice suddenly becomes soft and gentle: "Now lay your cheek snug up against the stock . . . both eyes wide open. Take a deep breath . . . then let out half of it . . . and now slowly squeeze down on the trigger." Wade is initiating Theron into the autoerotic pleasures of phallic sublimations, which are necessary to "heterosexual" masculinity.

Andrea Dworkin has remarked that older men hate boys because "boys still have the smell of women on them."[42] As "Hannah's boy" Theron has been feminized, or more precisely, he has yet to be masculinized by his father. Wade's phallic power is something that can cast an aura by association with him; it can be learned, but ideally, it must seem to be a natural inheritance. ("Well, you're my father! How come I wasn't taught?" the mortified son wants to know.)

In the way that Minnelli movies understand—with their emphasis on decor and mise en scène—Wade starts with the way things *look*, with the *appearance* of masculinity. Like Teddy Roosevelt's house at Oyster Bay, Wade Hunnicutt's "den" is an almost parodic expression of masculinity. Gesture, too, follows the same pattern. Wade strides over to his refrigerator and helps himself to a beer, which he drinks directly from the bottle. He seats himself squarely, legs apart, in his huge, red, leather armchair. As *the* patriarch, he has (or must show) no fear of any threat of symbolic castration (we see it in the way he sits), and his mastery is expressed in small details such as the obedient dog under his caressing hand and the way Mitchum delivers Wade's manifesto of masculinity:

I had somethin' from my father that his father gave to him. I'm goin' to give it to you. It's late, but it's not too late. You know, one these days I'm goin' to die, Theron. You're goin' to come into 40,000 acres of land—cotton, beef, goats, timber. Takes a special kind a man to handle that—kind of man that walks around with nothing in his pockets—no identification—because every-

[42] Andrea Dworkin, *Pornography: Men Possessing Women* (New York: G. P. Putnam's Sons, 1979), 51.

20. Masculinity defined by decor: Wade Hunnicutt in his den. (Robert Mitchum in *Home from the Hill*.)

body knows who you are; no cash because anybody in town be happy to lend you anything you need; no keys because you don't keep a lock on a single thing you own; and no watch, because time waits on *you*. What I'm sayin' is you goin' to be known in these parts as a *man*! Or as a mama's boy.

The speech is extraordinary. It is all about a form of male narcissism—a kind of masculinity that is founded on a radical denial of difference. Wade is in a position to have everything in his image. As a man (a subject) in a man's world, Wade is mirrored in his fellow man. In *Home from the Hill* all the main characters are in the same position in relation to Wade Hunnicutt: as a super-patriarch, Wade puts all others to a greater or lesser degree in a subordinate position. If he owns everything—land, cotton, beef, goats, timber, people—he even, to some extent and in a limited sense, also owns time. Wade's world would appear to have been designed specifically for him.

But there are a few problems in Wade's world that just will not go away: Hannah, whom he still desires deeply, is frigid; his son Theron

Fathers what could be illegitimate child—
Rafe prevents this by marrying Libby
so Wade's order isn't passed on

is a problem—first because he is not enough of "a man" to inherit Wade's position in the family or larger community, and later because he hates his parents; and Rafe is anxious, to the point of rebelliousness, to be recognized. Wade is a wealthy man—this is what distinguishes him from other men—and yet it is in his wealth that the causes of the disturbance of the patriarchal system lie. As Luce Irigaray has written in considering a few points in Marx's analysis of value,

> Wealth amounts to a subordination of the use of things to their accumulation. Then would *the way women are used matter less than their number*? The possession of a woman is certainly indispensable to a man for the reproductive use value that she represents; but what he desires is to have them all. To "accumulate" them, to be able to count off his conquests, seductions, possessions, both sequentially and cumulatively, as measure or standard(s).[43]

This is what Hannah will not tolerate, and she understands perfectly that in opposing Wade's conception of masculinity which is so much a function of wealth, she frustrates the system that would relegate her to the status of a commodity. At the same time she increases her own value, while remaining an abstraction: "Shall I tell you why you still find me attractive after all these years? Because you can't have me. Because you never will." In this, her powers of self-perception show up his lack of them. In Wade Hunnicutt's empire, Hannah is the one thing he cannot have.

Hannah will not make of herself a mirror that reflects narcissistically for Wade what he wants to see, and yet, paradoxically—aside from her exceptional beauty and her will that is as stubborn as Wade's—she does just that and cannot help it. She is his match, and as Captain Wade Hunnicutt's wife she has a value that is unique, a value that comes into being in that suspension between Wade and all other men. As Irigaray notes, it is not woman's "usefulness" that counts the most (her reproductive use value—reproductive of children and of the labor force), for "woman's price is not determined by the properties of her body—although her body constitutes the *material* support of that price," but her "value on the market by virtue of one single quality: that of being a product of man's 'labor.' "[44] Even

stronger doesn't die—defies him in putting Rafe on grace

[43] Irigaray, *This Sex Which Is Not One*, 174.
[44] Ibid., 174.

the Hunnicutts' house, which (apart from the overwrought, red-dominated decor of Wade's den) reflects Hannah's taste, is only Hannah's house in the sense that she and it are products of Wade's labor. She herself is always dressed elegantly, in beige, and the house reflects this same understated sense of style. Her "Southern" grace is a peculiar thing: exquisite, hysterical, carefully mannered. We see the cost of it, though, in her watery, "tragic" eyes, and in the way she clutches her stomach (womb) when Theron leaves home, and again when Wade is shot.

In this society one cannot accumulate wives. Wade can only have one wife, which is why, inevitably, she among all women becomes exceptional. One can have many sons, however, but in betraying the system (according to which one can only have one wife) Wade finds himself with one son too many and no sons at all.[45] That betrayal prevents both his sons from taking their "rightful" places in the patriarchal system of bourgeois society.

In *Home from the Hill* we see a variation on (not really a reversal of) the folklore of the bastard child. While Rafe is the legal outcast, he is the one who enjoys Wade's companionship and intimacy; it is the legitimate son Theron who must grow up outside the sphere of paternal influence. Both sons, on different levels, are excluded from the world of symbolic exchanges between men. This perversion of the conventional "hom(m)o-sexual" law according to which society operates is what, ultimately, the narrative must put right, or this symbolic system of bourgeois patriarchal society will come to an end. Irigaray writes:

Consider the exemplary case of *father-son relationships*, which guarantee the transmission of patriarchal power and its laws, its discourse, its social structures. These relations, which are in effect everywhere, cannot be eradicated through the abolition of the family or of monogamous reproduction, nor can they openly display the pederastic love in which they are grounded. They cannot be put into practice at all, except in language, without provoking a general crisis, without bringing one sort of symbolic system to an end.[46]

[45] Guérif opens his chapter on *Home from the Hill* with this: "Adapté d'un roman de William Humphrey, auquel a été rajouté le personnage essentiel du fils bâtard, *Home from the hill* fait penser au résumé que donnait William Faulkner d'un de ses livres préférés, *Absalon, Absalon*: 'C'est l'histoire d'un homme qui voulait des fils. Il en eut un de trop et il fut détruit.'" (Guérif, *Vincente Minnelli*, 106.)

[46] Irigaray, *This Sex Which Is Not One*, 193.

Wade must have a son, and since Theron belongs to Hannah, he will love Rafe instead, until he is forced to recognize that their love is doomed and that he must try, before it is too late, to direct his paternal imperatives towards Theron. The pseudo-philosophy Wade offers Theron speaks for him nevertheless:

> From now on you gonna learn in the woods. . . . What I'm talking about is coming face to face with your own courage, your own cunning, your own endurance, because what every man hunts out there is himself. Now, if that's what you want, I'll help you.

His philosophy thus expressed does speak the narcissism of masculinity founded on a radical denial of sexual difference. Wade would have Theron believe that one's sense of masculine self derives from oneself, is an exclusive affair—that *the only mirror good enough is oneself*. The feminine in *Home from the Hill* is always essentially a failure to be masculine, and yet masculinity needs the "feminine" to give it reality.

It is through Libby Holstead that Theron will feel he has finally achieved a masculine identity, and it is no surprise that the scene in which he has Rafe ask Libby to accompany him (Theron) to the dance, follows the hunt scene in which he kills the wild boar. Wade's statement that every hunt is essentially a quest for selfhood suggests at least two related things. While the hunt is obviously a test of the hunter's "masculinity," it is clearly a symbolic effort to overcome and repress the homosexual impulse that is postulated by patriarchal society. Masculine homosexuality, we know, is forbidden in patriarchal society, even though the economy as a whole is based on it, because (as Irigaray observes) masculine homosexual relations "openly interpret the law according to which society operates."[47] Masculine homosexual relations are "incestuous" and have the effect of "short-circuiting the mechanisms of commerce." Irigaray suggests that "furthermore, they might lower the sublime value of the standard, the yardstick. Once the penis itself becomes merely a means to pleasure, pleasure among men, *the phallus loses its power*. Sexual plea-

---

[47] Ibid., 193. This law according to which society operates is effectively camouflaged by the hunt, which itself furnishes the metaphor for our society's master form of mediation (through the bodies of women). During an unsuccessful buck-hunt Rafe suggests to Theron that they give up hunting for the day and go into town to look for girls, which he describes as "a different kind of hunting!"

sure, we are told, is best left to those creatures who are ill-suited for the seriousness of symbolic rules, namely, women."[48]

After the hunt, the intense feeling between father and son must be mediated. Wade offers Theron an orange to suck on, to cut the brassy taste of fear in his mouth, which only another hunter so tested would know about, and Rafe hands him the boar's tail ("a kinda trophy") as the music on the soundtrack swells and Theron lies back, spent and smiling. Theron has been admitted to the masculine club of phallic-power brokers, but they—Wade, Theron, all phallus-bearers—cannot themselves also be the commodities exchanged on the market.

In the scene that follows, we see how Hannah will not acquiesce to the feminine position to which this masculine system subjects her. For the great barbecue that Wade gives in Theron's honor Wade dresses up in his white evening clothes and approaches Hannah for this symbolic mediation, at the same moment that Theron is knocking on Libby Holstead's door. Hannah resists her husband's advance, and Mr. Holstead refuses to let Libby go with Theron to the barbecue; both father and son fail to secure the woman's mediation for their narcissistic display of masculinity. Rafe, on the other hand, is surrounded by pretty, young women, and in the next shot Hannah tells Wade that she almost put a ribbon in her hair tonight. Why "almost"? one may ask. For Wade? For Theron? Indeed, she must ask herself what for, since she will not play the mirror to Wade's triumph, which is her loss.

Theron's progress towards a masculine identity is represented by Minnelli not just in good dialogue but in a remarkable economy of gesture and motif. After Theron kisses Hannah goodnight (for the last time) Wade tells her she has "done a good job—as far as it goes." She asks, "What else do you want him to be?" to which he replies, "My son." To be his father's son, Theron will have to turn away from his mother, to reject her as his chief figure of identification. Hannah can only hope that Theron will show Wade that he has a mind of his own, a spirit of independence that she believes she has given him. When Theron resists a kiss she offers him, she gives in: "Oh, I see. No more syrupy sentimentality? Just rough friendliness? All right."

[48] Irigaray, *This Sex Which Is Not One*, 193.

When Wade tells the tenant farmers that his son will handle the problem they have brought to him (the killing of the boar) Theron accidentally knocks over his glass of milk—a gesture that aptly signals that Hannah's job is done. One recalls the scene later when Theron comes home at two in the morning from seeing Libby, to find Hannah waiting up for him with a glass of hot milk and a lecture. "I don't like hot milk," he tells her. Both occasions mark new phases in the evolution of Theron's masculinity.

Until Theron discovers that Wade is Rafe's father, Wade is the unflawed embodiment of the phallic principle. He is the sublime standard, the one with the power to confer identity. It is important to note, however, that Rafe's overly casual, drawling speech when he is with Theron on the hunt hints at the effort Rafe must make to repress any homoerotic feeling for his brother, a feeling intensified by this experience that puts them both under the law of the Father, both straining for a satisfactory identity in relation to that law. The necessary mediator, as we have said, is invariably a woman. Some sort of circuit—an economy of desire—is created by the exchange of women between men:

Reigning everywhere, although prohibited in practice, hom(m)o-sexuality is played out through the bodies of women, matter, or sign, and heterosexuality has been up to now just an alibi for the smooth workings of man's relations with himself, of relations among men.[49]

The film includes a scene which is explicit as ironic commentary on this theme of the fates of "normal" men and women in bourgeois heterosexual society. Rafe stumbles upon Theron and Libby having a picnic (he, on the other hand, is still attached to his dead mother; he had been cleaning her grave in Reprobate's Field):

Rafe:	Sonny, I do believe I notice a change in you these last few weeks.
Libby:	Well, it's the feminine touch, Rafe.
Rafe:	Yeah, I hear tell it does wonders for growing boys.
Theron:	You ought to try it yourself, Rafe.
Rafe:	There's not a woman in the world put up with me. A man who sleeps with his boots on and drinks beer in the morning and keeps a skunk for a house pet is no fit company for a lady. Isn't that right, Miss Libby?

[49] Ibid., 172.

21. With Libby, Theron discovers something which he decides is "more fun than huntin'." Rafe is still not convinced. (George Peppard, George Hamilton, Luana Patten.)

Libby:	Oh, some girl'll take you in hand. She'd get you to dry dishes and pay life insurance just like everybody else.

[She is preening herself with affected care in a tiny hand mirror.]

Rafe:	I can hardly wait.
Libby:	Oh, yeah. One of these days you'll be taking the kids to the dentist and mowing the lawn. Don't you think you won't.
Theron:	Is that what I got in store for me?
Libby:	Very likely if you hang around me much.
Theron:	It's more fun than huntin'!

Clearly, the point of the scene—since these choices for a man are unattractive, whichever way you look at them—is that, as Adrian Stokes has put it, "the implicit concept of maleness is manic and overwrought."[50]

[50] Cited in Michael O'Pray, "Movies, Mania and Masculinity," *Screen* 23, no. 5 (November–December 1982): 63.

In many ways Theron represents the film's progressive voice. Although he winds up losing almost everything in order to gain an identity, his remark to Libby that "You can't knock around on your own; you gotta have friends, family," must be taken as the film's most urgent point. The hunter must *come home from the hill*. By the next time Libby wants to talk family, however, Theron has been profoundly disillusioned. After his showdown with Wade, Theron leaves home and takes a job at the cotton compress. It is a dramatic working-out of what every boy must do to find an identity for himself: work it out on his own, and experience the kind of hardship that favors consciousness. There is no escaping the family, however, for when Wade tries for a reconciliation he will seek Theron out even there—Wade owns the mortgage on the place, which he feels gives him the right to "five minutes of [Theron's] time." Later Theron tells Libby,

He says I'm his son; she says I'm her son; but nobody's ever said, 'our son.' They pull me in half like that every day of my life. That's what they call love, they call being a family. Well, I'll go along with her; I owe her that; that's what she had me for. But if this is what being part of a family can do to you, I'm never goin' to get married and have kids. I'm never goin' to do this to them!

The irony, of course, is that as he is saying this, Libby is pregnant with his child; he does not know it, and she will not tell him. When Libby's father finds out that she is pregnant, he tries to get Wade to agree to put pressure on Theron to marry her, but Wade, using an aptly economic metaphor, calls Libby "damaged goods." Wade's description of Libby is an acknowledgment of the system according to which women are like goods exchanged in a market controlled by men. It should also be observed that Wade probably chooses this metaphor because he is talking to Albert Holstead, a storekeeper—and it is the storekeepers, he knows subconsciously, who are becoming the new leaders in the changing economy of the American South. *Home from the Hill* operates in a nostalgic mode. It ambivalently acknowledges the spread of a broad middle class in America (the Holsteads' class), but it loves the Southern Gothic splendor of Wade's vanishing world.

The Southern setting of *Home from the Hill* is an interesting one for the familial themes it underscores. Wade and Hannah are associated with an Old South whose codes of behavior will be superseded by

the next generation. Theron and Rafe represent the spirit of reconciliation and union, but as in other Minnelli films, the masculine erotic
exchange takes place within a complex matrix of sexual and class differences. Theron and Rafe are split by class (that of their mothers),
and Wade both ignores and observes that class difference—consort-
ing with Rafe's mother, then consigning Rafe to her lower-class status. The old theme of the divided family (in the movies, at least as
old as *The Birth of a Nation*) finds its analog in the story of the American Civil War, played out on a regional field that has cultural resonances of almost generic power.

Of all the film's main characters it is Rafe who is our standard of
the normal. He is the natural son, brought up away from the Hunnicutt household. He is Theron's opposite, for Theron has everything
to learn about survival in the natural world. Rafe's private suffering,
with which the melodrama's audience traditionally identifies keenly,
makes him sensitive to the suffering of others. His entry into the
world of adult responsibilities was brutal. He tells Theron how, when
his mother died, "Chauncey [the loyal black Hunnicutt family re-
tainer] came down here and he said, 'You gotta learn to make out on
your own. These tears, crying and carrying on, is a waste of time.
Colored folks know that, and little white orphan boys gotta learn
that, too. So, hitch up your pants and *be a man*.' "[51] As a man without
a mother or wife, Rafe must internalize these roles for himself.

Rafe represents the self-sufficiency that is implicit in Wade's credo
of masculinity, and yet it is different—more truly self-reliant because
he is not a man of wealth. When she runs into him at the supermar-
ket, Libby wants to know who irons his shirts, and who sweeps under his bed. Most telling however (of her heterosexual, bourgeois assumptions), is her question "Who spends your money?" The utterly
conventional Libby expects a woman to be a product of man's labor.
She is, in effect, offering herself as a commodity that is ready for
another exchange between men. She is advertising herself as a good
mirror for a man, a woman who will give back a flattering image of
him.

According to melodrama's sense of justice, Rafe inherits everything. He gains the recognition of his father post mortem and some-

---

[51] I have already quoted the second half of this observation of Adrian Stokes': "There
is the phrase: 'Be a man' (never: 'Be a woman'), as if it were an exotic role, perhaps
because the implicit concept of maleness is manic and overwrought." (O'Pray, "Movies, Mania and Masculinity," 63.)

how further redresses his bastardy by taking Theron's wife and child. By marrying Libby, Rafe shares in the cult of the Father, originating from Wade, through Wade's legitimate son. He becomes the father of Theron's child, and he gains a mother when Hannah accepts his invitation to come and live with him and Libby; a symbolic exchange between Wade and Rafe, through Hannah, is effected.

From the chaotic, wrenching scene of Wade's death, Theron's destiny quickly unravels. In the end it is Rafe who comes home from the hill, and it is Theron who will walk off into the woods like some unquiet ghost. When Wade falls to the floor he calls for Rafe, and Theron runs to fetch him. On the way we see two boys, no doubt brothers, playfully fighting on a lawn; they are the brothers that Rafe and Theron never were, and yet now, all at once, Rafe and Theron are brothers too intensely. Rafe begs his father to utter the two words he has been waiting all his life to hear: "My son."

"He was my father, too!" Rafe yells, as the brothers fight to avenge his death. With a curious logic, Theron's last hunt (for the man who killed his father) takes place in the same woods where he killed the wild boar. After Theron has shot Albert Holstead, Rafe places his leather hunting jacket about Theron's shoulders in a gesture of fraternal love, reconciliation and farewell. In a reversal of roles, Theron has become the restless hunter, and Rafe has entered the fold of legitimate identity. The fathers are dead, and new fathers have taken their place. The final shot of the film signifies the bearing the past will always have on the future. The patriarchal system, for the time being, has recuperated the excesses which are generated by the repression that keeps the system in place. But a history has been cut in stone, and Theron is out there somewhere, not yet home from the hill. On the right side of the frame Hannah and Rafe walk off towards Rafe's car, and in the foreground, on the left side of the frame, Wade's tombstone holds a story:

> WADE HUNNICUTT
> HUSBAND OF HANNAH
> BELOVED FATHER OF
> RAPHAEL AND THERON

MINNELLI AND MELODRAMA: PROVISIONAL CONCLUSIONS

The phase in the evolution of the family melodrama represented by the Minnelli films discussed in this chapter is not over yet. For that matter, the kind of melodrama represented by Vidor's *Stella Dallas* and *Ruby Gentry* has not disappeared from the movie screen either, but television has provided a good home for the family melodrama in serial form, and fewer out-and-out melodramas (melodramas that without embarassment, and without being "camp," present themselves *as* melodramas) are made for the movie screen anymore.

The camp streak we occasionally see in Vidor (e.g., in *Beyond the Forest*) is not quite the same thing that we see in Minnelli, who succeeds, rather, in a bold and brilliant use of cliché.[52] Of the three films in this chapter, *Some Came Running* offers the best example of Minnelli's "readiness to risk strong, sentimental, even embarrassing scenes, to resort to and go beyond cliché."[53] Built into the formulaic, generic character of the American cinema is a great dependency on cliché. Indeed, "cliché is an organic part of cinema aesthetics,"[54] but in Minnelli we see a critique of the dominant ideology and modes of representation from within. By "fleshing out the cliché,"[55] Minnelli manages to be powerfully subversive and mainstream at the same time.

The "Hollywood formula for criticism of life," as Catherine de la Roche called it,[56] is a formula that has always been essentially melodramatic, and Minnelli took the formula and exaggerated its struc-

---

[52] For a brief introduction to the role of cliché in language, see Ruth Amossy, "The Cliché in the Reading Process," trans. Terese Lyons, *SubStance* 35 (1982): 34–45.

[53] David Morse, "Aspects of Melodrama," *Monogram* 4 (1972): 16–17.

[54] Jurij Lotman, *Semiotics of Cinema*, trans. Mark E. Suino (Ann Arbor: Michigan Slavic Contributions/University of Michigan, 1981), 90.

[55] Thomas Elsaesser, "Tales of Sound and Fury: Observations on the Family Melodrama," *Monogram* 4 (1972): 8.

[56] Catherine de la Roche, *Vincente Minnelli* (The New Zealand Film Institute and *Film Culture* [U.S.A.], June 1959), 20. Consider de la Roche's criticism of Minnelli's *Madame Bovary*, in which she remarks on the way Hollywood handles literary adaptation:

> To include *all* these leading motivations in a film would admittedly have been neither possible nor desirable. But the spirit of social criticism, Flaubert's passionate anti-romanticism, could have been preserved. It seems that unconsciously even more than consciously, and perhaps unavoidably, Flaubert's story was remodelled to fit the current Hollywood formula for criticism of life, that is, to shift emphasis from the general to the particular; (Emma is made the victim of her lovers—whose importance is therefore enhanced—more than of her own folly and consequently is more sinned against than sinning); to omit controversy; to glamorize the leading roles (Rodolphe is transformed from a rough, self-indulgent country squire into a refined cavalier); and to over-stress extenuating circumstances in the case of the heroine. (20)

tures to the point of their subversion.[57] Minnelli clearly knows the differences among formula, camp, and cliché. He was perhaps the first filmmaker to consciously give camp full-blooded expression in the cinema,[58] and one of the first to make films with a psychoanalytic understanding, through the conscious use of cliché. His use of cliché is a form of acknowledgment of mass culture—a way of remaining within and of it, and yet being able to see mass culture for what it is, with a kind of objectivity.

Minnelli prefigures what John Berger has called "the theater of in-difference,"[59] which is a new phenomenon of public and private life charged with a form of theatricality. Briefly, the theater of indiffer-ence is peopled by caricatures, not drawn on paper, but alive. The whole effort of the melodrama, as we have already said, is to find an underlying morality, to assert that it exists, articulate it. But in mod-ern society—mass society—who or what is the Law that organizes and makes sense of everything? The historical precondition for the theater of indifference, Berger tells us, is that

everyone is consciously and helplessly dependent in most areas of their life on the opinions and decisions of others. To put it symbolically: the theater is built on the ruins of the forum. Its precondition is the failure of democracy. The indifference is the result of the inevitable divergence of personal fanta-sies when isolated from any effective social action. The indifference is born of the equation between excessive mobility of private fantasy and social, po-litical stasis.[60]

Berger's words pull it all together, making clear the relationship between mass culture ("everyone . . . dependent . . . on the opin-ions and decisions of others . . . the failure of democracy"), and the crisis of individual identity ("personal fantasies . . . isolated from any effective social action"). Emma Bovary has "one kind of dream and

[57] When de la Roche goes on to remark that, "within the limitations of the formula *Madame Bovary* is a film of quality with no few very fine moments," she obviously does not fully appreciate that Minnelli has consciously used the formula to give the story a depth that the formula, almost by definition, discourages. Minnelli has not produced "a film of quality" *in spite of* the formula's thinning, flattening tendency (that results so often in films that are mediocre—films that are formulaic and "melodramatic" in the pejorative sense), but he has used the formula to transcend itself.

[58] Of *The Pirate*—the opera bouffe by Sam Behrman—Minnelli wrote (of his hope to make it into movie), "It was great camp, an element that hadn't been intentionally used in films up to now . . . I say intentionally." (Minnelli, *I Remember It Well*, 164.)

[59] John Berger, "The Theater of Indifference," *The Village Voice* (April 19, 1983), 37.

[60] Ibid., 37, 44. All following quotations from Berger are from page 44.

another kind of life," and in the Hirshes' lives, as Dave finds out, "appearances hide failure, words hide facts, and symbols hide what they refer to."

The villager who visits John Berger's city of the theater of indifference (a latter-day John Sims arriving in New York, for example) "has never seen people producing such a surplus of expression over and above what is necessary to express themselves. And so he assumes that their hidden lives are as rich and mysterious as their expressions are extreme." He walks in a magnificent melodramatic theater, as the spectator does when he or she watches a Minnelli movie. And what is simultaneously invisible and visible, is "that which, according to [the spectator's] imagination, must lie behind their expressions and behavior." The spectator "believes that what is happening in the city [film] exceeds his[/her] imagination. . . . Tragically, [s]he is right."

The difference Berger talks about corresponds with Minnelli's cliché: it is a performance of the banal, a theatricalization of the ordinary, in signifiers that make "large but unsubstantiable claims on meaning."[61] Minnelli knows that his way of telling a story makes claims on meaning that are "unsubstantiable." To some extent, that *is* the meaning. His represented object is an Oedipal drama, and his way of representing it reveals the depth of his understanding of how identity is constructed in our culture out of an organization of surfaces, objects, movements, texts—material indexes of the unconscious.

[61] Brooks, *The Melodramatic Imagination*, 199.

9. Affects and Ideals: An Afterword

THE FAMILY melodrama in Hollywood's first five decades records the evolution of the dominant way in which we conceive of identity in America. The individual subject, whether male or female, is inscribed in language, and language in our culture, we have come to recognize, is patriarchal. By patriarchal, to reiterate, we refer before anything else to the way in which men are able to dominate women, and the way in which, as a result of this, women are identified sexually.

Females are en-gendered as such through a process that Catharine MacKinnon describes in terms of "sexual attractiveness, which means sexual availability on male terms. . . . Gender socialization is the process through which women come to identify themselves as sexual beings, as beings that exist for men."[1] If the family melodrama has become a discourse on sexuality, as we contend it has, it is because identity itself in our culture springs from sexual origins. This presents women (so often the subject of the family melodrama) with a unique problem: there is only one sex in patriarchy, and this, articulated in male/masculine terms, is phallic.

As MacKinnon's insight makes clear, however, femininity is not *of an essence*. While it may be a woman's experience of sexuality that engenders her as female (not, as one would expect, the other way round), she need not be bound, as I see it, to a "feminine destiny" of subordination to/signification of male desire. Of course, by the time one becomes a *thinking* subject, it is too late to radically change one's desire, but there is hope—and it is not just for future generations. This study of the American film melodrama—of some fictional subjects in their discursive realities—has, to echo Victor Burgin's words, become an attempt to show "the *meaning* of sexual difference

---

[1] Catharine A. MacKinnon, "Feminism, Marxism, Method, and the State: An Agenda for Theory," *Signs* 7, no. 3 (Spring 1982): 530–31. Quoted in Teresa de Lauretis, *Alice Doesn't* (Bloomington: Indiana University Press, 1984), 166.

as, precisely, a *process of production*; as something mutable, something historical, and therefore something we can do *something* about."[2]

Before sex and sexuality, however, we have the problem and necessity of "the symbolic function." If there is no reality apart from its representation, its inscription in language (the play of differences that constitutes the Symbolic), then there can be no (point in trying to) escape from the Symbolic. What the melodrama attempts to do, however, is to mitigate and deflect a little the goal of language to regulate life according to its ultimately castrating masculine principles. The melodrama is a crusade against the symbolic function's *inhibiting* imperatives. The melodrama recognizes that while language can be a prison, it is reality nonetheless; what the melodrama can do is keep a measure of pleasure in symbolic operations, to make us all—women and men—as free as possible *in* language. The melodrama's formal basis in "realism" attests to the form's underlying belief in reality. What it does not believe in is the necessity of human misery, of the subjection, most especially, of women.

The melodrama's male protagonists (John Sims in *The Crowd*, Dave Hirsh in *Some Came Running*, Rafe and Theron in *Home from the Hill*) assert that the form's quarrel is ultimately not just with "sexuality," but with the stern face of the Law. The Law, in the family melodrama, is of course articulated in familial terms, and the problem there is that ever since the rise of industrialism—with its radical separation of life into public and private spheres—there has been a heavy burden on the private sphere of the familial to organize and satisfy libidinal drives. The bourgeois family cannot cope. Too much is asked of actual mothers and fathers (and children) in ordinary families. The family, I think these melodramas demonstrate, is, after all, an organizational structure that is too limiting, too constricting.

While it is quite obviously beyond the scope of the melodrama to transcend Oedipus—since the melodrama is defined by its familial structures—the problems represented in and signified by the melodrama point to Oedipus as an origin of those problems. Moreover, the familial story described by the myth of Oedipus is not universal and trans-historical (its ancient origins notwithstanding). We must—if we can—go beyond Oedipus, for, in Mark Poster's words,

---

[2] Victor Burgin, "Man, Desire, Image," *Desire*, ed. Lisa Appignanesi (London: ICA Publications, 1984), 34.

Oedipus reduces and shrinks the individual to the family. The internaliza-
tion of the father as super-ego prevents the individual from participating in
collective myth. Oedipus privatizes myth, emotion, fantasy and the unconscious, centering the psyche forever on Mama/Papa. . . . Far from a general
law, Oedipus is the special law of the modern psyche. It is bound up with
the nuclear family, not with kinship, and it goes far in revealing the psychic
dynamics of modern families. The neuroses analyzed by Freud are private
myths, individual religions; they are the fetishism, the magic of the nuclear
family, the myth of people without collective fetishes to relieve guilt. As long
as Freud maintains the universality of Oedipus there can be no real history
of the family since this requires above all an account of the change from kinship to private families.[3]

Since the melodrama is a textual and aesthetic solution to ideological contradictions as they are signified in social problems, the form
changes over time. Its semantic dimension changes as the dominant
ideology (slowly, but not imperceptibly) changes, and the syntactic
dimension of the form undergoes change constantly. If we ever get
beyond Oedipus, however, we may or may not still call the aesthetic
text that articulates ideological contradiction the melodrama. In order
to do that, we shall have to conceive of desire in altogether different
terms. Nevertheless, for better or for worse, the melodramatic imagination dominates in our culture and probably will continue to dominate for a long time to come. The American cinema—the most powerful myth-making institution of our time—took Freud's family, lock,
stock and barrel, as its comprehensive Law. Cinematic language itself
was, from the very start, as Nick Browne points out, linked to a particular subject matter: the family—"typically the threat of its dismem-
berment either by loss of a child or by the death, separation, or violation of a parent."[4] Browne observes that, starting with Griffith's
first film, *The Adventures of Dollie* (1908, in which a child is stolen by
gypsies), "either the formal and technical advances in cinema as a
medium are introduced, or their meaning is normalized, by reference
to some family drama." This family drama, furthermore, is always
"achieved in the mode of nostalgia." The nostalgic mode works to
repeat original family relations ("the boy finds only his mother in his
wife,"[5] etc.) which all have their origin, as this study demonstrates,

[3] Mark Poster, *Critical Theory of the Family* (New York: The Seabury Press, 1978), 25–
26.
[4] Nick Browne, "Griffith's Family Discourse: Griffith and Freud," *Quarterly Review of
Film Studies* 6, no. 1 (Winter 1981): 68.
[5] Poster, *Critical Theory of the Family*, 100.

in the Oedipus Complex—that is to say, in how the super-ego is formed by *castration*:

Castration . . . sets in motion a deep and permanent alteration of personality structure: the child internalizes the authority of the parents in the form of a super-ego. The super-ego, in turn, assures that the child will *forever be a member of the family*, will forever carry within the dictates and emotional representations of the father. It assures that even when the child goes outside the family to seek a mate the emotional meaning of the choice will echo heavily the parent of the opposite sex. It makes certain that the bourgeoisie, a group without strong kinship ties, will be able to transmit property through generations.[6]

The bourgeois sons and daughters who learn this lesson well (Emma Bovary, Frank and Agnes Hirsh in *Some Came Running*—characters in all the films in this study) must believe that their problems, and the realization of their desires, have everything to do with money and social position. But the family melodrama equivocates here. It wishes to demonstrate that this is *not* so, and in spite of itself asserts that it *is* so. The form is caught between progressive and reactionary impulses—between locating real causes, and identifying symptoms.

One of the progressive impulses of the form, as I see it, is the way, not unlike the amorous state, the melodrama offers a respite from "resentment, our daily lot, [which] is opaque, exacting."[7] To borrow Julia Kristeva's words, it "allows us to dream another subjectivity: one which combines affects and ideals, the 'ego and the other' and, from these assumed contradictions, fashions open systems capable of innovation. Which is to say, of life."[8] The family melodrama holds that the ego and the other are forged in a familial context and that there, in the family, where we first start learning the symbolic function, affect's sources and the determinants of our ideals lie. In the forms's use of music, especially, we identify an impulse to fly free of the codifications of the Symbolic, and in the stories we see the sufferings and triumphs of characters who, by their actions or their mere being, critique or protest the Law. All this is part of the progressive

---

[6] Ibid., 100.

[7] Julia Kristeva, "*Histoires d'Amour*—Love Stories," *Desire*, ed. Lisa Appignanesi (London: ICA Publications, 1984), 21.

[8] Ibid., 21.

function; melodrama offers, in some sense, resistance to the restrictive demands of familial functions.

Since all stories are different, and yet all the same, everyone's differences with the Law are different, and yet the same. Conclusions and decisions, in other words, in the face of evidence that there is "something we can do" about the Law, will be different. The characters in the films in this study try various things—fantasy, masochism and self-sacrifice, mastery of the masculine system, marriage, murder, and death. But as for causes and origins, who can say? If we are not to deny history (the relationship between monotheism, capitalism and sexuality), and if the films can only tell us stories, then what can be done to realize melodrama's dream of "another subjectivity"?

As we are in a post-Industrial era—far from the imperatives of early monotheism and of capitalism—we might look to the family and reformulate its structure, for the familial relation has become metaphorical for all others, and that is the problem. The melodrama, as an aesthetic, theatrical articulation of this relation, offers us a place to begin to "do something about" it. We must go into the wings of this stage where the machines that produce the play's effects are hidden. Those effects, to echo Christian Metz once more, are perfectly real, which is why we might take more active, conscious control of their production—to reduce human misery.

If the melodrama sees the world as a stage, and the stage as a world, it is because there is an affinity between the familial (melodrama's controlling structure) and the theatrical. When Deleuze and Guattari observe that there is an affinity between psychoanalysis and the theatrical and structural representation it makes visible, they repeat two of André Green's reasons for this affinity that they find especially striking: "the theater raises the familial relation to the condition of a universal metaphoric structural relation, whence the imaginary place and interplay of persons derives; and inversely, the theater forces the play and the working of machines into the wings, behind a limit that has become impassible (exactly as in fantasy the machines are there, but *behind the wall*)."[9]

---

[9] Gilles Deleuze and Félix Guattari, *Anti-Oedipus: Capitalism and Schizophrenia*, trans. Robert Hurley, Mark Seem, and Helen R. Lane (Minneapolis: University Of Minnesota Press, 1983), 307. They are referring to André Green's *Un oeil en trop* (Paris: Editions de Minuit, 1969).

This study has taken us a little way "behind the wall," where we have found some of the machines of ideology and art working to create effects (which are perfectly real) in family drama. It is not that the art of bourgeois ideology denies the difficulties and the human misery in the world, but that it disguises why they are there. In Dana Polan's words, "Art doesn't deny this malaise; it merely hides and denies it bases in historical forces."[10]

We need, then, a critical theory of the family, a social and historical theory of the subject, which will provide a basis for reform; and whether we choose to take up Deleuze and Guattari's schizo-analysis[11] or their notion of *le devenir femme,*[12] or decide with Dorothy Dinnerstein that our children must be raised equally by mothers and fathers, or believe with early Julia Kristeva that those of us who are denied entry to social experience shall gain it "by listening; by recognizing the unspoken in speech, even revolutionary speech; by calling attention at all times to whatever remains unsatisfied, repressed, new, eccentric, incomprehensible, disturbing to the *status quo*"[13]—we shall, like the family melodrama, be talking about the hope for a better future.

[10] Dana Polan, "A Brechtian Cinema? Towards a Politics of Self-Reflexive Film," *Jump Cut* 17 (1978); reprinted in *Movies and Methods*, vol. II, ed. Bill Nichols (Berkeley: University of California Press, 1985), 668.

[11] To borrow Charles Stivale's summing-up of the tasks of schizo-analysis as they are defined in *Anti-Oedipus*: "(1) the destructive task, 'a whole scouring of the unconscious, a complete curettage,' by undoing 'the Oedipal trap of oppression'; (2) the first positive task, 'discovering in a subject the nature, the formation or the functioning of *his* desiring-machines, independently of any interpretations'; and (3) the second positive task, 'whereby schizo-analysis schizophrenizes the investments of the unconscious desire of the social field.' " (Charles Stivale, "The Literary Element in *Milles Plateaux*: The New Cartography of Deleuze and Guattari," *SubStance* 44/45 [1984]: 32.)

[12] Becoming-woman: to become a minority, "in order to resist the dominant mode of representation represented by any majority." (Alice Jardine, "Woman in Limbo: Deleuze and His Br[others]," *SubStance* 44/45 [1984]: 46–60.)

[13] Julia Kristeva, *About Chinese Women*, trans. Anita Barrows (New York: Urizen Books, 1977), 38.

Filmography

WAY DOWN EAST (1920)

Production: D. W. Griffith Inc.; released by United Artists
Direction: D. W. Griffith; Assistant Director, Elmer Clifton
Scenario: Anthony Paul Kelly, elaborated by D. W. Griffith, from the stage
    play by Lottie Blair Parker and Joseph R. Grismer
Cinematography: G. W. Bitzer, Henrik Sartov
Editing: James and Rose Smith
Art direction: Charles O. Seessel, Clifford Pember
Technical direction: Frank Wortman
Decorative titles: Victor Georg
Music (composed and selected): Louis Silvers, William F. Peters
Running time: 165 minutes (13 reels)
Principal characters: Anna Moore (Lillian Gish); Anna's mother (Mrs. David
    Landau); Mrs. Tremont (Josephine Bernard); Diana Tremont (Mrs.
    Morgan Belmont); Diana's sister (Patricia Fruen); the eccentric aunt
    (Florence Short); Lennox Sanderson (Lowell Sherman); Squire Bartlett
    (Burr McIntosh); Mrs. Bartlett (Kate Bruce); David Bartlett (Richard Bar-
    thelmess); Martha Perkins (Vivia Ogden); Seth Holcomb (Porter
    Strong); Reuben Whipple (George Neville); Hi Holler (Edgar Nelson);
    Kate Brewster (Mary Hay); Professor Sterling (Creighton Hale); Maria
    Poole (Emily Fitzroy)

THE MOTHER AND THE LAW (1919)

Production/distribution: D. W. Griffith Inc. (1914)/Wark Producing Company
    (1919)
Direction: D. W. Griffith
Scenario: D. W. Griffith
Cinematography: G. W. Bitzer; Assistant Cameraman, Karl Brown
Editing: James and Rose Smith
Music: D. W. Griffith, Joseph Carl Breil
Running time: 112 minutes (7 reels)
Principal characters: The Dear One (Mae Marsh); her father (Fred Turner); the
    Boy (Robert Harron); Arthur Jenkins (Sam de Grasse); Mary T. Jenkins
    (Vera Lewis); the "Uplifters" (Mary Alden, Pearl Elmore, Lucille
    Brown, Luray Huntley, Mrs. Arthur Mackley); the Friendless One (Mir-
    iam Cooper); the Musketeer of the Slums (Walter Long); a friend of the
    Musketeer (Tully Marshall); the kindly policeman (Tom Wilson); the

Governor (Ralph Lewis); the Judge (Lloyd Ingraham); attorney for the Boy (Barney Bernard); Father Farley (Rev. A. W. McClure); the kindly neighbor (Max Davidson)

BROKEN BLOSSOMS (1919)

Production: D. W.Griffith, Inc.; released by United Artists
Direction: D. W. Griffith
Scenario: D. W. Griffith, based on "The Chink and the Chinaman" in *Limehouse Nights* by Thomas Burke
Cinematography: G. W. Bitzer; special effects, Henrik Sartov; additional photography, Karl Brown
Editing: James Smith
Technical advice: Moon Kwan
Music arranged by: Louis F. Gottschalk and D. W. Griffith
Running time: 90 minutes (6 reels)
Principal characters: Lucy Burrows (Lillian Gish); the Yellow Man (Richard Barthelmess); Battling Burrows (Donald Crisp); his manager (Arthur Howard); Evil Eye (Edward Peil); the Spying One (George Beranger); a prizefighter (Norman "Kid McCoy" Selby)

THE CROWD (1928)

Production: Metro-Goldwyn-Mayer Pictures
Direction and story: King Vidor; scenario by V. A. Weaver, Harry Behn; titles by Joe Farnham
Cinematography: Henry Sharp
Editing: Hugh Wynn
Set design: Cedric Gibbons, Arnold Gillespie
Running time: 95 minutes
Principal characters: Mary (Eleanor Boardman); John (James Murray); Bert (Bert Roach); Jane (Estelle Clark); Jim (Daniel G. Tomlinson); Dick (Dell Henderson); Mother (Lucy Beaumont); Junior (Freddie Burke Frederick); Daughter (Alice Mildred Puter)

STELLA DALLAS (1937)

Production: Samuel Goldwyn; released by United Artists
Associate production: Merrit Hulburd
Direction: King Vidor
Screenplay: Sarah Y. Mason and Victor Heerman; based on the novel by Olive Higgins Prouty and dramatization by Harry Wagstaff Gribble and Gertrude Purcell
Cinematography: Rudolphe Maté
Editing: Sherman Todd
Art direction: Richard Day

Costumes: Omar Kiam
Sound: Frank Maher
Music: Alfred Newman
Running time: 104 minutes
Principal characters: Stella Dallas (Barbara Stanwyck); Stephen Dallas (John
    Boles); Laurel Dallas (Anne Shirley); Helen Morrison (Barbara O'Neil);
    Ed Munn (Alan Hale); Mrs. Martin (Marjorie Main); Charlie Martin
    (George Walcott); Miss Phillibrown (Ann Shoemaker); Richard Gros-
    venor (Tim Holt); Mrs. Grosvenor (Nella Walker); Con Morrison
    (Jimmy Butler); John Morrison (Jack Egger); Lee Morrison (Dickie
    Jones)

RUBY GENTRY (1952)

Production: Joseph Bernhard and King Vidor; released by 20th Century-Fox
Direction: King Vidor
Screenplay: Silvia Richards; story by Arthur Fitz-Richard
Cinematography: Russel Harlan
Editing: Terry Morse
Art direction: Dan Hall; set decoration, Ed Boyle
Music: Heinz Roemheld, David Chudnow
Running time: 77 minutes
Principal characters: Ruby Gentry (Jennifer Jones); Boake Tackman (Charlton
    Heston); Jim Gentry (Karl Malden); Jud Corey (Tom Tully); Dr. Saul
    Manfred (Bernard Phillips); Jewel Corey (James Anderson); Letitia Gen-
    try (Josephine Hutchingson); Tracy McAuliffe (Phyllis Avery); Judge
    Tackman (Herbert Heyes); Ma Corey (Myra Marsh); Cullen McAuliffe
    (Charles Cane); Neil Fallgren (Sam Flint); Clyde Pratt (Frank Wilcox)

MADAME BOVARY (1949)

Production: Pandro S. Berman; released by MGM
Direction: Vincente Minnelli
Screenplay: Robert Ardrey, based on the novel by Gustave Flaubert
Cinematography: Robert Planck
Editing: Ferris Webster
Set design: Cedric Gibbons, Jack Martin Smith; set decoration, Edwin B. Wil-
    lis, Richard A. Pefferle
Women's costumes: Walter Plunkett
Men's costumes: Valles
Sound: Douglas Shearer
Music: Miklos Rozsa
Choreography: Jack Donohue
Running time: 114 minutes
Principal characters: Emma Bovary (Jennifer Jones); Gustave Flaubert (James
    Mason); Charles Bovary (Van Heflin); Rodolphe Boulanger (Louis Jour-

dan); Léon Dupuis (Christopher Kent); J. Homais (Gene Lockhart); L'Heureux (Frank Allenby); Mme. Dupuis (Gladys Cooper); Major Tuvache (John Abbot); Hippolyte (Henry Morgan); Dubocage (George Zucco); Félicité (Ellen Corby); Rouault (Edward Franz); Guillaumin (Henri Letondal); Mme. Lefrançois (Esther Somers); Pinard (Frederic Tozere); Marquis d'Andervilliers (Paul Cavanagh); Justin (Larry Simms); Berthe (Dawn Kinney); Priest (Vernon Steele)

SOME CAME RUNNING (1958)

Production: Sol C. Siegel; released by MGM
Direction: Vincente Minnelli; Assistant Director, William McGarry
Screenplay: John Patrick, Arthur Sheekman, based on the novel of the same title by James Jones
Cinematography: William H. Daniels, in CinemaScope and Metrocolor
Editing: Adrienne Fazan
Art direction: Urie McCleary, William A. Horning; set decoration, Henry Grace, Robert Priestley
Makeup: William Tuttle
Costumes: Walter Plunkett
Sound: Franklin Milton
Music: Elmer Bernstein
Running time: 136 minutes
Principal characters: Dave Hirsh (Frank Sinatra); Bama Dillert (Dean Martin); Ginny Moorehead (Shirley MacLaine); Gwen French (Martha Hyer); Frank Hirsh (Arthur Kennedy); Edith Barclay (Nancy Gates); Agnes Hirsh (Leora Dana); Dawn Hirsh (Betty Lou Keim); Rosalie (Carmen Philips); Raymond Lanchak (Steven Peck); Professor Gates (Larry Gates); Jane Barclay (Connie Gilchrist); Smitty (Ned Weaver); Wally Dennis (John Brennan); Bus driver (William Lockbridge); Hotel porter (Chuck Courtney); Student (W. W. Grabowski); Virginia Stevens (Janelle Richards); Mrs. Stevens (Geraldine Wall); Al (William Shallert); Ted Harperspoon (Don Haggerty); Dewey Cole (Denny Miller); Slim (George E. Stone); Judge Baskin (Anthony Jochim); Sister Marie Joseph (Marion Ross); Joe (Ric Roman); Sheriff (Roy Engel)

HOME FROM THE HILL (1960)

Production: Edmund Grainger, for Sol C. Siegel; released by MGM
Direction: Vincente Minnelli; Assistant Director, William McGarry
Screenplay: Harriet Frank, Jr. and Irving Ravetch, based on the novel by William Humphrey
Cinematography: Milton Krasner, in CinemaScope and Technicolor
Editing: Harold F. Kress
Art direction: George W. Davis, Preston Ames; set decoration, Henry Grace, Robert Priestley

Makeup: William Tuttle
Costumes: Walter Plunkett
Sound: Franklin Milton
Music: Bronislau Kaper; musical direction, Charles Wolcott
Special effects: Robert R. Hogue
Running time: 148 minutes
Principal characters: Wade Hunnicutt (Robert Mitchum); Hannah Hunnicutt
  (Eleanor Parker); Rafe Copley (George Peppard); Theron Hunnicutt
  (George Hamilton); Albert Holstead (Everett Sloane); Libby Holstead
  (Luana Patten); Sarah Holstead (Anne Seymour); Opal Bixby (Con-
  stance Ford); Chauncey (Ken Renard); Dr. Reuben Carson (Ray Teal);
  Melba (Hilda Haynes); Tenant farmers (Guinn "Big Boy" Williams, Dub
  "Cannonball" Taylor, Orville Sherman, Dan Sheridan, Denver Pyle,
  Charlie Briggs); John Ellis (Tom Gilson)

Bibliography

MELODRAMA

Affron, Charles. *Cinema and Sentiment*. Chicago: University of Chicago Press, 1982.

Allen, Robert C. *Speaking of Soap Operas*. Chapel Hill and London: University of North Carolina Press, 1985.

Amengual, Barthélémy. "Propos pédants sur le mélodrame d'hier et le faux mélo d'aujourd'hui." *Les Cahiers de la cinémathèque* 28 (1979): 12–15.

Ang, Ien. *Watching Dallas: Soap Opera and the Melodramatic Imagination*. Trans. Della Couling. London and New York: Methuen, 1985.

Arlen, Michael J. "On Giving the Devil His Due." *New Yorker*, 12 March 1979; reprinted in *The Camera Age*. New York: Farrar, Straus & Giroux, 1981, 297–306.

Bargainnier, Earl F. "Melodrama as Formula." *Journal of Popular Culture* 9, no. 3 (Winter 1975): 726–33.

Basinger, Jeanine. "When Women Wept." *American Film* 2 (September 1977): 52–57.

Belton, John. "Classical Style, Melodrama, and the Cinema of Excess: Griffith and Borzage." In *Cinema Stylists*. Metuchen, N.J.: The Scarecrow Press, 1983, 160–94.

Bentley, Eric. "Melodrama." In *The Life of the Drama*. New York: Atheneum, 1967, 195–218.

Bermel, Albert. "Where Melodrama Meets Farce." In *Melodrama. See* Gerould 1980, 173–78.

Beylie, Claude. "Propositions pour le mélo." *Les Cahiers de la cinémathèque* 28 (1979): 7–11.

———, and Max Tessier. "Mélo, mon beau souci." *Cinéma 71* 161 (December 1971): 41–59.

Booth, Michael R. *English Melodrama*. London: Herbert Jenkins, 1965.

Bourget, Jean-Loup. "Aspects du mélodrame américain." *Positif* 131 (October 1971): 31–43.

——— "Faces of the American Melodrama: Joan Crawford." *Film Reader* 3 (February 1978): 24–33.

———. *Le Mélodrame hollywoodien*. Paris: Stock, 1985.

Bowman, David. "Detective Melodrama on TV." *Journal of the University Film Association* 27, no. 2 (1975): 40.

Brooks, Peter. *The Melodramatic Imagination: Balzac, Henry James, Melodrama, and the Mode of Excess*. New Haven: Yale University Press, 1976.

Burgoyne, Robert. "Narrative and Sexual Excess." *October* 21 (Summer 1982): 51–61.

Les Cahiers de la cinémathèque 28 (1979). Special issue on melodrama.

Carroll, Noël. "The Moral Ecology of Melodrama: The Family Plot and *Magnificent Obsession.*" In *Melodrama. See* Gerould 1980, 197–206.

Cawelti, John G. "Melodrama." In *Adventure, Mystery, and Romance: Formula Stories as Art and Popular Culture.* Chicago: University of Chicago Press, 1973, 44–47.

Cook, Pam. "Melodrama." In *The Cinema Book.* Ed. Pam Cook. New York: Pantheon Books, 1986, 73–84.

Corrigan, Robert W. "Melodrama and the Popular Tradition in Nineteenth-Century British Theater." In *Laurel British Drama: The Nineteeth Century.* Ed. R. W. Corrigan. New York: Dell, 1967, 7–22.

——. "Melodrama: The Drama of Disaster." In *The World of Theater.* Glenview, Ill.: Scott, Foresman, 1979, 103–15.

Creed, Barbara. "The Position of Women in Hollywood Melodrama." *Australian Journal of Screen Theory* 4 (1978): 27–31.

Cunningham, Stuart. "The Force-Field of Melodrama." *Quarterly Review of Film Studies* 6, no. 4 (Fall 1981): 347–64.

Davies, Robertson. *The Mirror of Nature.* Toronto: University of Toronto Press, 1982.

De Cordova, Richard. "A Case of Mistaken Legitimacy: Class and Generational Difference in Three Family Melodramas." In *Home Is Where the Heart Is. See* Gledhill 1987, 255–67.

Doane, Mary Ann. "*Caught* and *Rebecca*: The Inscription of Femininity as Absence." *Enclitic* 5, no. 2/6, no. 1 (Fall 1981/Spring 1982a): 75–89.

——. "The 'Woman's Film': Possession and Address." In *Re-Vision: Essays in Feminist Film Criticism.* Ed. Mary Ann Doane, Patricia Mellencamp, Linda Williams. Los Angeles: AFI Monograph Series, 1983, 67–82.

——. "The Clinical Eye: Medical Discourses in the 'Woman's Film' of the 1940s." *Poetics Today* 6, no. 1/2 (1985): 205–27.

——. *The Desire to Desire: The Woman's Film of the 1940s.* Bloomington: Indiana University Press, 1987.

Durgnat, R. E. "Ways of Melodrama." *Sight and Sound* 21, no. 1 (August–September 1951): 34–40.

Ehrenstein, David. "Melodrama and the New Woman." *Film Comment* 14, no. 5 (September-October 1978): 59–62.

Elsaesser, Thomas. "Tales of Sound and Fury: Observations on the Family Melodrama." *Monogram* 4 (1972): 2–16.

Fell, John. "Dissolves by Gaslight." In *Film and the Narrative Tradition.* Norman: University of Oklahoma Press, 1974; reprinted Berkeley (University of California Press, 1986), 12–36.

——. "Melodrama, the Movies, and Genre." In *Melodrama. See* Gerould 1980, 187–95.

——. "Melogenre." *North Dakota Quarterly* 51, no. 3 (Summer 1983): 100–10.

Feuer, Jane. "Melodrama, Serial Form and Television Today." *Screen* 25, no. 1 (January–February 1984): 4–16.

Finch, Mark. "Sex and Address in *Dynasty*." *Screen* 27, no. 6 (November–December 1986): 24–42.

Fischer, Lucy. "Two-Faced Women: The 'Double' in Women's Melodrama of the 1940s." *Cinema Journal* 23, no. 1 (Fall 1983): 24–43.

Gerould Daniel. "Russian Formalist Theories of Melodrama." *Journal of American Culture* 1, no. 1 (Spring 1978): 151–68.

———. ed. *Melodrama*. New York: New York Literary Forum, 1980.

———. "The Americanization of Melodrama." In *American Melodrama*. Ed. Daniel Gerould. New York: Performing Arts Journal Publications, 1983: 7–29.

Gledhill, Christine, ed. *Home Is Where the Heart Is: Studies in Melodrama and the Woman's Film*. London: British Film Institute, 1987.

Goimard, Jacques. "Le Mélodrame: le mot et la chose." *Les Cahiers de la cinémathèque* 28 (1979): 17–65.

Grimstead, David. *Melodrama Unveiled: Theater and Culture 1800–1850*. Chicago: University of Chicago Press, 1968.

Harper, Sue. "Historical Pleasures: Gainsborough Costume Melodrama." In *Home Is Where the Heart Is. See* Gledhill 1987, 167–96.

Heilman, Robert Bechtold. *Tragedy and Melodrama*. Seattle: University of Washington Press, 1968.

———. "Tragedy and Melodrama: Alternate Forms." In *The Iceman and the Arsonist, and the Troubled Agent*. Seattle: University of Washington Press, 1973, 22–62.

Jacobs, Lea. "Censorship and the Fallen Woman Cycle." In *Home Is Where the Heart Is. See* Gledhill 1987, 100–12.

Journal of the University Film and Video Association 35, no. 1 (Winter 1983). Special issue on melodrama.

Kaplan, E. Ann. "The Case of the Missing Mother: Maternal Issues in Vidor's *Stella Dallas*." *Heresies* 16 (1983a): 81–85.

———. "Mothering, Feminism and Representation: The Maternal in Melodrama and the Woman's Film 1910–40" (1983c). In *Home Is Where the Heart Is. See* Gledhill 1987, 113–37.

———. "Theories of Melodrama: A Feminist Perspective." *Women and Performance* 1, no. 1 (1983d): 40–48.

Kauffmann, Stanley. "Melodrama and Farce: A Note on a Fusion in Film." In *Melodrama. See* Gerould 1980, 169–72.

Kehr, David. "The New Male Melodrama." *American Film* (April 1983): 43–47.

Kleinhans, Chuck. "Notes on Melodrama and the Family under Capitalism." *Film Reader* 3 (February 1978): 40–47.

Kuhn, Annette. "Women's Genres." *Screen* 25, no. 1 (January–February 1984): 18–28.

LaPlace, Maria. "Producing and Consuming the Woman's Film: Discursive

Struggle in *Now Voyager.*" In *Home Is Where the Heart Is. See* Gledhill 1987, 138–66.

Lebrun, Michel. "Les 'Figures imposées' du mélo." *Les Cahiers de la cinémathèque* 28 (1979): 90–93.

Lippe, Richard. "Melodrama in the Seventies." *Movie* 29/30 (Summer 1982): 122–27.

McConnell, Frank. "The World of Melodrama: Pawns." In *Storytelling and Mythmaking: Images from Film and Literature.* New York: Oxford University Press, 1979, 138–99.

Meisel, Martin. "Speaking Pictures." In *Melodrama. See* Gerould 1980, 51–68.

Merritt, Russell. "Melodrama: Postmortem for a Phantom Genre." *Wide Angle* 5, no. 3 (1983): 25–31.

Mitry, Jean. "Le Mélodrame." In *Histoire du cinéma.* Paris: Universitaires, 1981, 593–627.

Modleski, Tania. *Loving With a Vengeance: Mass-Produced Fantasies for Women.* New York: Methuen, 1982.

———. "Time and Desire in the Woman's Film." *Cinema Journal* 23, no. 3 (Spring 1984): 19–30.

Morse, David. "Aspects of Melodrama." *Monogram* 4 (1972): 16–17.

Movie 29/30 (Summer 1982). Special issue on melodrama.

Mulvey, Laura. "Douglas Sirk and Melodrama." *Australian Journal of Screen Theory* 3 (1977): 26–30.

———. "Notes on Sirk and Melodrama." *Movie* 25 (Winter 1977–78): 53–56.

———. "Melodrama In and Out of the Home." In *High Theory/Low Culture.* Ed. Colin MacCabe. New York: St. Martin's Press, 1986: 80–100.

Neale, Steve. "Melodrama and Tears." *Screen* 27, no. 6 (November–December 1986a): 6–22.

Nichols, Bill. "Revolution and Melodrama." *Cinema* (U.S.) 6, no. 1 (1970): 42–47.

Nowell-Smith, Geoffrey. "Minnelli and Melodrama." *Screen* 18, no. 2 (Summer 1977): 113–18.

Pollock, Griselda; Nowell-Smith, Geoffrey; and Heath, Stephen. "Dossier on Melodrama." *Screen* 18, no. 2 (Summer 1977): 105–19.

Rahill, Frank. *The World of Melodrama.* University Park, Pa.: Pennsylvania State University Press, 1967.

Rodowick, D. N. "Madness, Authority, and Ideology in the Domestic Melodrama of the 1950's." *The Velvet Light Trap* 19 (1982b): 40–45.

Roelens, Maurice. "Mélodrame, cinéma, histoire . . ." *Les Cahiers de la cinémathèque* 28 (1979): 4–5.

———. "La Mise à mort." *Les Cahiers de la cinémathèque* 28 (1979): 110–15.

Rosenberg, James. "Melodrama." In *The Context and Craft of Drama.* Ed. Robert W. Corrigan and James L. Rosenberg. San Francisco: Chandler, 1964, 168–85.

Schatz, Thomas. "The Family Melodrama." In *Hollywood Genres: Formulas, Filmmaking and the Studio System.* New York: Random House, 1981, 221–67.

Sefani, Pierre. "Les Gens du voyage." *Les Cahiers de la cinémathèque* 28 (1979): 94–99.

Seiter, Ellen. "Men, Sex and Money in Recent Family Melodramas." *The Journal of the University Film and Video Association* 35, no. 1 (Winter 1983): 17–27.

Smith, James L. *Melodrama*. London: Methuen, 1973.

Sypher, Wylie. "Romeo and Juliet are Dead: Melodrama and the Clinical." In *Melodrama*. *See* Gerould 1980, 179–86.

Tessier, Max. "Le Mélodrame, genre ou vision du monde." *Cinéma 71* 161 (1971): 44–49.

Thomson, David. "Woman's Realm and Man's Castle." In *America in the Dark: Hollywood and the Gift of Unreality*. New York: William Morrow, 1977, 192–223.

Vardac, A. Nicholas. *Stage to Screen: Theatrical Origins of Early Film: David Garrick to D. W. Griffith*. New York: Da Capo Press, 1987. Originally published as *Stage to Screen: Theatrical Method from Garrick to Griffith*. Cambridge: Harvard University Press, 1949.

Vicinus, Martha. " 'Helpless and Unfriended': Nineteenth-Century Domestic Melodrama." *New Literary History* 13, no. 1 (Autumn 1981): 127–43.

Viviani, Christian. "Who is Without Sin? The Maternal Melodrama in American Film, 1930–39." *Wide Angle* 4, no. 2 (1980): 4–17.

Walker, Janet. "Hollywood, Freud and the Representation of Women: Regulation and Contradiction, 1945–early 60s." In *Home Is Where the Heart Is*. *See* Gledhill 1987, 197–214.

Walker, Michael. "Melodrama and the American Cinema." *Movie* 29/30 (Summer 1982): 2–38.

Wegner, Hart. "Melodrama as Tragic Rondo: Douglas Sirk's *Written on the Wind*." *Film/Literature Quarterly* 10, no. 3 (1982): 155–61.

Williams, Linda. "'Something Else Besides a Mother': *Stella Dallas* and the Maternal Melodrama." *Cinema Journal* 24, no. 1 (Fall 1984): 2–27.

Wide Angle 4, no. 2 (Spring 1981). Special issue on melodrama.

Yeck, Joanne L. "The Woman's Film at Warner Bros., 1935–1950." Ph.D. Dissertation, University of Southern California, 1982.

DIRECTORS AND FILMS DISCUSSED IN THIS STUDY

D. W. Griffith

Altman, Rick, ed. "Special Issue: Essays on D. W. Griffith." *Quarterly Review of Film Studies* 6, no. 1 (Winter 1981).

———. "*The Lonely Villa* and D. W. Griffith's Paradigmatic Style." *Quarterly Review of Film Studies* 6, no. 2 (Spring 1981): 123–34.

Belton, John. "The Art of the Melodramatic Style: D. W. Griffith and *Orphans of the Storm*." *Silent Picture* 16 (1972): 28–32.

———. "*True Heart Susie*." *The Silent Picture* 17 (Spring 1973): 25–29.

Brown, Karl. *Adventures With D. W. Griffith*. New York: Da Capo Press, 1973.

Cadbury, William. "Theme, Felt Life, and the Last-Minute Rescue in Griffith After *Intolerance.*" *Film Quarterly* 28, no. 1 (1974): 39–49.

Cardullo, Bert. "*Way Down East*: Play and Film." In *Indelible Images: New Perspectives on Classic Films*. Lanham, Md.: University Press of America, 1987, 15–21.

Casty, Alan. "The Films of D. W. Griffith: A Style for the Times." *Journal of Popular Film* 1 (Spring 1972): 67–69.

Dorr, John. "The Griffith Tradition." *Film Comment* 10 (March–April 1974): 48–54.

Eisenstein, Sergei. "Dickens, Griffith and the Film Today." In *Film Form*. Ed. and trans. Jay Leyda. New York: Harcourt Brace, 1949, 195–255.

Geduld, Harry M., ed. *Focus on D. W. Griffith*. Englewood Cliffs, N.J.: Prentice-Hall, 1971.

Gish, Lillian, with Pinchot, Ann. *The Movies, Mr. Griffith, and Me*. Englewood Cliffs, N.J.: Prentice-Hall, 1969.

Kepley, Vance. "Griffith's *Broken Blossoms* and the Problem of Historical Specificity." *Quarterly Review of Film Studies* 3 (1978): 37–48.

Kozloff, Sarah R. "Where Wessex Meets New England: Griffith's *Way Down East* and Hardy." *Film/Literature Quarterly* 13, no. 1 (Spring 1985): 35–41.

Lennig, Arthur. "*Broken Blossons*, D. W. Griffith, and the Making of an Unconventional Masterpiece." *Film Journal* 2 (Fall–Winter 1978): 2–9.

Lesage, Julia. "Artful Racism, Artful Rape: Griffith's *Broken Blossoms.*" *Jump Cut* 26 (1981); reprinted in *Home Is Where the Heart Is. See* Gledhill 1987, 235–54.

Petric, Vlada. "David Wark Griffith." In *Cinema: A Critical Dictionary*. Ed. Richard Roud. New York: Viking, 1980, 449–62.

Schickel, Richard. *D. W. Griffith: An American Life*. New York: Simon & Schuster, 1984.

Wagenknecht, Edward, and Slide, Anthony. *The Films of D. W. Griffith*. New York: Crown Publishers, 1975.

King Vidor

Amengual, Barthélémy. "Entre l'horizon d'un seul et l'horizon de tous: sur *La Grande Parade* et *La Foule.*" *Positif* 161 (September 1974): 31–42.

Baxter, John. *King Vidor*. New York: Monarch Press, 1976.

Carbonnier, A. "King Vidor ou l'ambivalence du désir." *Cinéma 82* 288 (December 1982): 28–36.

Cebe, G. "*Ruby Gentry.*" *Cinéma 82* 281 (May 1982): 82–83.

Cohn, Bernard. "Entretien avec King Vidor." *Positif* 161 (September 1974): 13–22.

Combs, Richard. "King Vidor." In *Cinema: A Critical Dictionary*. Ed. Richard Roud. New York: Viking, 1980, 1026–35.

Denton, Clive. "King Vidor: Texas Poet." *The Hollywood Professionals* 5 (New York: Barnes, 1976): 7–55.

Deutelbaum, M. "King Vidor's *The Crowd.*" *Image* 17, no. 3 (1974): 20–25.

Durgnat, Raymond. "King Vidor." *Film Comment* 9, no. 4 (July-August): 10–49; and no. 5 (September–October 1973): 16–51.

Ellis, M. "In the Picture: Crowd Music." *Sight and Sound* 50, no. 4 (1981).

Greenberg, Joel. "War, Wheat and Steel: An interview with King Vidor." *Sight and Sound* 37, no. 4 (Autumn 1968): 192–97.

Henry, Michael. "Le Blé, l'acier et la dynamite: de *An American Romance* à *Ruby Gentry*, ou l'après-guerre de King Vidor." *Positif* 163 (November 1974): 41–48.

Kaplan, E. Ann. "The Case of the Missing Mother: Maternal Issues in Vidor's *Stella Dallas*." *Heresies* 16 (1983): 81–85.

Legrand, G. "King Vidor, sur deux notes." *Positif* 259 (September 1982): 69–72.

Nacache, Jacqueline. *"Ruby Gentry." Cinéma 82* 281 (May 1982): 82–83.

Positif 161 and 163 (September and November 1974). Special issues on King Vidor.

Rothman, William. "In the Face of the Camera." Review of *Cinema and Sentiment*, by Charles Affron. *Raritan* 3, no. 3 (Winter 1984): 116–35.

Sarris, Andrew. "Films in Focus: The Remembered Vitality of King Vidor." *The Village Voice*, 28 November 1982.

Schickel, Richard. *The Men Who Made the Movies*. New York: Atheneum, 1975: 131–60.

Segond, Jacques. "The Bad and the Beautiful: Sur *Stella Dallas* et *The Wedding Night*." *Positif* 163 (November 1974): 37–40.

Sherman, Eric. "King Vidor (1895–1982)." In *American Directors*. Vol. 1. Jean-Pierre Coursodon with Pierre Sauvage. New York: McGraw-Hill, 1983, 347–50.

Silver, Charles. "Program Notes." New York: Museum of Modern Art, 1972.

Vidor, King. *A Tree Is a Tree*. New York: Harcourt Brace, 1952.

———. *On Film Making*. London: W. H. Allen, 1973.

Viviani, Christian. "La Garce ou le côté pile." *Positif* 163 (November 1974): 51–54.

Williams, Linda. " 'Something Else Besides a Mother': *Stella Dallas* and the Maternal Melodrama." *Cinema Journal* 24, no. 1 (Fall 1984): 2–27.

Vincente Minnelli

Anderson, Lindsay. "Minnelli, Kelly and *An American in Paris*." *Sequence* 14 (1952): 36–38.

Bathrick, Serafina. "The Past as Future: Family and the American Home in *Meet Me in St. Louis*." *The Minnesota Review*, New Series 6 (Spring 1976): 132–39.

Bitsch, Charles and Domarchi, Jean. "Entretien." *Cahiers du cinéma* 74 (August–September 1957): 4–14.

Bourget, Jean-Loup. "L'Oeuvre de Vincente Minnelli." *Positif* 310 (December 1986): 2–12.

Britton, Andrew. "*Meet Me in St. Louis*: Smith, or the Ambiguities." *Australian Journal of Screen Theory* 3 (1978): 7–25.

Byron, Stuart. "With Minnelli, the Melodrama Lingers On." *The Real Paper*, 12 December 1973.

Carey, Gary. "Vincente Minnelli and the 1940s Musical." In *Cinema: A Critical Dictionary*. Ed. Richard Roud. New York: Viking, 1980, 689–96.

Casper, Joseph Andrew. *Vincente Minnelli and the Film Musical*. London: The Tantivy Press, 1977.

Chaumeton, Etienne. "L'Oeuvre de Vincente Minnelli." *Positif* 12 (November–December 1954): 36–45.

Cook, J. "*On a Clear Day You Can See Forever*." *Movie* 24 (Spring 1977): 61–62.

Coursodon, Jean-Pierre. "Vincente Minnelli." In *American Directors*. Vol. II. New York: McGraw-Hill, 1983, 232–41.

Cunningham, S. "Stock, Shock, and Schlock." *Enclitic* 5, no. 2/6, no. 1 (Fall 1981/Spring 1982): 166–71.

Curtis Fox, Terry. "Vincente Minnelli: The Decorative Auteur." *The Village Voice*, February 6, 1978: 37.

Domarchi, Jean and Douchet, Jean. "Rencontre avec Vincente Minnelli." *Cahiers du cinéma* 128 (February 1962): 3–13.

Durgnat, Raymond. "Film Favorites: *Bells Are Ringing*." *Film Comment* 9 (March–April 1973): 46–50.

Dyer, R. "Lana: Four Films of Lana Turner." *Movie* 25 (Winter 1977–78): 30–52.

Elsaesser, Thomas. "Vincente Minnelli." *Brighton Film Review* 15 (December 1969): 11–13; no. 18 (March 1970): 20–22; reprinted in *Genre: The Musical*. Ed. Rick Altman. London: Routledge & Kegan Paul, 1981: 8–27.

Galling, Dennis Lee. "Vincente Minnelli." *Films in Review* 15 (March 1964): 129–40.

Genné, Beth. "Vincente Minnelli's Style in Microcosm: The Establishing Sequence of *Meet Me in St. Louis*." *Art Journal* (Fall 1983): 47–54.

Guérif, François. *Vincente Minnelli*. Paris: Edilig, 1984.

Harcourt-Smith, Simon. "Vincente Minnelli." *Sight and Sound* 21, no. 3 (January–March 1952): 115–19.

Hogue, Peter. "*The Band Wagon*." *The Velvet Light Trap* 11 (Winter 1974): 33–34.

Johnson, Albert. "The Films of Vincente Minnelli." *Film Quarterly* 12 (Winter 1958): 21–35, and no. 13 (Spring 1959): 32–42.

Lippe, Richard. "*A Matter of Time*." *Movie* 27/28 (Winter 1980/Spring 1981): 70–73.

Mayersberg, Paul. "The Testament of Vincente Minnelli." *Movie* 3 (October 1962): 10–13.

McVay, Douglas. "The Magic of Minnelli." *Films and Filming* (June 1959): 11.

Minnelli, Vincente, with Arce, Hector. *I Remember It Well*. Garden City, N.Y.: Doubleday, 1974.

Morris, George. "The Minnelli Magic." *The Soho Weekly News*, January 19, 1978: 19–21.

Nowell-Smith, Geoffrey. "Minnelli and Melodrama." *Screen* 18, no. 2 (1977): 113–18.

Schickel, Richard. *The Men Who Made the Movies*. New York: Atheneum, 1975: 243–68.

Serebrinsky, Ernesto, and Garaycochea, Oscar. "Vincente Minnelli interviewed in Argentina." *Movie* 10 (June 1963): 23–28.

Shivas, Mark. "Minnelli's Method. Minnelli Talks about *The Four Horsemen of the Apocalypse*." *Movie* 1 (June 1962): 17–24.

Siegel, J. E. " 'Love is the exception to every rule, is it not?' ": The Films of Vincente Minnelli and Alan Jay Lerner." *Bright Lights* 3, no. 9 (1980): 7–11.

Simsolo, Noël. "Sur quelques films de Minnelli." *La Révue du cinéma* 365 (October 1981): 97–116.

Telotte, J. P. "Self and Society: Vincente Minnelli and Musical Formula." *Journal of Popular Film and Television* 9, no. 4 (1982): 181–93.

Török, Jean-Paul, and Quincey, Jacques. "Vincente Minnelli ou le peintre de la vie rêvée." *Positif* 50/51/52 (March 1963): 56–74.

Truchaud, François. *Vincente Minnelli*. Paris: Editions Universitaires, 1966.

Vidal, Marion. *Vincente Minnelli*. Paris: Editions Seghers, 1973.

Wood, Robin. "Minnelli's *Madame Bovary*." *CineAction!* 7 (Winter 1986–87): 75–80.

Related Books and Articles

Affron, Charles. *Star Acting: Gish, Garbo, Davis*. New York: Dutton, 1977.

Althusser, Louis. *Lenin and Philosophy and Other Essays*. Trans. Ben Brewster. New York: Monthly Review Press, 1971.

Andrew, Dudley. *Concepts in Film Theory*. New York: Oxford University Press, 1984.

———. *Film in the Aura of Art*. Princeton: Princeton University Press, 1984.

Barthes, Roland. *Critical Essays*. Trans. Richard Howard. Evanston, Ill.: Northwestern University Press, 1972.

———. *S/Z*. Trans. Richard Miller. New York: Hill and Wang, 1974.

———. *The Pleasure of the Text*. Trans. Richard Miller. New York: Hill and Wang, 1975.

———. *Image-Music-Text*. Trans. Stephen Heath. New York: Hill and Wang, 1977.

Baxter, Peter. "On the History and Ideology of Film Lighting." *Screen* 16, no. 3 (Autumn 1975): 83–106.

Bazin, André. *What is Cinema?* 2 vols. Trans. Hugh Gray. Berkeley: University of California Press, 1967.

Benjamin, Walter. "The Work of Art in the Age of Mechanical Reproduction." In *Illuminations*. Ed. Hannah Arendt, trans. Harry Zohn. New York: Schocken Books, 1969, 217–51.

Bergman, Andrew. *We're in the Money: Depression America and Its Films*. New York: New York University Press, 1971.

Bersani, Leo. *A Future for Astyanax: Character and Desire in Literature*. Boston: Little, Brown & Co., 1976.

Bordwell, David; Staiger, Janet; and Thompson, Kristin. *The Classical Holly-wood Cinema: Film Style and Mode of Production to 1960*. New York: Columbia University Press, 1985.

Braudy, Leo. *The World in a Frame: What We See in Films*. Garden City, N.Y.: Anchor Press/Doubleday, 1976.

Brooks, Peter. "Freud's Masterplot: A Model for Narrative." In *Reading for the Plot: Design and Intention in Narrative*. New York: Alfred A. Knopf, 1984, 90–112.

Brownlow, Kevin. *The Parade's Gone By*. New York: Alfred A. Knopf, 1968.

Caughie, John, ed. *Theories of Authorship*. London: Routledge & Kegan Paul, 1981.

Chodorow, Nancy. *The Reproduction of Mothering*. Berkeley: University of California Press, 1978.

Coward, Rosalind. *Patriarchal Precedents: Sexuality and Social Relations*. London: Routledge & Kegan Paul, 1983.

———. *Female Desires: How They Are Sought, Bought, and Packaged*. New York: Grove Press, 1985.

———, and Ellis, John. *Language and Materialism: Developments in Semiology and the Theory of the Subject*. London: Routledge & Kegan Paul, 1977.

Cowie, Elizabeth. "Fantasia," *m/f*, no. 9 (1984): 71–104.

De Lauretis, Teresa. *Alice Doesn't: Feminism, Semiotics, Cinema*. Bloomington: Indiana University Press, 1984.

———. "Oedipus Interruptus." *Wide Angle* 7, no. 1–2 (1985): 34–40.

Deleuze, Gilles, and Guattari, Félix. *Anti-Oedipus: Capitalism and Schizophrenia*. Trans. Robert Hurley, Mark Seem, and Helen R. Lane. Minneapolis: University of Minnesota Press, 1983.

Dinnerstein, Dorothy. *The Mermaid and the Minotaur: Sexual Arrangements and Human Malaise*. New York: Harper & Row, 1977.

Doane, Mary Ann. "Misrecognition and Identity." *Ciné-Tracts* 3, no. 3 (Fall 1980): 25–32.

———. "Woman's Stake: Filming the Female Body." *October* 17 (Summer 1981): 23–36.

———. "Film and the Masquerade: Theorizing the Female Spectator." *Screen* 23, no. 3/4 (September–October 1982b): 74–87.

Douglas, Ann. *The Feminization of American Culture*. New York: Avon Books, 1977.

Dyer, Richard. "Entertainment and Utopia." *Movie* 24 (Spring 1977): 2–13; reprinted in *Movies and Methods*, Vol. II. Ed. Bill Nichols. Berkeley and Los Angeles: University of California Press, 1985, 220–32.

Flinn, Carol. "The 'Problem' of Femininity in Theories of Film Music." *Screen* 27, no. 6 (November–December 1986): 56–72.

Flitterman, Sandy. "Woman, Desire, and the Look: Feminism and the Enunciative Apparatus in Cinema" (1978); reprinted in *Theories of Authorship*. See Caughie 1981, 242–50.

———. "That 'Once-Upon-a-Time . . .' of Childish Dreams." *Ciné-Tracts* 13 (Spring 1981): 14–25.

Foucault, Michel. *The History of Sexuality, Volume I: An Introduction.* Trans. Robert Hurley. New York: Random House, 1978.

Freud, Sigmund. *The Interpretation of Dreams.* Trans. James Strachey. London: The Hogarth Press and The Institute of Psycho-Analysis, 1953.

Gledhill, Christine, "Developments in Feminist Film Criticism" (1978); reprinted in *Re-Vision: Essays in Feminist Film Criticism.* Ed. Mary Ann Doane, Patricia Mellencamp, Linda Williams. Los Angeles: AFI Monograph series, 1983, 18–48.

———."Recent Developments in Feminist Film Criticism." 1977; reprinted in *Film Theory and Criticism*, 3rd ed. Ed. Gerald Mast and Marshall Cohen. New York: Oxford University Press, 1985, 817–45.

Gorbman, Claudia. "The Drama's Melos: Max Steiner and *Mildred Pierce.*" *The Velvet Light Trap* 19 (1982): 35–39.

Guattari, Félix. *Molecular Revolution.* Trans. Rosemary Sheed. Harmondsworth, Middlesex: Penguin Books, 1984.

Habegger, Alfred. *Gender, Fantasy, and Realism in American Literature.* New York: Columbia University Press, 1982.

Hansen, Miriam. "Pleasure, Ambivalence, Identification: Valentino and Female Spectatorship." *Cinema Journal* 25, no. 4 (Summer 1986): 6–32.

Haskell, Molly. *From Reverence to Rape: The Treatment of Women in the Movies.* London: New English Library, 1975.

Heath, Stephen. "Difference." *Screen* 19, no. 3 (1978): 50–112.

———. *Questions of Cinema.* Bloomington: Indiana University Press, 1981.

———. *The Sexual Fix.* London: Macmillan Press, 1982.

Hirsch, Marianne. "Mothers and Daughters" (Review Essay). *Signs: Journal of Women in Culture and Society* 7, no. 1 (Autumn 1981): 200–22.

Irigaray, Luce. *This Sex Which Is Not One.* Trans. Catherine Porter. Ithaca, N.Y.: Cornell University Press, 1985.

Kalinak, Kathryn. "The Fallen Woman and the Virtuous Wife: Musical Stereotypes in *The Informer, Gone With the Wind*, and *Laura.*" Film Reader 5 (1982): 76–82.

Kaplan, E. Ann, ed. *Women in Film Noir.* London: British Film Institute, 1978.

———. "Missing Mothers." *Social Policy* 14, no. 2 (Fall 1983b): 151–61.

———. *Women and Film: Both Sides of the Camera.* New York: Methuen, 1983e.

———. "Feminist Film Criticism: Current Issues and Problems." *Studies in the Literary Imagination* 19, no. 1 (Spring 1986): 7–20.

Kay, Karyn, and Peary, Gerald, eds. *Women and the Cinema: A Critical Anthology.* New York: Dutton, 1977.

Kleinhans, Chuck. "Types of Audience Response: From Tear-Jerkers to Thought-Provokers." *Jump Cut* 4 (1974): 21–23.

Klinger, Barbara. " 'Cinema/Ideology/Criticism' Revisited: The Progressive Text." *Screen* 25, no. 1 (January–February 1984): 30–44.

Koch, Gertrude. "Exchanging the Gaze: Re-Visioning Feminist Film Theory." *New German Critique* 34 (Winter 1985): 139–53.

Kristeva, Julia. *About Chinese Women*. Trans. Anita Barrows. New York: Urizen Books, 1977.

———. "Woman Can Never Be Defined." In *New French Feminisms*. Ed. Elaine Marks and Isabelle de Courtivron. New York: Schocken Books, 1981, 137–41.

———. *Histoires d'amour*. Paris: Editions Denoël, 1983.

———. "Histoires d'Amour—Love Stories." In *Desire*. Ed. Lisa Appignanesi. London: ICA Documents, 1984, 18–21.

———. "Julia Kristeva in Conversation with Rosalind Coward." In *Desire*. Ed. Lisa Appignanesi. London: ICA Documents, 1984, 22–27.

Kuhn, Annette. *Womens's Pictures: Feminism and Cinema*. London: Routledge & Kegan Paul, 1982.

Lacan, Jacques. *Encore: Le Séminaire XX*. Paris: Seuil, 1975.

———. *Ecrits: A Selection*. Trans. Alan Sheridan. New York: Norton, 1977.

———. *The Four Fundamental Concepts of Psycho-Analysis*. Ed. Jacques-Alain Miller, trans. Alan Sheridan. New York: Norton, 1978.

———. *Le Séminaire, Livre II*. Paris: Seuil, 1978.

———. *Feminine Sexuality*. Ed. Juliet Mitchell and Jacqueline Rose, trans. Jacqueline Rose. New York: Norton, 1983.

Laplanche, J., and Pontalis, J.-B. *The Language of Psycho-Analysis*. Trans. Donald Nicholson-Smith. New York: Norton, 1973.

Lasch, Christopher. *The Culture of Narcissism*. New York: Norton, 1978.

Mayne, Judith. "Feminist Film Theory and Film Criticism." *Signs: Journal of Women in Culture and Society* 11, no. 1 (Autumn 1985): 81–100.

McNiven, Roger D. "The Middle-Class American Home of the Fifties: The Use of Architecture in Nicholas Ray's *Bigger Than Life* and Douglas Sirk's *All That Heaven Allows*." *Cinema Journal* 22, no. 4 (Summer 1983): 38–57.

Metz, Christian. *The Imaginary Signifier: Psychoanalysis and the Cinema*. Trans. Celia Britton, Annwyl Williams, Ben Brewster, and Alfred Guzzetti. Bloomington: Indiana University Press, 1977.

Mitchell, Juliet. *Psychoanalysis and Feminism*. New York: Random House, 1974.

Mulvey, Laura. "Visual Pleasure and Narrative Cinema." *Screen* 16, no. 3 (Autumn 1975): 6–18.

———. "Afterthoughts on 'Visual Pleasure and Narrative Cinema' Inspired by *Duel in the Sun* (King Vidor, 1946)." *Framework* 15/16/17 (1981): 12–15.

Neale, Stephen. *Genre*. London: British Film Institute, 1980.

———. "Sexual Difference in Cinema—Issues of Fantasy, Narrative and the Look." *The Oxford Literary Review* 8, no. 1–2 (1986b): 123–132.

O'Pray, Michael. "Movies, Mania and Masculinity." *Screen* 23, no. 5 (November–December 1982): 63–70.

Panofsky, Erwin. "Style and Medium in the Motion Pictures" (1934, revised 1947); reprinted in *Film Theory and Criticism*. 3rd ed. Ed. Gerald Mast and Marshall Cohen. New York: Oxford University Press, 1985, 215–33.

Poster, Mark. *Critical Theory of the Family*. New York: The Seabury Press, 1978.

Robbe-Grillet, Alain. *For a New Novel: Essays on Fiction*. Trans. Richard Howard. New York: Grove Press, 1965.

Rodowick, D. N. "The Difficulty of Difference." *Wide Angle* 5, no. 1 (1982a): 4–15.

Rose, Jacqueline. "Femininity and Its Discontents." *Feminist Review* 14 (June Rodowick 1983): 5–21.

———. *Sexuality in the Field of Vision*. London: Verso, 1986.

Rubin, Martin. "The Voice of Silence: Sound Style in John Stahl's *Back Street*." In *Film Sound: Theory and Practice*. See Weis and Belton 1985, 277–85.

Sedgwick, Eve Kosofsky. *Between Men: English Literature and Male Homosocial Desire*. New York: Columbia University Press, 1985.

Silverman, Kaja. "Masochism and Subjectivity." *Framework* 12 (1980): 2–9.

———. "Suture" [Excerpts]. In *Narrative, Apparatus, Ideology*. Ed. Philip Rosen. New York: Columbia University Press, 1986, 219–35. Excerpted from chapter 5 of Kaja Silverman, *The Subject of Semiotics*. New York: Oxford University Press, 1983.

———. "Lost Objects and Mistaken Subjects: Film Theory's Structuring Lack." *Wide Angle* 7, no. 1–2 (1985): 14–29.

Sontag, Susan. "Notes on 'Camp.' " In *Against Interpretation*. New York: Dell, 1966, 275–92.

Studlar, Gaylyn. "Masochism and the Perverse Pleasures of the Cinema" (1984); reprinted in *Movies and Methods*. Vol. II. Ed. Bill Nichols. Berkeley and Los Angeles: University of California Press, 1985, 602–21.

Thompson, Kristin. "The Concept of Cinematic Excess." In *Eisenstein's "Ivan the Terrible": A Neoformalist Analysis*. Princeton: Princeton University Press, 1981, 287–302; reprinted in *Narrative, Apparatus, Ideology*. Ed. Philip Rosen. New York: Columbia University Press, 1986, 130–142.

Waldman, Diane. " 'At last I can tell it to someone!': Feminine Point of View and Subjectivity in the Gothic Romance Film of the 1940s." *Cinema Journal* 23, no. 2 (Winter 1983): 29–40.

Walker, Janet. "Psychoanalysis and Feminist Film Theory: The Problem of Sexual Difference and Identity." *Wide Angle* 6, no. 3 (1984): 16–23.

Weeks, Jeffrey. *Sexuality and its Discontents*. London: Routledge & Kegan Paul, 1985.

Weis, Elisabeth, and Belton, John, eds. *Film Sound: Theory and Practice*. New York: Columbia University Press, 1985.

Willemen, Paul. "Voyeurism, The Look and Dwoskin." *Afterimage* 6 (Summer 1976): 40–50.

Wood, Robin. "The American Family Comedy: From *Meet Me in St. Louis* to *The Texas Chainsaw Massacre*." *Wide Angle* 3, no. 2 (1979): 5–11.

Zaretsky, Eli. *Capitalism, the Family, and Personal Life*. New York: Harper & Row, 1976.

Index